PUBLICATIONS
OF THE FACULTY OF ARTS
OF THE UNIVERSITY OF MANCHESTER
NO. 22

A FRENCH SOCIOLOGIST LOOKS AT BRITAIN

Gustave d'Eichthal and British society in 1828

A FRENCH SOCIOLOGIST LOOKS AT BRITAIN

Gustave d'Eichthal and British society in 1828

Translated and edited by
BARRIE M. RATCLIFFE
and
W. H. CHALONER

MANCHESTER UNIVERSITY PRESS

ROWMAN AND LITTLEFIELD

© University of Manchester 1977

Published by
MANCHESTER UNIVERSITY PRESS
Oxford Road
Manchester M13 9PL

ISBN 0 7190 1283 X

North America
ROWMAN AND LITTLEFIELD
Totowa, N.J. 07512

Library of Congress Cataloging in Publication Data
Eichthal, Gustave d', 1804–1886.
A French sociologist looks at Britain.

(Publications of the Faculty of Arts of the
University of Manchester; No. 22.)
Includes 'Gustave d'Eichthal (1804–1886): an
intellectual portrait', by B. M. Ratcliffe (p. 109).
Includes bibliographical references and index.
1. Great Britain – Social conditions. 2. Great
Britain – Economic conditions. 3. Sociologists –
France – Biography. 4. Eichthal, Gustave d', 1804–
1886. I. Ratcliffe, Barrie M. Gustave d'Eichthal
(1804–1886): an intellectual portrait. 1977. II.
Title. III. Series: Victoria University of
Manchester. Faculty of Arts. Publications; No. 22.
HN388.G7E4   1977   309.1'73'074   77–1899
ISBN 0–87471–963–1

Printed in Great Britain by
Western Printing Services Ltd, Bristol

CONTENTS

PREFACE

This monograph, we hope, will serve a dual purpose: the publication of an unusually well-qualified and perceptive French observer's notes on the British economy and society in 1828 and of an intellectual portrait of the observer himself, a writer whose preoccupations, career and accomplishments make him typical of the 1830 generation in Paris. The first part, therefore, consists of d'Eichthal's notes which we have jointly introduced, translated and annotated, and the second part is a memoir of d'Eichthal by Barrie M. Ratcliffe.

Our work was made possible because most of Gustave d'Eichthal's personal papers have survived. The rôle he played in the Saint-Simonian movement can be ascertained from the large manuscript collections at the Bibliothèque de l'Arsenal, the Saint-Simonian papers presented to the Bibliothèque Nationale by Alfred Pereire and the papers and published works on and by Saint-Simonians bequeathed to the Bibliothèque Thiers by d'Eichthal himself. His notes on Britain together with the rest of his private papers, diaries and voluminous correspondence form the Fonds d'Eichthal at the Arsenal.

Our work was greatly facilitated by the courteous help accorded by Mlle Hélène Michaud, *conservateur* at the Bibliothèque Thiers, Mme F. B. Py, *conservateur adjoint*, and Mme Monique Cazeaux at the Bibliothèque de l'Arsenal as well as by the counsel of a number of colleagues and friends, and particularly T. Ashworth, François Crouzet, A. J. Graham, E. R. R. Green, R. G. Kirby, I. J. Prothero, A. J. Robertson, and Walter M. Stern. We are happy to acknowledge our debt to them as we are to Elisabeth Dyckhoff and Edwina Cubie for their expert typing of a wayward manuscript.

University of Manchester
May 1976

W.H.C.
B.M.R.

EDITORS' INTRODUCTION

The gradual unfolding of the process termed the Industrial Revolution in Britain in the late eighteenth and early nineteenth centuries inevitably attracted many observers, businessmen, engineers and industrial spies, whose activities have been investigated in some detail during the past twenty years.[1] At first such visitors were content to record mainly industrial and topographical matters, but from the mid-1820s some of them began to pay more attention to British social conditions and particularly to the social impact of the Industrial Revolution.[2] One of the first, if not the first, of these more philosophical observers was Gustave d'Eichthal, whose account of his visit to England and Scotland in 1828, although printed in part as early as 1902[3] has hardly been used by British

[1] W. O. Henderson, *Britain and Industrial Europe, 1750–1870*, 1st ed. Liverpool, 1954, 2nd rev. ed. Leicester, 1965; W. O. Henderson, *J. C. Fischer and his Diary of Industrial England, 1814–51*, London, 1966; W. O. Henderson, *Industrial Britain under the Regency: The Diaries of Escher, Bodmer, May and de Gallois, 1814–18*, London, 1968; E. T. Svedenstierna, *Svedenstierna's Tour: Great Britain, 1802–3; The Travel Diary of an Industrial Spy*, ed. M. W. Flinn, trans. E. L. Dellow, Newton Abbot, 1973; C. von Oeynhausen and H. von Dechen, *Railways in England, 1826 and 1827*, trans. E. A. Forward, London, 1971.

[2] See A. de Tocqueville, *Journeys to England and Ireland*, ed. J. P. Mayer, London, 1958 (a visit in the mid-1830s) and the list given on p. xix, n. 2 in F. Engels, *The Condition of the Working Class in England*, trans. and ed. W. O. Henderson and W. H. Chaloner, 2nd ed. Oxford, 1971. A number of visitors came from France in the 1820s (see Ethel Jones, 'Les Voyageurs français en Angleterre de 1815 à 1830', thèse présentée pour le Doctorat de l'Université de Paris, Paris, 1930, especially pp. 315–17). Among these were some who were especially concerned with the state of society and the economy. In 1815 Jean-Baptiste Say visited Britain; in 1817, 1819 and 1824 Simonde de Sismondi made visits; Adolphe Blanqui came in 1823 and Say's son, Horace, came in 1828.

[3] 'Condition de la classe ouvrière en Angleterre (1828), notes prises par Gustave d'Eichthal', edited by Eugène d'Eichthal, *Revue historique*, Paris, vol. LXXIX, 1902, pp. 63–95.

historians.[4] It might even be claimed, in view of his ties with Comte, that he was the first sociologist to observe the Industrial Revolution in Britain. He came, as did his compatriot Alexis de Tocqueville five years later, to give himself 'the intellectual pleasure of watching a great people in the throes of revolutionary change' and he recorded his impressions about the state of British society and politics in his diary, notes and correspondence.

The difficulties faced by a foreign observer were manifold. Language acted as a barrier to understanding. The emerging industrial economy and society were complex, and to understand them was a subtle and elusive task. As Cavour wrote to Paul Emile Maurice in 1835:

> L'Angleterre est le pays qui est le moins facile à voir en courant, car les ressorts de la société ne sont pas à la surface du sol; ils sont profondément enracinés dans le sein de la nation, et pour les découvrir il faut de longues et pénibles recherches.[5]

The quality of a foreign visitor's comments depended not only on his insight, on his sensibility as an observer, but also on the length of his stay, the people he met, the places he visited. Gustave d'Eichthal stayed in Britain almost a year, from April to December 1828. Much of this time was spent in London with occasional visits to friends at Bucklebury in Berkshire but he also made a two-month trip to the industrial north and to Scotland between 1 September and 1 November. He came to Britain with certain advantages. Though only twenty-four years old he had already travelled extensively in Germany and Austria and he already spoke English with some fluency. He had good contacts in London, for Isambard Kingdom Brunel, who was then working on the Thames tunnel project, had been a fellow pupil at the Lycée Henri IV and d'Eichthal came armed with letters of introduction to a number of his father's business contacts. He came, too, as the disciple of

---

[4] Exceptions are D. Read, *Peterloo*, Manchester, 1958, p. 5 and D. Bythell, *The Handloom Weavers*, Cambridge, 1969, p. 70.

[5] Cited by Rosario Romeo, *Cavour e il suo tempo (1810–1842)*, Bari, 1969, p. 500. For a discussion of the ways in which French travellers' views were limited by prevailing myths about British character and society, myths elaborated during the Restoration, see Pierre Reboul, *Le Mythe anglais dans la littérature française sous la Restauration*, Lille, 1962. The problems of Anglo-French understanding (and misunderstanding) are succinctly sketched out in François Crouzet, 'Problèmes de la communication franco-britannique aux XIXe et XXe siècles', *Revue historique*, vol. CCLIV, 1975, pp. 105–34.

Auguste Comte whose early work was just beginning to be known in England. In London he met a group of young English intellectuals, including Roebuck, Chadwick, Buller, Elphinstone, Erskine Perry, W. Eyton Tooke and John Stuart Mill.[6] He also met and had long discussions with Francis Place, the Radical, and his account of these adds vivid touches to our knowledge of an individual who has been written about with undue solemnity. In Edinburgh he met Blackwood and McCulloch and in Birmingham he had contacts with the Parkes family. In the industrial towns of the north he met leading industrialists and bankers such as Benjamin Gott the Leeds woollen manufacturer and John Kennedy the Manchester cotton-spinner. Many of those who made d'Eichthal's acquaintance seem to have thought highly of him. Francis Place, for instance, was very favourably impressed, and, after dining with him early in 1829, Adolphe d'Eichthal wrote to his brother:

> ... c'est surtout Mons. Place que je pourrais appeler ta *conquête*. Je ne te souhaite rien de plus que de faire beaucoup de prosélytes comme lui.[7]

It was, however, with W. Eyton Tooke, son of the merchant and economist, and John Stuart Mill that d'Eichthal formed especially close relationships. It was d'Eichthal who introduced Mill to Comte by presenting him with a copy of the *Système de politique positive*[8] and who encouraged Mill's growing interest in French affairs. D'Eichthal later described their relationship thus:

> mes relations avec Mill ... ont eu une grande influence sur sa vie (lui-même l'atteste) et aussi sur la mienne. Dans une certaine mesure c'est lui qui m'a ouvert l'Angleterre comme je lui ai ouvert la France. Ce qui nous rapprochait ce n'étaient point des idées abstraites. C'était notre nature et nos désirs d'apôtre.[9]

[6] Manuscript notes in the hand of Gustave d'Eichthal, Fonds d'Eichthal, *Bibliothèque de l'Arsenal*, 13756, fo. 90.

[7] Letter from Adolphe d'Eichthal to Gustave d'Eichthal, 22 January 1829, Fonds d'Eichthal, *Bibliothèque de l'Arsenal*, 13746, fo. 158.

[8] Journal de Gustave d'Eichthal, entry for 3 February 1864, Fonds d'Eichthal, *Bibliothèque de l'Arsenal*, 14721.

[9] Letter from Gustave d'Eichthal to Dr Henry, 26 November 1873, Fonds d'Eichthal, *Bibliothèque de l'Arsenal*, 13756, fo. 76. Mill acknowledged his debt to d'Eichthal in his *Autobiography* as well as in a letter he wrote to d'Eichthal in September 1866, Fonds d'Eichthal, *Bibliothèque de l'Arsenal*, 14722. On the relationships between Bentham, Coleridge, Comte and J. S. Mill, see F. R. Leavis's introduction to *Mill on Bentham and Coleridge*, London, 1950, pp. 1–18.

Mill, for his part, was also favourably impressed by d'Eichthal, so favourably, indeed, that when he and a number of friends planned to set up their own newspaper, with Edwin Chadwick as editor, towards the end of 1829, he wrote to d'Eichthal suggesting that he become the paper's French correspondent:

> As this newspaper will pay very particular attention to French affairs, and will endeavour, as one of its grand objects, to make its leaders understand not only French politics but the whole social state of France, including all that is doing in the world of literature and philosophy by that active and important member of the European community, and in short to explain the character of that general movement which is taking place in the human mind all over the continent of Europe but especially in France, we shall be very anxious to have a first rate correspondent at Paris, capable of supplying (along with the general news of the day in politics, literature and philosophy) sound and enlarged views on all these subjects. I imagine there is scarcely any person except yourself who, with the other necessary qualifications, possesses that knowledge of England which a Frenchman writing for Englishmen would need and I am speaking in the sentiments of all my expected collaborators when I request, that if we succeed in realising our scheme, you will undertake this department of it. . . .[10]

Mill's project was never realised, however, and, in any case, d'Eichthal was already too closely involved in the Saint-Simonian sect.

His visit to Great Britain was important for Gustave d'Eichthal in a number of ways. The knowledge he gained and the contacts he made were to serve him in good stead when he came to England on a proselytising mission for the Saint-Simonians in 1831-2. It was in England in 1828 that he completed the monograph on government finance he published in May 1829 which first brought him into contact with the Saint-Simonians.[11] This work was greatly

---

[10] Letter from John Stuart Mill to Gustave d'Eichthal, 7 November 1829, Fonds d'Eichthal, *Bibliothèque de l'Arsenal*, 13756, fo. 9. For a Discussion of the importance Mill attached to the reporting of French affairs, see Iris W. Mueller, *John Stuart Mill and French Thought*, Urbana, Ill., 1956, pp. 22–4.

[11] *Lettres à MM. les Députés composant la commission du budget, sur la permanence du système de crédit public, et sur la nécessité de renoncer à toute espèce de remboursement des créances sur l'état*, Paris, 1829, 83 pp. This book was finished by November 1828 and d'Eichthal showed it to various English friends, including Eyton Tooke. See his letter to Louis d'Eichthal,

influenced by what d'Eichthal saw in Britain and by the conversations he held with bankers and economists. In the book he praised the savings bank movement in England and Scotland and suggested the establishment of similar institutions in France as a means of improving the standard of living of the working class.[12] More important, the major thesis he put forward—the desirability of government loans, and the absurdity of a Sinking Fund—owed much to the House of Commons Finance Committee under the chairmanship of Sir Henry Parnell, whose first report had been instrumental in the abolition of Britain's Sinking Fund in July 1828.[13]

Even before he left the country d'Eichthal had decided to write a book on Britain and in the early months of 1829 he was writing to Place, to Eyton Tooke, to Mill, and to his brother requesting further information on aspects of British life.[14] He was encouraged to publish his impressions by Mill who wrote to him in March:

> I am glad to hear that you are busily engaged in writing on the subject of England and am not surprised to learn that you find a great number of unexpected difficulties in giving an account of the state of society here. As there is nobody even in England who is by any means qualified to treat so immense a subject with anything like completeness, it would be very wrong in you to be discouraged by finding that there is a great deal which you do not know—it is sufficient if you know, as I am satisfied you do, very much on the subject of England which is known to few, perhaps to none of your countrymen.[15]

---

14 November 1828, Fonds d'Eichthal, *Bibliothèque de l'Arsenal*, 14383, fo. 13. D'Eichthal described the success of his book in a letter to Place, 19 June 1829, B.M. MSS, 37950.

[12] *Lettres à MM. les Députés . . .* , pp. 34–5.

[13] D'Eichthal noted the work of the committee in his diary in July 1828, Fonds d'Eichthal, *Bibliothèque de l'Arsenal*, 14383, fo. 8.

[14] He questioned Place on the separation of powers and on the workings of the House of Commons, Richard K. P. Pankhurst, *The Saint-Simonians, Mill and Carlyle: A Preface to Modern Thought*, London, n.d. (1957), pp. 11–12. He questioned Tooke on English law and banking and he questioned Mill on parliamentary accounts, letters from Tooke and Mill to d'Eichthal, 19 April and 15 May 1829, Fonds d'Eichthal, *Bibliothèque de l'Arsenal*, 13756, fos. 2 and 3. Letter from Gustave d'Eichthal to Francis Place, n.d. (early 1829), B.M. Add. MSS, 35153.

[15] Letter from John Stuart Mill to Gustave d'Eichthal, 11 March 1829, Fonds d'Eichthal, *Bibliothèque de l'Arsenal*, 13756, fol. 1.

Not only did d'Eichthal find that writing a book on Britain was a more arduous task than he had anticipated, but other factors hindered his work: he had to help nurse his mother during an illness,[16] and his growing involvement in Saint-Simonism sapped his enthusiasm for other matters. By September 1829 he was writing to his brother that he was unsure as to whether he would have the strength to finish the book[17] and by the end of the year he was wholly committed to Saint-Simonism. All he managed to complete was the first part of the book which consisted of general observations and a discussion of the British political system,[18] and though the manuscript has not survived we know that both Mill and Eyton Tooke were enthusiastic about the chapters they read.[19]

The text that follows is taken from the diary d'Eichthal kept and the notes he made during his stay in Great Britain.[20] It appears in English for the first time and though part was published in French in the *Revue historique* in 1902 by d'Eichthal's eldest son, this was marred by errors and omissions. The diary he kept is not all equally interesting or valuable and towards the end of his trip to Scotland and northern England his entries are shorter—often indeed tantalisingly brief—and more disjointed, the consequence perhaps of the pace of his journey. A number of the persons he met and interviewed are identified in his notes under incorrect forms of their surnames.[21] It cannot be denied that some of his reflections are oversimplifications and that he gets some things plainly wrong. Some of his comments are obviously influenced by the Radicals and Philosophical Radicals he knew in London. His conclusions about British politics, his comparisons between the British situa-

[16] Letter from Gustave d'Eichthal to his brother Adolphe, 3 July 1829, Fonds d'Eichthal, *Bibliothèque de l'Arsenal*, 14407, fo. 8.
[17] Letter from Gustave to Adolphe d'Eichthal, 1 September 1829, Fonds d'Eichthal, *Bibliothèque de l'Arsenal*, 14407, fo. 12.
[18] Letter from Gustave to Adolphe d'Eichthal, n.d. (1829), Fonds d'Eichthal, *Bibliothèque de l'Arsenal*, 14407, fo. 24.
[19] Letter from John Stuart Mill to Gustave d'Eichthal, 8 October 1829, Fonds d'Eichthal, *Bibliothèque de l'Arsenal*, 13756, fo. 4; Gustave d'Eichthal to his brother, 1 September 1829.
[20] These are to be found in the Fonds d'Eichthal, *Bibliothèque de l'Arsenal*, 14401 (papiers divers et correspondence de Gustave d'Eichthal), 14381, 14382 and 14383 (journal tenu par Gustave d'Eichthal pendant son voyage en Angleterre), and 14384 (correspondance reçue par Gustave d'Eichthal pendant son voyage en Angleterre en 1828).
[21] Examples are 'Dorthé' for Doherty, 'Done' for Dunn, 'Grieg' for Greg.

tion and the condition of France on the eve of the Revolution and his belief in the urgent need for reform, in both central and local government, bear this out.[22]

It can be claimed, however, that d'Eichthal brings an intelligent eye to various aspects of British society. He noted differences in national character between the English and the French and the English and the Scots and he took an interest in British politics and the arts. But he came here because he felt Britain to be in the vanguard of history. He therefore came to study the impact that industrialisation was having on society and to this end he toured the manufacturing areas, interviewed employer and employed, collected newspaper cuttings and statistics on the cost of living, wages, drunkenness and prostitution. He came to discover the impact economic change had had on religious beliefs and practices among the different classes of British society and was interested in British education, and especially the meagre facilities—from charity schools to mechanics' institutes—available for the working class.[23] In his quest d'Eichthal was guided both by the knowledge of banking and commerce acquired during his apprenticeship in Paris, Berlin and Le Hâvre and by the industrialists, bankers and intellectuals he met who furnished him with reflections, information and their services as guides.

He summed up his general impressions in a letter he wrote to Auguste Comte at the end of his stay in Britain:

> There are so many things I would like to tell you about that in truth I don't know where to start. I have just been to Scotland and Lancashire. I have made as careful a study as I can and can accurately describe the state of society in these areas. As for the industrial aspect, you can imagine I felt only one thing, admiration, they make machines in this country as we plant cabbages in ours. They are afraid of nothing, so plentiful are funds; they raze hills, fill in valleys, to open up communications they dig tunnels under towns and they don't consider such things worthy of mention. The physical condition of the working class is very uneven.

[22] In his belief in the necessity for reform d'Eichthal was unusual amongst French observers who discussed British politics at this time. See Ethel Jones, *op. cit.*, p. 197.

[23] During the Restoration, and especially during commercial crises, a number of French observers commented on, and sought to explain, the persistence of widespread poverty in Britain despite the new wealth and industrialism. See Pierre Reboul, *op. cit.*, pp. 175–80 and, for a discussion of Sismondi, pp. 220–6.

A spinner in a cotton factory earns at least 20*s* a week and this can be taken as typical of the wages of many workers in the towns. It is a more than adequate wage, considering that meat, clothing, rent and fuel are not expensive in this country, bread and beer are but they do without the latter. While the majority of workers earn at least 16*s*, weavers only get 8*s* to 10*s* a week and agricultural labourers sometimes much less. The disparity of weavers' wages results, I think, from the very nature of their condition. For they are wretched everywhere. The advantage of working at home and being self-employed attracts a greater number of workers to this trade than to any other. Moreover, they have to face the competition of the Irish who were weavers in their own country and who bring their skills to England. The Irish have not yet been able to enter cotton mills, at least in any great number, or even other trades. As for agricultural labourers, their distress results from two factors: first, the Poor Laws, since every man has the right to aid from his parish and his parish alone. When he finds himself unemployed he does not seek work elsewhere, even in another trade, but applies to his parish and thus population increases out of line with the demand for labour; the second reason for agricultural labourers' distress is the difficulty of changing one's job because of workers' combinations which restrict entry into trades, and then there is the competition of the Irish who monopolise the public works which local agricultural labourers used to carry out. The six million pounds spent every year just for the care of the poor indicate quite clearly that some sections of the population are suffering.

I took great pains to discover the moral and intellectual condition of the British for we are used to hearing the most contradictory assertions on this subject. After careful study I have found that these assertions were all true because they apply to different sections of the population. The great majority are still decidedly bigoted and superstitious and though, as you might imagine, there are a number of individuals among them whose conduct is quite exemplary, the vast majority are addicted to drink, the English worker's most degrading vice, for however little they earn, a man who knows them well told me, they always find enough to get drunk on Saturday night. A much smaller proportion have raised themselves above popular prejudice and among these you find some very outstanding individuals. This development is most obvious in Scotland. Nowhere is the church more powerful or more intolerant—this goes so far that public conveyances cannot operate on a Sunday—and any man who dared make a direct attack on religious views would be stoned to death. However the same thing is happening there as is happening in Germany, they are slowly linking religion with science and as every denomination is independent this change can take place without hindrance. You see posters announcing that there will be a meeting in some chapel to hear a lecture on astronomy or chemistry. The newspapers affirm the need to give some instruction in the sciences on a Sunday, and Mr Owen has given an excellent example in giving elementary scientific education in his establishment at New Lanarck [sic]. Similar things can be seen in England, as I myself saw in Manchester, though on a lesser scale. I have heard the confidences of several well-informed workers and I especially enjoyed meeting a young man of French extraction who, orphaned at an early age, has risen to a very respectable rank in society by his perseverance and who has one of the finest minds I have ever encountered.[24]

A similar development is taking place or rather has been taking place for a long time among the upper classes. The setting up of two universities in London will open a new era in the intellectual history of England. In every town of any importance you also find Philosophical Societies, intended to cultivate the sciences and which usually have a large membership. Every town, too, has a Mechanics' Institution, as yet poorly attended by the working class though well frequented by the small shopkeepers, but which are expanding daily.

I will not say anything to you about English politics. You are as aware as I am of the odd and monstrous aspects of their constitution. The worst aspect, however, is not well known. This is the power given to the petty aristocracy in local government and in the administration of justice. People are beginning to be fully aware of this cause of suffering and we will probably live long enough to see its abolition.

I like and admire the English character. Recently someone drew my attention to one of the most striking characteristics when he pointed out that an Englishman never talked about things he did not know about except sometimes in the case of politics. You would not believe what a love of peace there is in this country, a more profound and sincere feeling would be inconceivable. Recent events and all our French blustering have not affected their friendly disposition.[25]

[24] This was Rowland Detrosier (1800–34) whom d'Eichthal met in Manchester. For Detrosier see Gwyn A. Williams, *Rowland Detrosier, a Working-class Infidel, 1800–34*, Borthwick Papers, No. 28, York, 1965.

[25] Letter from Gustave d'Eichthal to Auguste Comte, 17 October 1828,

Comte replied to d'Eichthal, gently admonishing him for what he felt to be his Anglophilia:

> I found your comments on England most interesting; they fit in exactly with what my own reflections had already shown me. I confess I share your predilection for the character of this nation which can be seen in level-headed and well-bred individuals. I particularly like the caution and *positivité* (allow me this neologism) of their leading thinkers. However, I think you must have found the state of mind of this people very backward from the theoretical point of view and strangely given to consider things only in the light of their immediate, material usefulness. Especially, with your knowledge of Germany, you must have been struck by this serious defect. It seems to me that our French genius, if one considers its present state among the more intelligent amongst us, unites the two great opposite qualities of these two geniuses of the north, or at least is eminently qualified to effect the union. . . .[26]

D'Eichthal's enthusiasm for the British 'esprit d'association', for the achievements of their middle class in industry and trade also led the young and radical John Stuart Mill to reproach him for failing to see that the British commercial and industrial prowess had, Janus-like, its other face.[27]

> You were very naturally struck with the superiority of the English to the French in all those qualities by which a nation is enabled to turn its productive and commercial resources to the best account. But this superiority is closely connected with the very worst point in our national character, the disposition to sacrifice everything to accumulation, and that exclusive and engrossing selfishness which accompanies it. I am well aware how much of this is owing to our political institutions, under which everything is accessible to wealth and scarcely anything to poverty. But I fear that the commercial spirit, amidst all its good effects, is almost sure to bring with it wherever it prevails, a certain amount of this evil, because that which necessarily occupies every man's time and

---

see 'Matériaux pour servir à la biographie d'Auguste Comte: correspondence d'Auguste Comte et Gustave d'Eichthal', edited with an introduction by Pierre Laffitte, *Revue occidentale*, 1896, 2nd series, vol. xii, pp. 358–61.

[26] Letter from Auguste Comte to Gustave d'Eichthal, 9 December 1828, Pierre Lafitte, *loc. cit.*, pp. 168–73.

[27] In 1835 Cavour described England as 'habité par une race mâle et puissante, grand dans le bien comme dans le mal', cited by Rosario Romeo, *op. cit.*, p. 501.

thoughts for the greater part of his life, naturally acquires an ascendancy over his mind disproportionate to its real importance; and when pursuit of wealth in a degree greater than is required for comfortable subsistence—an occupation which concerns only a man himself and his family—becomes the main object of his life, it almost invariably happens that his sympathies and his feelings on interest become incapable of going much beyond himself and his family.

... Our middle class moreover have but one object in life, to ape their superiors; for whom they have an open-mouthed and besotted admiration, attaching itself to the bad more than to the good points, being those they can most easily comprehend and imitate. It is true that those who wish to do good, are here enabled, by that *esprit d'association* which you so much admire, to effect more, in proportion to their numbers, than they do in France. It is a great fault in your nation to surround themselves as you say with an atmosphere of personal vanity, which makes them desire to get all the honor of everything to themselves, and not to call in the co-operation of others lest they should be compelled to share the credit with them. The fault of your public men certainly is a desire for display. Here it is not so much anxiety of that kind.[28]

Mill's strictures may well be justified, though d'Eichthal's enthusiasm was shared by many other foreign observers around this time. Some of his observations, some of the places he visited were similar to other foreign visitors. Thus he visited London Docks, which attracted a number of observers who gazed in wonder at their animation and size.[29] If d'Eichthal was enthusiastic about the large number of charitable organisations set up on private initiative, so were a number of other French visitors at this time.[30] Like his fellows he noted with interest the hold of religion, especially in Scotland, and commented on the rigours of the British Sunday which Stendhal described as 'ce jour destiné à honorer le ciel est la meilleure image de l'enfer que j'aie jamais vue sur la terre'. He, too, found a lack of enthusiasm for their pastoral duties amongst the Anglican clergy. Nevertheless, there is much in his diary that is interesting and valuable. While most of the foreign observers found British society profoundly religious, d'Eichthal found that

[28] Letter from John Stuart Mill to Gustave d'Eichthal, 15 May 1829, Fonds d'Eichthal, *Bibliothèque de l'Arsenal*, 13756, fo. 2.

[29] Ethel Jones, *op. cit.*, pp. 203–4.

[30] *Ibid.*, pp. 206–7.

for some of the middle classes religious observance was a façade of respectability rather than an act of conviction. D'Eichthal also paid more attention to the condition of the working class, their education, wages, habits than did others. In part his observations mirror contemporary preoccupations like Catholic Emancipation, finally achieved in the year of his visit, reform of the suffrage and local government, the condition of the working class, the reform of the Poor Law and more transitory and fashionable interests like phrenology and popular sermonisers of the day. It could be claimed that d'Eichthal was to some extent a prisoner of his preoccupations and that some of his comments, such as those on the condition of the workers, are too often those of the employers he met or of Francis Place, whose personal knowledge of the proletariat of the new industrialism was notoriously deficient. However, his observations on diverse aspects of a rapidly-changing society are of interest because of his own qualities as an observer, the length of his stay and the wide spectrum of people he met, from bankers and merchants to Radicals and artisans.

BRITISH SOCIETY IN 1828
Gustave d'Eichthal's
Journal and Notes

1 LONDON

29 April In my opinion London is not different from Paris because its streets are busier, and I would claim that the contrary is the case. London's main streets, in the City and the West End, are splendid and very lively, but the others, especially outside the City itself, are silent. Much has been said about the excellence of English machinery, and I think the finest machine is the populace of London. Here everything is done with as little friction and loss of time as possible. Here you do not find the horde of carriages carrying businessmen from one end of the city to the other every morning that you do in Paris. Since everything here is done at a fixed hour and place, many journeys are saved. In the same way the great numbers of dealers in all kinds of second-hand goods who throng the streets of Paris every morning are not to be seen here. Goods are either delivered at home or bought at fixed places. Messengers, boot-blacks and public conveniences are not to be seen either. It appears that on the whole no one is concerned about public well-being. In the inns guests are treated with indifference. There is nothing that resembles our cafés and restaurants. Bath-houses are few in number, though nearly every family has its own bath. In a word, it is impossible to be received with greater cordiality than one usually is by Englishmen in their own homes or in a more surly manner by innkeepers. At ten o'clock in the evening all the shops are closed, except for the numerous cake shops. Carriages and horses travel at a set speed which not even cabs can be persuaded to exceed even by the offer of more money. Carriages for public hire generally have worn-out horses, though there are exceptions, and their turn-out is not as good as I expected. When you take a coach to the outskirts of London you are liable to wait quite a while until the coach is full, and the coachmen make lengthy stops en route.

We went to visit London Docks, built between 1802 and 1805. The original basin can take five hundred ships and is entirely surrounded by warehouses. A second basin has just been completed, below the first and not as large, and a third is planned. The two basins, which occupy twenty and fourteen acres respectively, cost £3 million, of which £800,000 was spent on the second. It is said that the wine celllars of the older basin can hold eighty-one million pipes of wine. We noticed that in the warehouses currently under construction they are using iron pillars with a through section shaped like a cross which have the same strength as solid columns of the same diameter but which cost a quarter less.

We had an introduction to Mr Palmer,[1] engineer of the basin, but in his absence we were shown round by his deputy and then by his foreman.

30 April   We took a boat on the Thames and for *2s* we were taken to Horseferry Stairs. We were going to visit one of the establishments of the London Gas Company situated at Horseferry Road.[2] The works is very impressive and very similar to Mr Pauwels'[3] in Paris, except that the latter is not yet finished.

---

[1] Henry Robinson Palmer worked for many years with Thomas Telford (obituary notice, *The Gentleman's Magazine*, vol. XXII, November 1844). Besides directing the construction of the new London Docks, he also helped Brunel with the Thames tunnel (L. T. C. Rolt, *Thomas Telford*, London, 1958, p. 189; L. T. C. Rolt, *Isambard Kingdom Brunel*, London, 1957, pp. 38–9.
[2] This was the Peter Street gasworks (later renamed Horseferry Road gasworks) of the Gas Light and Coke Co., founded in 1812 (S. Everard, *The History of the Gas Light and Coke Company, 1812–1949*, London, 1949, pp. 38, 97). The French feminist Flora Tristan visited it in 1839 (Jean Baelen, *La Vie de Flora Tristan*, Paris, 1972, pp. 144–8, and C. N. Gattey, *Gauguin's Astonishing Grandmother*, London, 1970, pp. 127–9).
[3] There were two Pauwels in the Parisian gas industry. Pauwels *père* set up a gasworks at No. 20 rue de la Tour-du-Temple in 1822. D'Eichthal is most probably referring to the larger gasworks which Pauwels *fils* was building at 97 faubourg Poissonnière. See *L'Industrie du gaz en France, 1824–1924*, edited on the occasion of the centenary of the French gas industry and the fiftieth anniversary of the founding of the Société technique de l'industrie du gaz, Paris, 1924, pp. 52–8.

The Horseferry works has nineteen gasometers, the largest of which are 44 ft in diameter and 18 ft high. We were told that it supplied 600,000 cubic feet of gas to 24,000 burners and that as much as 720,000 cubic feet of gas had been manufactured in twenty-four hours. We noticed water tanks under the furnaces which serve as a safety precaution and to help the combustion of all the gases in the furnace. Our guide gave us these figures as averages: nine of coke burned to carbonise twelve of coal; twelve of coke resulting from the reduction of nine of coal . . .

1 May We went to visit the tunnel under the Thames with Mr Meyer from Bremen and one of his friends. It has now reached the middle of the river.[4] £150,000 has been spent and as much again will be needed.

Afterwards we went to the West India Docks, which consist of two basins, one for loading and one for unloading. The first basin has an area of thirty acres and can accommodate three hundred vessels, while the second has twenty-four and can accommodate two hundred. We admired the buildings where goods are unloaded and stored as well as the various machines for handling the goods, such as a little trolley for carrying sugar casks, a hook balance to weigh them and a handspike to pull them down, etc.

We attended the dinner given by the Society for Foreigners in Distress. The Duke of Clarence[5] presided and spoke very fluently and even good-naturedly. An annual donation of £100 from the King of France gave him the occasion to talk about him at length. The Duke frequently asserted that he wanted to see a permanent peace between the European powers. M. de Polignac[6] replied in a like manner and was loudly applauded.

You would have to have attended a great number of these dinners to be able to appreciate their usefulness. There is a great deal of drivel in everything that is said at them. They are nevertheless a means of spreading useful ideas, which are always slow to spread. They serve as a centre, as a meeting-place. As for the dinner itself,

[4] The tunnel was not completed until 1842. See D. Lampe, *The Tunnel*, London, 1965.

[5] The future King William IV (1830–7). The Duke of Clarence was patron of the Society of Friends of Foreigners in Distress which held its anniversary dinner at the City of London Tavern, Bishopsgate (*The Times*, 3 May 1828).

[6] French ambassador in London from 1823 to 1829.

it was execrable, badly served, and for wine there were only a few bottles of bad wine and some sherry and port. . . .

2 and 3 May M. Schaezler came for us in a post-chaise to go to Windsor. We went over Hammersmith suspension bridge, a magnificent monument, especially striking for its gracefulness and lightness. To reach Windsor we crossed a beautiful green plain divided up by hedges, as is, I am told, all the countryside in England. We dined at the Castle Inn at Windsor, which was not particularly clean. The ancient or semi-ancient Windsor Castle is not at all remarkable. The old apartments we saw are less than memorable. We were told that those which have recently been renovated and which we did not see are magnificent and that the changes have already cost £1,200,000 and a further £200,000 or £300,000 will still be needed.[7] What was more interesting was the view we had from the great tower, a superb panorama.

Whilst we were going through Windsor Park on our way to Winkfield we saw the giraffe given to the King of England by the Pasha of Egypt. It seems it came to England too young and that it suffered greatly on the voyage, for it is absolutely 'out of joint'.[8]

It was not long before we arrived at Winkfield, at the house of the parson, Mr de Rham,[9] and we quickly realised that what is said about members of the Anglican Church is true.

Mr de Rham is a worthy and charming fellow, but his personality is hardly what we would expect of a man of the cloth. He is very intelligent and well informed, but he has all the humour and the easy manners of a man of the world. Yet he appeared to attach great importance to carrying out the duties of his ministry. He invited us to hear him preach, which he did very well. He gave us

---

[7] The best short account of these alterations is to be found in C. Hibbert, *George IV, Regent and King, 1811–1830*, London, 1973, pp. 269–74. They eventually cost about £900,000. See also A. L. Rowse, *Windsor Castle in the History of the Nation*, London, 1974, pp. 180–98.

[8] According to C. Hibbert, the giraffe 'took the public's fancy' in the summer of 1827, *op. cit.*, p. 278.

[9] William Lewis Rham (1778–1843) was born in Utrecht but came to England while still young. He took holy orders and was vicar at Winkfield from 1808 until his death. He is chiefly remembered for his interest in agriculture, on which he wrote a number of papers. In 1835 he set up a school of industry at Winkfield to teach agricultural methods. (*Dictionary of National Biography*; W. L. Rham, *The Dictionary of the Farm*, London, 1850, also contains a notice of Rham, pp. vii–xii).

a long explanation of the liturgy and the day's service, and finally he told us about the advantages the Protestant religion enjoyed over Catholicism. Bidding us farewell, he asked us to excuse the modest hospitality of his parsonage. He left me uncertain, I confess, as to whether he really wanted to play his rôle of clergyman or whether a real conviction of the importance of his clerical dignity went with his remarkable lack of every other antiquated idea. The second supposition seems the most likely, for so often do men need to have a self-respect that they always find a way of seeing everything that is in their own interest in a favourable light.

Mr de Rham has two benefices, one of which is served by a curate, and which together are worth at least £800.

For dinner he served us vegetables he had been given as tithes. For the most part, however, he has made arrangements to be paid in money, by instalments which are at most seven years. Although he is an intelligent man and this is proof of his desire to be conciliatory, he complained a lot about the rows that his tithes caused him and I found no difficulty in believing him.

From what he said, the conduct of his parishioners is far from exemplary. Doubtless he exaggerated when he told us that sometimes when a girl got married people were heard to exclaim, 'What! She is getting married and she is not pregnant!' The only thing is that when a girl has a child she is constrained, under threat of punishment, to name the guilty party, who is obliged either to marry her or to provide an allowance for the child, who otherwise would be a burden on the parish.

As for the Poor Laws, he told me that in his parish things had greatly improved. Any man with a wife and four children who earns less than 10s a week is entitled to relief from the parish. On the grounds that they are overburdened with taxes, the English masses insist on receiving relief. 'I have as much right to relief from the parish as you have to your tithes', a man from the lower classes told him. It does seem, however, that methods of allocating relief have been improved. The poor rate has been much reduced, and instead of giving the poor relief in money they are made to work on the roads, etc. Mr de Rham has had quite a nice little house built with a pretty garden, and he has two horses, one of which is a pony, a cook and a manservant.

We left Winkfield at two o'clock on Sunday; we skirted Windsor Park and went up St Ann's hill, near Chertsey. From here we had a panoramic view, like that from Windsor Castle, only much more beautiful. . . .

5 May Mr Thomas Tooke had invited me to the dinner of the Society for Political Economy. I saw there Mr Parnell, chairman of the committee on finances, Messrs Malthus, McCulloch, Mill (who took the chair), Cazenove, Torrens and Colonel Thompson.

The dinner passed in a very seemly and quiet manner. No toasts were made. During the dinner there was a lot of discussion of Cobbett's pamphlet against Lord Grenville, which is apparently written in a remarkably acrimonious and biting style.[10]

After dinner two major questions were discussed: (1) whether the rate of profit is lowered by the taxes levied to repay the National Debt; (2) whether the National Debt should be paid off, and what methods might be used to do this.

In the various discussions Mr Tooke always seemed to me to be markedly superior to the others, for he always viewed the question in a realistic way, which is the great strength of businessmen. After him, I was most impressed with Mr Mill. Everything he says is to the point, and he expresses himself marvellously. Torrens is also a man of great intelligence, with a good grasp of the problem, but he has an appalling fear of the disasters that would occur if the National Debt were not repaid. Malthus seemed to me to be a little slow of apprehension. He regards the State as burdened with the Debt where the capital has been destroyed. An accident has deformed his mouth and makes speaking difficult. McCulloch speaks in a broad Scottish accent, has deep-set dark eyes, is very witty and is bald, though still young. He appears to me to have more wit than good judgement, for he quite misunderstood several points.

On the first question it was decided that capitalists' profits were in no way reduced by taxation, these profits being understood as the difference between costs and annual receipts, and supposing that the taxes raised are used to pay off the Debt, but that profit earned by individual capitalists was reduced.

I entirely agree with this view, but the way in which the principle is stated is not quite correct. Properly speaking, it is not the

---

[10] This was William Cobbett's *Noble Nonsense!; or, Cobbett's Exhibition of the Stupid and Insolent Pamphlet of Lord Grenville*, London (1828). William Wyndham, Baron Grenville (1759–1834) had published the first part of an *Essay on the Supposed Advantages of a Sinking Fund*, London, early in 1828.

interest of individuals that is reduced by the levying of these taxes, but since a proportion of all funds is in fact mortgaged to the State's creditors they receive the interest on this. If as well as the taxes the need to pay this interest were also abolished, capitalists would be made richer at the expense of fund-holders but the rate of profit on capital would in no way be increased.

As for the second question, it was fairly generally agreed that the existence of the National Debt did not make the State one penny richer or poorer, if for the present you put aside the expense of levying the taxes that it makes necessary. There was also a general fear concerning the difficulties that might arise during war-time. There was talk of bankruptcy, of ruin, of the example of Holland, etc., and there seemed to be quite general agreement that the National Debt should be got rid of. The English reached this conclusion a good hundred years ago and still have not gone any further. It is the story of the council of mice which wanted to bell the cat. Following much discussion about liquidating the Debt by increasing taxes, Messrs Torrens and Mill spoke at great length and with great seriousness about transferring wealth to stockholders, but Mr Tooke soon criticised this idea by showing the practical difficulties involved in such a scheme. Discussion ended at 10.30 without a way having been found of getting rid of this abominable debt, and the English will long have to groan under the burden which they claim is crushing them.[11]

12 May   We went to visit the exhibition of paintings at Somerset House.[12] . . . There was nothing of note at this exhibition except for the portraits by Sir Thomas Lawrence. Whatever faults this artist may have, it cannot be denied that he has considerable talent for posing his subjects and for producing a likeness. Besides, every noble lord feels he has to have himself, his wife and his children painted by Lawrence, and I was told that he is frequently paid 800 or 1,000 guineas for one of his paintings. Historical paintings are few in number compared with portraits, and I did not see

[11] It was while he was in England that d'Eichthal began to write his book on government finance where he denied that the National Debt was a burden and advocated further government borrowing. This work was published in May 1829 as *Lettres à MM. les Députés composant la commission du budget* . . .

[12] This was the annual Royal Academy exhibition (*The Times*, 6 May 1828).

a single one that I considered memorable. I was rather surprised to see the title of a painting showing a mare in heat written in French.[13] In the catalogue it was entitled *L'Amour du Cheval*. What a chaste people the English are! However, it is not very tactful to any Frenchmen who might perchance go to the exhibition. There was a time when Boileau wrote:

> Le lecteur français veut être respecté
> Du moindre sens impur la liberté l'offense.

This indeed is only one of a thousand examples of English prudery. There are many words which seem very innocent but which are banished from polite conversation. These ladies would need a Molière to correct all the words. What is certain is that their theatre is in no way less free than ours and that they even seem to like *risqué* allusions. It has to be said, though, that under their skirts dancers wear the type of pantaloons worn by Turks, which are cleverly contrived.

To return to the exhibition, we also saw there a small number of sculptures, several of which were very good. When you have been through Westminster and seen all the magnificent monuments to be found in the Abbey you realise that the English are as superior to us in sculpture as we are to them in painting.

After leaving Somerset House we went to see the exhibition near Pall Mall of gouaches or watercolours, I do not know which of the two is the correct term.[14] We were as happy with this exhibition as we had been unhappy with the other. We saw seascapes and landscapes by Copley Fielding and Robson, townscapes by Nash, paintings of Normandy towns by Prout, interiors and subject pictures by Hunt, and pictures of churches by C. Wild. Most of these little paintings look surprisingly well, and it is astonishing how much can be done with such little colour and finish. I believe that watercolours should always be exhibited as they are here: apart from oil paintings. Every painting needs an atmosphere to produce the best effect, and arrangements for showing a watercolour are not the same as for an oil painting.

[13] This was exhibit 302, one of a number of animal paintings by J. Ward. *The Times* said of this that 'everything offensive—and there might have been in vulgar hands much of this description—is avoided and the drawing and execution are beyond all exception of the very first degree'.

[14] This was the exhibition held by the Society of Painters in Watercolours which opened on 20 April.

In the evening I went to Drury Lane with a young American from our table at the hotel. The auditorium is very beautiful and there are no balconies. Like all London theatres, it is very well maintained; dust covers are put on the columns and the fronts of the boxes after each performance. The auditorium is redecorated almost every year—it is more necessary to do this in London than elsewhere. The theatres are usually badly lit, the chandelier is too small and badly placed. On the first row of boxes there are fittings lit by gas or candles. The theatres manufacture their own lighting from oil, and no bad smell is given off. Box tickets cost 7s, stall tickets 3s 6d, and it costs ——[15] in the gallery above, which is where all the rabble go, or what they call here 'John Bull'. It is in fact the ruling element in the audience and it commands respect. Intervals here are only a few minutes long. Since ladies are in the pit, especially respectable women from the middle class, the pit cannot play the same role as it does in Paris. Theatres, moreover, are the haunt of prostitutes, who parade to and fro in the foyers and corridors. They are not allowed in the first-tier boxes, however.

I was at Drury Lane for six hours, from seven in the evening until one o'clock in the morning. First of all I saw *William Tell*, a five-act drama, the main theme of which, as far as I recollect, is taken from Schiller, whilst another part of the play, which has not the slightest connection with the rest, has practically the same plot as *The Barber of Seville*. In this hotch-potch Macready, who played Tell, was very impressive. His acting is very elaborate, and one is too aware of it, but he never shocks and is often convincing, for he is always restrained and a master of his rôle.[16] But he was poorly supported, especially by the two actresses who figured in the secondary plot, and looked like two aged marionettes. . . .

The dress of London ladies can be gauged from the attire of actresses. In this regard most actresses are well dressed, though among them are to be found a few dresses and especially hairstyles that recall the ladies of 1815. A stay in London bears out this assertion.

The second play was called *The Dumb Savoyard and his Monkey*.

---

[15] Blank in the text.
[16] Macready was in J. Sheridan Knowles' play at the Drury Lane until 23 May (*Macready's Reminiscences and Selections from his Diaries and Letters* by Sir Frederick Pollard, New York, 1875, p. 250). Macready had played Tell in Paris in April and had been much applauded (Alan S. Downer, *The Eminent Tragedian*, Cambridge, Mass., 1966, p. 115).

I will be forgiven for forgetting how many acts it had. It is just the vehicle for the antics of a man dressed in a monkey costume. However, Monsieur —— is very inferior to Mazurier, and *Toco* is a masterpiece of good sense compared with the *Dumb Savoyard*. The sets for the play are extremely elaborate, which is a marked taste with the English, and it must be said that they usually pay more attention to stage setting than we do, except at the Opéra. In this play an ingenious way of multiplying the scenery has been devised. When the boat is supposed to be moving the backcloth moves but the boat does not. The evening ended with an extravaganza. This is what it passed for, but an extravaganza should not have two acts, which is what *Don Juan* in London has. The play also has the defects of being pure caricature without any humour at all. The English always like their comedy heavy.

I will now describe Covent Garden, which I saw the following day. *School for Scandal* was being presented. Kemble played Charles Surface, Warde Joseph Surface, ——[17] Sir Peter Teazle and Miss Chatterley Lady Teazle. The central plot has some similarities with *Tartuffe* but the characters are placed higher up the social scale and have the language and manners of high society. The play can thus be acted only by players of good breeding, and in this respect the actors I saw left nothing to be desired. I doubt whether at the moment one could see a play so well acted in Paris. The second piece, *The Invincibles*, is a copy of a French play which, I think, is called *Les Femmes en garnison*. Its principal merit lies with a group of seven pretty women who, to be with their lovers, join the army and go on parade. Those I saw did very well. The play is spiced, in the English manner, by the presence of a retired Irish soldier serving in the French army who regales the audience with all the maxims and phrases generally ascribed to his countrymen.

Finally on Thursday I went to Coburg's Theatre at the other end of Waterloo bridge. Here they put on roughly the same kind of melodramas that we have in France and of about the same quality. I saw half a real melodrama, *The Spanish Banditti*, and half another, *Henry IV; or, The Old Time of Paris*. I was a little put out by the swaggering air given to our worthy king, but I was pleased with the way in which his personality was depicted and above all appreciated by the audience. Included in the play were the best known of Henri IV's sayings, and they were as favourably received

[17] Blank in the text.

by this foreign audience as they would have been by my com-
patriots. The play's author did not forget the help Elizabeth sent to
Henri IV, and a review of the English army was depicted. The
announcement of this episode—made by placard—doubtless helped
to create a favourable disposition towards Henri IV among the
audience, for the English love to find themselves everywhere. The
curtain at Coburg's Theatre depicts the death of Nelson. The
composition of the picture is good, and the last moments of Nelson
dying victorious are perfectly portrayed. I must confess that this
patriotic painting was what interested me most at Coburg's
Theatre.[18]

14 May This was the day Mr Donat had fixed to visit an infant
school with us. The average age of the pupils is about four years
and they belong to the poorest class in London. They are brought
to the school more to keep them amused and to take them off their
parents' hands than to instruct them, though they do learn to read,
count and sing. The school is run by two women and certainly only
women are capable of giving the necessary care to children of this
age, since they alone have the required patience. We were delighted
with the behaviour, the happy, contented appearance of these little
children. Particular attention is given to teaching the children to
behave correctly towards one another, and this certainly should be
the most important objective in every school of whatever level,
though in practice it is regarded as of minor importance. Parents
are asked above all to send their children to school clean. They
come at 9.30 in the morning and leave at 5.00 in the evening, having
worked five hours out of seven or eight. This school, like all schools
in England, is maintained by private subscription.

On leaving the school Mr Donat was kind enough to take us to
one of these poor quarters of London hemmed in between rich
areas. This particular quarter takes its name from the Houndsditch
which runs behind Mr Donat's house. We went down Petticoat
Lane[19] and several of the adjacent streets. This area is the haunt

---

[18] Most French visitors to London at this time made pilgrimages to the
theatre, for British theatre, and above all Shakespeare and actors like
Kean, Kemble and Macready, were growing in popularity in the Paris of
the 1820s, J. L. Borgerhof, *Le Théâtre anglais à Paris sous la Restauration*,
Paris, 1912.

[19] The popular name for Middlesex Street, London E1, now noted for
its Sunday morning street market.

of the most dreadful vice and poverty. It is claimed in London that you cannot pass through these streets without being jeered, assaulted and robbed, chiefly because of the large numbers of poor prostitutes who throng the alleyways of these streets and the people they attract. Mr Donat says that this is not true, at least nowadays. He advised us, however, to button up our frock-coats, for fear that our white waistcoats made us appear too much like gentlemen, and, as an extra precaution, he had us carry in our hands one of the little books of the Society for Foreigners in Distress, of which he is a member. It was in this capacity that he took us into several dwellings of the poor. Although these were foreigners we were able to judge the natives from seeing their houses since they had all lived some time in England and had even married here. We saw Dutchmen, Germans, an Arab and above all a large number of Jews who seemed to control the commerce of the colony. I repeat that these streets are peopled only by the poor, people who are prevented from earning enough for their upkeep from their labour through illness, some vice or other circumstances of whatever kind. Workers in employment, except for a few unfortunate Irishmen, do not live here.

The streets are of disgusting appearance. They are either very badly paved or entirely unpaved. In many parts there are no drains, and several streets are extremely narrow. In short, I think it is worse than anything I have ever seen in Paris, except that even in these streets you do not find the practice of throwing rubbish on to the public highway as you do in Paris. The lack of improvements in these localities doubtless stems from the absence of any central administration in London. Since each parish is left to its own devices, the poorest of them cannot meet the needs of their inhabitants.

The interiors of the houses I saw were what could be called clean, bearing in mind there was so much poverty. In each room there was a complete set of kitchen utensils. Tea drinking is quite widespread among this class. Mr Donat is sure that tea is a cheaper beverage than any other These people are believed to eat a lot of potatoes They no longer eat any but wheaten bread, and I think the same is true in all the towns where the middle class eats this quality of bread. I have seen this myself in Paris and Le Hâvre. Would it not be an economy to eat a cheaper bread?

In this quarter rent for a single room is 2s a week. Supposing the rent is equivalent to one tenth of total expenditure, which is an underestimation, this would be 20s a week or £56 a year (1,400 francs). This sum, however, is not sufficient, certainly for a family with children. At least it would not be in Paris, where a family could not subsist or live decently on less than 1,500 to 2,000 francs.

We would have liked to visit the homes of the silk workers which are nearby at Spitalfields. Except during times of commercial crisis, when their poverty is sometimes extreme, these are a much more prosperous group than the one we have just described. But since they are currently up in arms because there is talk of lowering the duties on imported silks and are seeking a meeting with the government to make representations, Mr Donat, fearing they might accost him, declined to act as our guide. It seems that these workers understand the questions they discuss as well as anyone and that nobody knows how to secure a reply from the government better than they.

15 May I accompanied Adolphe to Woodford. All I will note about this little trip is the ease with which the English on top of stagecoaches enter into conversation, at least with foreigners, especially on political questions. A gentleman whom I had addressed asked if I were French and immediately began to hold forth on the reasons why the two countries would always be rivals. It was not long before he came to the question of Catholic Emancipation and he spoke about it most moderately. Mr Hookes at Woodford had already talked to me about it from the point of view of a member of the Established Church, as had Mrs Hookes as an intelligent woman. It seems to me that the problem, reduced to its most simple form by the opposition papers, 'Are we strong enough to prevent the Catholics from taking up arms to gain their rights?', is beginning to be widely understood. Equally, it is felt that the first step that needs to be taken is to remove the absolute interdiction on any government agreement with Rome. It is generally realised that Catholic Emancipation is only the prelude to more important changes in the constitution and that it is more than anything else an indication of the declining importance of the Established Church.

16 May At three o'clock I went to the Mansion House to see the public examination of pupils from the National Schools of the City of London, which took place in the Egyptian Hall, a superb hall surrounded by a colonnade. The public, made up in large part of ladies, were seated on stepped seats (three tiers) placed against the columns. At the head of the hall, along with several high-ranking persons and the little Duke of Cumberland, were the bishops of London, Chester and ——. The children from the different classes of all the schools were summoned one after the other. Some of the pupils wore uniforms while others did not, and those who did not were rather poorly dressed. The entire examination turned on the Catechism and the Bible, apart from one simple bit of arithmetic. When each class had been examined separately, all the children— about a thousand altogether—were brought in, a prayer was said and then the Bishop of London made a speech. In this country clergymen do not wear a calotte but a wig, and a very comical one which is short and resembles those worn by elderly figures of fun in our comedies. The Bishop of London wears his peruke down over his eyes. He has very little eloquence and it was clear that his colleagues and his listeners were on the rack, while for my part I had difficulty preventing myself bursting into laughter. He ended his speech, as do his *confrères* on the Continent, complaining about the frequent attacks made on religion and by expressing satisfaction that in such trying times his young listeners appeared so well versed in the principles of the Established Church. Indeed, the National Schools in London have Anglican religious instruction, while instruction in the other schools is non-denominational.

22 May ... The French are a fraternal people and, the Jesuits excepted, we bear no one any malice. But here it is distressing to find oneself among a people torn by so many different enmities. There are, first of all, those who are Europeans and those who are insular. There are the English, the Scots and the Irish. There are the Catholics and the Protestants and among the latter there are the upper and lower clergy and the Established Church and Dissenters. There is the aristocracy and the middle class. There are the country gentlemen and the commercial interest. There are masters and men. There are, finally, those who own property and those who do not, not forgetting the Hindus in the East Indies and the Negroes in the West Indies who also have their spokesmen in this hubbub of recriminations. And though for the moment these diverse interests seem to have adjourned the battle and engage only

in skirmishes, it is still a sorry sight for a lover of peace. Evidence
of this civil war is to be seen everywhere, even when you go out for
a walk. You see fine hedges and beautiful gardens but everywhere
there are notices that warn that a spring-trap or gun awaits any
unfortunate who might be tempted to go over the wall, or else
threats of legal action are used against those who might do any
damage and a reward offered to the informer who reports the
malefactor.

23 May We went with Adolphe to see the Asylum for the Orphan
Children of Clergymen near the other end of Regent's Park.[20] Fifty
children are taught in this school, thanks to private subscriptions.
This happened to be the day of the public examination. First we
saw the boys and noticed how well-behaved they were. Afterwards
we saw the little girls and we were immediately struck by their
dress, which was extremely plain and even unusual. They wore a
simple chemise, made of brown material with short sleeves and cut
low on the chest, and their hair was short and sleek. The custom
of not overdressing young girls is undoubtedly one of the reasons
for the beauty of English women. Nevertheless, it can be imagined
that the orphans' uniform I have described is not at all becoming
and some of the girls had to be really beautiful to appear to be so
in that garb. While we were there the examination dealt with
Roman history; there were a large number of different questions
on this subject and the pupils always showed a great deal of intelligence in their replies.

25 May Adolphe returned to Woodford and I went to call for
Chasseloup so we could go a walk together. To get there I had to
go through Drury Lane, Broad Street and High Street, an area
with a very impoverished population. In London such areas are
situated right in the middle of the finest parts of town, because not
long ago they formed quarters which major rebuilding has subsequently radically altered. The inhabitants are of disgusting
appearance, nothing could be more unhealthy, dirtier or more
repugnant. In the alehouses were large crowds, chiefly composed of
women. These women are a sight to be seen as they gulp down

[20] The Clergy Orphan School, run by the Rev. Thomas Wharton and
Mrs Jones, held its annual public examination on 23 May (*The Times*,
27 May 1828).

their glasses of gin, whisky, toddy and cheap brandy, and some of them smoke pipes. Two or three men and as many women were asleep on the pavement.

Last evening on our way back from Clapham we witnessed a no less curious but more interesting spectacle. It is on a Saturday evening that workers do their shopping for the following day and even for all the next week and the butchers', bakers', greengrocers' and ironmongers' shops were a most fascinating sight.

I went with Chasseloup to Primrose Hill, behind Regent's Park, which overlooks the park and all London. Regent's Park . . . is just one immense lawn with a path bordered by clumps of trees all round. It is now almost entirely surrounded by a wall of fine buildings which have been built recently, a large number of which are still for rent. This wall of buildings can be fully appreciated from Primrose Hill, since the green of the park can be seen and the view is magnificent. It reminds me of those Indian and Persian buildings which are often seen in engravings. The view of the immense London plain is also very beautiful but a clear day is needed to enjoy it, and these are rare accidents in this country. Views of London have one advantage over those of Paris, and that is that the greenery is more beautiful and that since there are no stone quarries on the outskirts of the city, outlying villages do not form a mass of white.

We went as far as Hampstead where we boarded a stagecoach that brought us back to London. I entered into conversation with the driver who assured me he hated piety and the pious, nine-tenths of whom he said were the greatest ne'er-do-wells in the world. He was then kind enough to show me a tavern which was the haunt of all the boxers and where you can learn the place of the next fight, which is always kept secret for fear of the magistrates.

26 May I attended the dinner given by the Westminster electors to celebrate their success in the elections.[21] The meal was given at the Crown and Anchor Tavern on the corner of the Strand. The price of a ticket was 14s and some three hundred people were there. Sir Francis Burdett was in the chair, with Hobhouse, his fellow member of Parliament, by his side.[22] This is the classic territory

[21] This was the twenty-first anniversary dinner (*The Times*, 27 May 1828).

[22] For John Cam Hobhouse (1786–1869), later Baron Broughton of

of the Radical or Reforming party. The dinner was very good and was disposed of remarkably quickly. It was quite clear that no one would be able to make a clean sweep of all abuses better than these people.[23]

The meal over, which it quickly was, the health of the people was drunk, then that of the King, *provided he behaved*, then that of Burdett. Afterwards Burdett climbed on top of the table, the usual rostrum at this kind of dinner, and harangued the gathering. It would take too long to repeat in detail all he and his colleagues, Hobhouse and Dawson[24] (an Irish member), said. All I can assure you[25] is that they are absolutely right and that, moreover, I found in their speeches nearly all the conclusions I have reached during my stay in England, several of which I have previously written about in letters to you.

Sir F. Burdett, Westminster's favourite son, though noble blood and £40,000 in private income greatly moderates his radicalism, felt it necessary this year to hold forth a little longer.

You would not believe the way in which he and the others described the House of Commons: a nest of intrigue, a corruption, the reef where the best intentions are broken etc. 'It is a relief', said Burdett, 'to leave that assembly of actors and to find myself among such enlightened people, so solicitous for the public good as the electors of Westminster.' He then drew their attention to the Catholic question, a question which should rather be called a Protestant question because it is most important for the welfare of the majority of the nation. Would not Emancipation mean that the army of 35,000 men currently maintained in Ireland would no longer be needed and would it not better relieve the country than any finance committee? 'In the House of Commons', he went on, 'we have committees, inquiries, reports of all kinds, we discuss and we publish! All this is pure deception; for ever inquiries but never reforms.' Then he came to the subject of the different kinds of privilege and monopoly to be found in England: the aristocracy, the House of Commons, the country gentlemen, the Church, the

---

Broughton de Gyfford, see M. Joyce, *My Friend H*, London, 1948, where there is an account of the disorderly nature of the Westminster political dinner of 1827 (pp. 193–4) and Robert E. Zegger, *John Cam Hobhouse: A Political Life, 1819–1852*, Columbia, Miss., 1973.

[23] 'table nette' in the text.

[24] Alexander Dawson, M.P. for County Louth in Ireland.

[25] These remarks are addressed to d'Eichthal's father.

municipalities, the Parish overseers, the poor of the Parish, all of which exist on some kind of monopoly. It appears that the lowest are the highest and that their numbers have multiplied rapidly all over England. He concluded by declaring that a reform of the electoral system was the only way to put an end to this system of deception.

Hobhouse in turn climbed on to the table and with the grestures and delivery of an actor spoke in a more openly radical style. The most biting part of his speech was a very lively survey of the four administrations that have followed each other in the last year and which are about to be succeeded by a fifth. 'It would appear', he said, 'that our ministers are elected like the Popes, on account not of their ability but of their poor health. Lord Liverpool dies, Mr Canning dies. Lord Harrowby turns down a post through ill health, the Duke of Portland gives the same reason. Lord Goderich accepts after wanting to step down because of his poor health six months before and after six weeks he is forced to resign, and who is chosen? A man who six months previously had declared in Parliament itself that he ought to be regarded as mad if ever he accepted the post (the Duke of Wellington)! Does England not have men capable of holding the reins of government then? Undoubtedly, but at present ability is not taken into consideration. It is the number of votes a man has in the one House and the other, it is one's attitude for or against the Catholics etc. The wishes of the people count for nothing.' Finally, he apologised for his silence in the House of Commons. 'What can five or six individuals do', he said, 'against an overwhelming majority? If you always stand with your fists clenched ready to strike, your blow will be ineffective at the decisive moment and your posture will be ridiculous.'

In his turn the famous Hunt spoke.[26] As his purpose was to annoy F. Burdett by reminding him of his old opinions, which had been much more radical than they are today, he had great difficulty making himself heard above the baronet's friends. But in the end his challenges were so temperate and polite that he finally managed to make himself heard. What has happened to the time when the honourable baronet, on the hustings of St James, called the House

<hr>

[26] Henry Hunt (1773–1835) the Radical reformer; see *Dictionary of National Biography*. There is no modern life of Hunt, but there is a good deal about his character and conduct in R. Walmsley, *Peterloo: The Case Reopened*, Manchester, 1969.

of Commons 'that house on the other side of the street' where he
said 'he was ashamed to enter, having no liking for keeping bad
company at all hours of the night'?[27] Speaking of the Whigs and
Tories he said that 'they had crucified the constitution between
two thieves'. He then reproached Sir Francis with more important
wrongs than changes in language and he sat down with more signs
of approval than when he had stood up. Hunt is very handsome
with a fine head of fair hair, a very gentle face, the exact appearance of a parasite. For several years he has been a polish manufacturer and has become much more moderate.

Sir Francis Burdett rose amidst thunderous applause and, since
he is an orator of charm and grace, he found no difficulty in overcoming Hunt's feeble attack.

Mr Dawson, member for Louth in Ireland, topped off the evening. He expressed satisfaction that Catholic Emancipation was near
to being attained, for as long as this preliminary issue was not
settled all the other improvements were impossible. He was particularly pleased to see this question settled for good so as to put
an end to all religious strife and quibbling. 'What do they matter
to us, transubstantiation and all the substantiations in the world,
purgatory and Papacy, and all those fads! Let every man go to
Heaven in his own way and let us attend to matters temporal. Let
us concern ourselves with the taxes, the government, the finances
and the industry of this world. And let us leave the priests to settle
their quarrels as they will.' I believe that nothing was better received that evening. There is good reason for being surprised by
the success of such opinions when you see the apparent respect the
English show for religious matters. But in fact religion is a matter
of habit for most people. They go to church for something to do on
a Sunday, as we go for walks, and because it is not the done thing
to stay away. On the other hand those who are dependent on the
clergy for relief also affect a religious exterior. There is a great deal
of sham in all this. A young Englishman said to Adolphe the other
day, 'we are still under the thumb of Cromwell but this will not
last much longer.'

The fact is that for the last six years the English people seem to
have been little concerned about the future. They are busy with

[27] The words Hunt actually used were 'the house over that way' which
he claimed Sir Francis Burdett declared he did not wish to enter because
'he disliked bad company and bad hours' (*The Times*, 27 May 1828).

their own affairs, and precisely because individual prosperity is quite good it is impossible to attempt a reform. It is known, Hobhouse said, that the administration is just a team of mules that the aristocracy uses to tow its own waggon. So long as circumstances do not alter, the nature of the different administrations is of little import since they can do neither much good nor much harm. Only Canning had succeeded in breaking the power of this phalanx of enemies of the commonweal who used their extensive power to block every proposed reform. But Canning died in the effort! However, this apparent apathy among the general public is more apparent than real. The liberal reforming party is to be found here as it was in France on the eve of the Revolution, and so is the system of privilege which extends from the aristocracy right down to the village. The struggle is between these two parties. For the past year petty intrigues have been able to make and unmake ministries without the national interest counting for anything in any of these arrangements. Yet the slightest difficulty in England's affairs would breath life into this party and I would be very surprised if they did not end up here with another Constituent Assembly, though I would not wish to claim that the excesses of the French Revolution will be repeated. It is the memory of these excesses which up to now has halted the advance of Reform, but the abuses of the present system, ever more widely felt, could well give them victory in the first crisis to hit England. The aristocracy is fully aware of this and of the number of slights it has had to suffer from foreign powers to remain at peace. The Radicals are also fully aware of this and I regret I cannot give you a translation of the issue of Cobbett's paper which follows the one I have quoted, where commenting on M. Laffitte's speech he pours sarcasm on the English government by describing its foreign policy over the last six years.

A period of peace and calm is the only way that reform could be made gradually but this is just when those with privilege are least inclined to make concessions. There is a striking instance of this in the latest government changes. The Tories have thrown out Mr Huskisson and his friends in a shameful way, and it appears that they want to replace them by what are called High Tories. Tories of the 'order of Melchizedek' as *The Times* called them. The latter are the equivalent of our Ultras and will do anything to follow the same path.

I persist in believing that England will not play a major rôle in the affairs of the Continent. It is too preoccupied with domestic questions. At the Radicals' dinner I attended, not a single word was said on foreign policy except to ask what was to become of England with such a government when storms were brewing.

If the Aberdeens and those whose names are being mentioned really enter the government they will be helpful for Metternich, but I doubt that they will be for long.

29 May In company with Mr William Hawes,[28] master soap-boiler, I went over the houses of several of his workpeople.

As a rule, these houses have a cellar and three storeys above ground, but not more than one or two windows in each storey. As a rule, too, the worker and his family retain the use of the ground floor and the cellar, and let out the upper floors. At the rear is a small courtyard, but so tiny as hardly to deserve the name. The houses are clean but scantily furnished; the beds do not have much bedding. In practically all these houses a clock on the mantelpiece or on the wall seems to be an object of prime necessity. They have privies which are kept clean.

In the poverty-stricken hovel, occupied by an Irishman, about which I shall speak later, I saw meat and potatoes prepared for his son's dinner. It appears that even the Irish, who earn the lowest wages of all, and who are not very thrifty, eat meat once a day. The Irish are notorious for dirt and untidiness. Those I saw, with two exceptions (and the wife of one of these was an Englishwoman), did not deserve this reputation, at least not in my opinion. Their rooms were very neat and tidy.

As for the better-class English workmen, they eat meat with every meal (maybe about a pound); they also consume two pounds of bread [each] per day.

The length of the working day is generally from six o'clock in the morning to six o'clock in the evening, making ten hours of actual work,[29] to which one or two further hours [of overtime] in

---

[28] William Hawes (1805–85), along with his brother Benjamin (1797–1862) and their father Benjamin Hawes senior (1770–1860), operated the family soapworks in Upper Ground Street, Blackfriars. F. Boase, *Modern English Biography*, vol. I, 1892, 2nd impression, 1965. Benjamin Hawes senior was governor, i.e. chairman, of the Gas Light and Coke Co. from 1851 to 1860 (Everard, *op. cit.*, pp. 191–201).

[29] I.e. allowing two hours for meals.

the evening are usually added. The lowest paid workers in the employ of Mr Hawes get 18s, those of next highest grade, 21s, and so on up to the skilled engineers and foremen, whose normal wage may be as high as 36s a week; with overtime and night work this may be increased to 40s or 50s.

1st [*visit*]. House of an engineer working a ten-hour day and earning 36s a week. Although he is very often ill, he has perhaps £40 to £50 saved up; the rent of his house is 10 guineas a year or 4s 6d a week. His bedroom and kitchen appeared to be extremely comfortable.

2nd [*visit*]. House of an engineer earning 24s a week, including overtime and night work; rent of his house 5s a week; he rents off the first floor at 3s a week and two beds on the second floor, both of which are occupied by two men, who each pay 18d a week.[30]

3rd [*visit*]. W——,[31] a foreman, showed us his house, part of which serves as a shop kept by his wife. They are what you might call very respectable people. There are six rooms from the ground floor upwards, of which he lets out four, keeping for his own use the kitchen and ground floor. His rent is £26 per annum. It would be £32 or £33 if a seedy neighbourhood did not tend to reduce rents in that street.

4th [*visit*]. Finally we saw two hovels occupied by Irishmen; their wives and their lodgers were most disgusting creatures, and the greatest filth pervaded the rooms. They let out the two upper rooms. There were two men to a room and each paid 1s 6d a week. The loose life of these men was the cause of their poverty. W—— told me that a man and his wife with four children could easily live on 80 guineas a year, provided that the wife was a good housekeeper.

Elementary schools. The Benevolent Society of St Patrick, near Old Bargehouse. This Society was founded by Irish noblemen for the children of the poor Irish living in London. The school contains between 200 and 250 boys and 100 girls. The annual expenditure is about £1,500, of which £800 comes from dividends on Government stock and £700 in subscriptions.

The children are provided with stockings, shoes and even their clothes; they are [eventually] put out as apprentices for a considera-

[30] '18s' in original, which is clearly an error for '18d'.
[31] Illegible in the text.

tion of £5 and receive £5 on coming out of their time, if they have behaved themselves properly. These children come from all parts of London. Considering that they come from the most poverty-stricken class in the metropolis, they appear to be in very good health and are not badly dressed. They attend school from 9 a.m. to 2 p.m.; they learn reading, writing and arithmetic; anything that smacks of religious instruction is avoided and children from all communions are admitted.

Mr Palmer, engineer of the London Docks,[32] tells me that, among the workers in manufacturing industry, three classes are to be distinguished corresponding to degrees of skill; that the new class in the manufacturing towns is quite brutalised, and that it is much inferior with respect to intelligence and manners to the working class which he knew formerly.

He told me that the Spitalfield operatives, the silk weavers, are really a kind of self-employed small master; and that they are, indeed, intelligent and well-informed; but that if power-weaving of silk is introduced, and there have been attempts made at this already, it will be on the cards that these workers will be forced down to the level of cotton weavers.

The wages of the workers at St Katherine's Docks are 21s for six days' labour for twelve hours a day. The journeymen employed in Mr Hawes' soapery get the same rate. M. Castellain's[33] gardener at Clapton, the same. Wages rise in proportion to the greater skill of the worker to 24s–28s and more.

M. [Marc Isambard] Brunel complains of the extravagant tastes of the workers. They give their children hot rolls and fresh butter for lunch, which means an enormous consumption of fresh butter. They must have tea, sugar, etc.

The wages of menservants vary from 20s to 25s, those of cooks from 16s to 20s, those of maids from 21s to 16s. But the custom of boarding means that their real wages are in fact much higher. They must have roast meat, puddings, etc. In a house where soup featured on the bill of fare every day, I was told that boiled beef never appeared on the servants' table. I was [also] told that servants would never agree to filling up teapots used by their master and mistress, they must have a fresh brew, together with best quality sugar, etc.

I was told that when workers marry, as they often do, girls who

[32] See above p. 14, n. 1.   [33] See below, p. 45, n. 45.

have been in service, this leads them to adopt the same expensive tastes. These same day-labourers who receive a guinea a week are forced to pay 3s a week for a room. The cheap truckle beds in Petticoat Lane cost 2s a week.

The wages of a good journeyman tailor are 36s a week.

Prices of various things in London. A three-storey house two windows across in Bridge Street, Blackfriars, rents at £260 [per annum] with taxes; a house with three storeys and three windows at each level, in Richmond Terrace, Whitehall, £600. A family house in the ordinary West End streets costs at least £200 [per annum]. A coat costs £4 10s, a fancy overcoat £4 10s, a nice waistcoat in goatskin 18s, a good pair of trousers from 21s to 24s. These prices are not those of a fashionable tailor, where you will pay as much as they like to charge. A pair of riding boots costs £2 2s, a pair of shoes 12s to 15s, but you can see in ordinary shoemakers' shops [ready-made] shoes for sale at 8s or 9s a pair and they seem quite substantial and well made.

Note on laundry charges

A shirt	5d
Cravat	2d
Handkerchief, socks	1d
Waistcoat	4d
Trousers	6d

You can hardly dine at a tavern (without wine) for less than 3s or 4s.

You can live 'en pension', with your own bedroom and plenty of food for £70 a year.

A bedroom and drawing room in Arundel Street or thereabouts costs no less than 25s or 30s [a week]. People who let out furnished rooms almost always provide meals when desired. The charge is generally 1s 6d for lunch and 3s for dinner, or £1 10s a week.

30 May   London Debating Society at the Freemasons Tavern.[34] I was taken here by Mr Tooke and John [Stuart] Mill. The subject of debate was: *legislation against cruelty to animals.*[35]

[34] On the foundation in 1825 of the London Debating Society and on Mill's part in its debates, see John Stuart Mill, *Autobiography*, London, 1873, pp. 125–9.

[35] This was a matter much discussed in the 1820s. The only law for the protection of animals was Richard Martin's Act, passed in 1822. The

The person who initiated the discussion began by examining the following definition of the purpose of government: *the greatest happiness of the greatest number*, and after having spoken against it, came down in favour of the following definition: *the maintenance of the social order*. Given this proposition, government ought to intervene to stop acts of cruelty to animals, if these acts might cause some harm to society; if these acts of cruelty merely encouraged a propensity which could lead to the commission of criminal acts, this propensity could not be under the control of government. In addition, this propensity could not be corrected by a system of repression, given that the speaker took it for granted that every penal system has the effect of encouraging rather than discouraging crime.

The next speaker seized this opening to deal with the Church, and to praise Lord Eldon and Viscount Castlereagh, to the greatest amusement of the meeting.

A third speaker spoke against the legislation [against cruelty to animals] for the following three reasons: (1) that the punishment inflicted on the individual was proportionately greater than the hurt inflicted on society; (2) that the penalties were ineffectual; (3) that the end could be achieved by other means, namely by a good education.

A fourth participant made the point that *for the moment* (it was useless to speak of what the state of affairs might be in the future) the mass of the people were not sufficiently educated for it to be possible to persuade them to treat animals gently; that a law could be useful and that the existing law had had some effect. The ridiculous Irish custom of attaching horses' tails [to the plough] would still exist if it had not been suppressed by law; that people in London who caught cats for the sake of their skins deserved to be punished, not because of the fact they made a trade of it but because they left the skinned carcasses in the streets and thereby affronted the public gaze by a disgusting spectacle.

A fifth speaker called for a definition of the word cruelty: should the hunting and shooting of the great landlords be classed as acts of cruelty? did the fights between animals which drew such crowds of people differ in any essential from such recreations?

Royal Society for the Prevention of Cruelty to Animals was founded in 1824. See Shevawn Lynham, *Humanity Dick: A Biography of Richard Martin, M.P., 1754–1834*, London, 1975.

A sixth member complained that up to now no one had spoken of the *rights of animals*; and observed that philosophers had recognised in animal natures mental faculties very like those of human beings; and that if it were claimed that the inferior quality of faculties of animals deprived them of all rights, the same reasoning could be extended to cover a part of the human race.

Mr Mill spoke last; he admitted that the law was right and proper in principle, but he regarded its enforcement as impracticable, because it was very often impossible to determine up to what point ill-treatment was more or less necessary. But Mr Mill did not confine himself to stating his opinion in these perfectly reasonable terms. He took up one by one all the points raised in the course of the evening, even those which had only a tenuous connection with the subject under debate, and on each he gave an expression of opinion full of good sense and moderation and quite divorced from dogmatic principles. In this way he reviewed what had been said on the subject of the rights of animals, on the rights of man over them, on the effect of penalties, of changes in moral attitudes and legislation, etc. Never before have I heard a speech in which I would not have wished to quarrel with one iota.

I attended another meeting of this society on Friday 13 June [1828]. The question under debate was: *Should the government of India be left in the hands of the [East India] Company?* Such at least is what I took to be the question for it was not clearly posed by anyone. I discovered the same general defect as on the first occasion, that is to say, a fondness for indulging in generalities and a great disregard for facts, springing no doubt from the ignorance of the members. I found the same hostility towards the government and also the same fondness for raising cheap laughs and giving an amusing turn to the discussion, which, I must confess, surprised and charmed me. Speakers never missed an opportunity for some declaration of truly liberal principles and to have a dig at opponents.

1 June   I had been invited to lunch by Mr Benjamin Hawes, Mr Brunel's son-in-law. He is director of a savings bank and had been kind enough to promise me some information on this subject. At present the total amount of government bonds held by savings banks amounts to £14,000,000 which is one-fiftieth of all bonds. As in France, domestic servants, and women especially, constitute the largest group of depositors. Since the English savings banks have not taken the wise precaution of transferring the bonds to their depositors, as have ours, they are quite often exposed to heavy demands for withdrawals. It is true, though, that if the bonds fall in value, the government rather than the banks bears the loss since it credits them with the full amount of their investment. Mr Hawes told me that they are currently assailed with withdrawal requests and do not really know the reason for this. It is possibly because the popular press is raising fears of war.

After lunch I went to Westminster Abbey with Mrs Hawes and heard an extremely boring sermon on the concept of God in three natures. Whatever might be said about them, preachers in England are very interested in dogma and some of the laity also seem to be very interested in it. In the Edinburgh papers you see accounts of Mr Irving's sermons where he explains the Apocalypse and compares the Flood with baptism,[36] and supplements to the *Dublin Gazette* are devoted to the deliberations of the assembly of Protestant theologians on the 'Perpetuity of the Visible Church'.

After church Mr and Mrs Hawes took me first to the studios of the sculptors Westmacott and Chantrey and then to the studio of Varley, the painter in watercolours.[37] Westmacott is famous, among other things, for doing the bad, execrable statue of Achilles in Hyde Park,[38] erected in honour of the Duke of Wellington by English ladies. I saw several good things in his studio but nothing outstanding. The most remarkable thing was an eighteen-foot vase on which a representation of the Battle of Waterloo had been sculpted in bas-relief. The marble used to make this vase had been bought by Bonaparte for a similar purpose and had fallen into English hands. At Chantrey's[39] studio I saw a lot of good busts and several

[36] Edward Irving (1792–1834), Scottish preacher of considerable oratory and millennarian outlook. Early in 1828 Irving published his *Lectures on Baptism* and in May undertook a tour of Scotland, proclaiming the imminence of the Second Coming. His sermons attracted much attention in the press (*Dictionary of National Biography*).

[37] This was more likely to have been John Varley (1778–1842) who had opened a studio and gallery at 10A Great Titchfield Street in 1817 (which he left in 1830) than Cornelius Varley (1781–1873), his brother (see *Dictionary of National Biography*), although Cornelius did paint watercolours (*Industrial Archaeology*, vol. XI, 1974, pp. 170–3).

[38] Sir Richard Westmacott (1775–1856) sculpted the bronze statue of Achilles in 1822. It was copied from the original on Monte Cavallo in Rome.

[39] Sir Francis Legatt Chantrey (1781–1841) was most famous for his portrait sculptures.

good funerary figures. Varley is one of the best painters in water-colours in London and I found his works just as pleasurable as those of his fellow painters I have already described. The English are equally good at painting landscapes in oils and they have the great merit of not overworking their paintings, which is a very common fault in France and which greatly harms the result.

I dined with Mr Brunel and after dinner felt a slight feverish attack coming on. I would not mention this fact had it not brought me into contact with English medicine. They have no knowledge here of infusions or laxatives, which would not fit in with the regular diet of the English. On returning to my hotel that evening I requested a glass of sugared water and was asked whether I would not rather take some wine, and the following day I was constantly offered tea and coffee. Although I realised that my indisposition was only the result of tiredness I was afraid I would not recover quickly enough to be able to go to Ascot. I therefore called Mr Green, for whom we had a letter of introduction. He treated me with relaxative and sudorific potions because these are the fashion here and because they are found to be the most effective treatment. Indeed, by the Tuesday evening I was again looking forward to the trip planned for the next day. I therefore decided to complete the cure by having . . . a you know what![40] It was first objected that a doctor's prescription was necessary. I was then told that no one knew where to find the apparatus. Finally when I insisted my hostess sent to her doctor's for one, but imagine how surprised I was when I was brought a kind of *bagpipe*, for the thing looked more like a bagpipe than anything in the world. If in this country they do not make you believe chalk is cheese, they make you undergo changes no less unbelievable. I had too little faith in my own dexterity to put it to the test with that implement and I went to bed promising myself that in future I would be satisfied with potions in England and that when in Rome I would do as the Romans do.

It seems to me beyond doubt that sooner or later there must be reforms in England, for the institutions of the country are as bad as public opinion is powerful and well-informed. Privilege and monopoly are the basis of the entire constitution. There is the monopoly of the aristocracy or the House of Lords, the monopoly of the gentry or the House of Commons. These are virtually the only

[40] An enema.

families who profit from the funds allocated to the army, the navy or the Church, and they therefore do all in their power to ensure there is no reduction in these allocations which for the army and for the navy amount to 300 million and 150 million in pensions every year. There are the privileges of the county gentlemen who make all England pay more than 20 sous for a four-gallon loaf. There are the privileges of the clergy who, apart from their fixed incomes, still levy their tithes, and the Protestants, whose sumptuous establishment in Ireland is paid for by Catholics. There is the privilege of the municipalities, oligarchically organised, who in many cases exploit their position for their own benefit, and that of the plantation owners and the East India Company who cost England I do not know how many millions every year. Finally, the keystone of this whole edifice of privilege, which in my opinion has made its survival possible for so long, is the privilege enjoyed by the poor who *have a right* to relief from the rich, according to the level of their wages and the number of children in their families. At the moment this costs the State between 150 and 175 million [francs] a year.[41]

I am well aware that, despite the existence of all these detestable institutions, certain factors, which are very difficult to determine, have given such a hitherto unparalleled vigour to human activity that the power and capital of the country have grown incessantly and, as a result above all of the strength of public opinion, which acts as a check on a large number of abuses, one can live tolerably well in England, though there is also a great deal of suffering.

It is clear to me that a very large proportion of the country is strongly in favour of a change in the present system of government. And however strong the resistance of those with privilege, it is impossible to say how long the present system will last. For 150 years, when they have been able to set the Continental nations against each other at will, their policy has been to dazzle the country with conquests. Today, however, they can no longer use this stratagem because European nations are too well aware of their real interests and because the English people have no desire to pay any more subsidies. Even apart from their current concerns, the English have the most profound and sincere desire for peace, a desire which is quite genuine, deeply felt and entirely without

[41] I.e., £6 million–£7 million. The rate of exchange at this time was approximately 25 francs to the £ sterling.

ulterior motive. They love peace because it is in the spirit of the times and because war is repugnant to them. Even if it were announced tomorrow that the Russians were in Constantinople, the news would be received with the most complete indifference.

From the moment when the aristocracy were no longer regarded, rightly or wrongly, as the architects of national greatness, their prestige would be considerably reduced, while the attention of the public would no longer be diverted by foreign policy and would concentrate all its attention on reform at home. There is clear proof of this. It should not be forgotten that reforms relating to the power of the aristocracy, the law and the Church were begun during the Cromwellian period, reforms interrupted by the Restoration. It is not sufficiently understood in France that at the time of the French Revolution the reform movement re-emerged with new strength. The scaffold was needed to halt it. But even more than the scaffold the excesses of the French Revolution helped to check the movement, and this sad episode is an arsenal where, like their French counterparts, the party of privilege can draw its weapons. This is what I recently read in a paper, *The Plain Englishman*,[42] published several years ago and intended to inculcate the people with sound doctrines. The writer begins a series of articles on the French Revolution[43] with these words:

> The freedom with which revolutionary doctrines are now maintained seems to show that the horrible evils resulting to every nation which has adopted them are well nigh forgotten in England; for else the recollections of those awful events which took place in France would be sufficient to check their progress in this country. We have for some time contemplated the expediency of recalling to the memory of our readers some of the principal transactions of the French Revolution, in order to show what

[42] *The Plain Englishman* (London, 3 vols.), a periodical publication, ran from 1820 to 1823. It was founded by Charles Knight and E. H. Locker as an antidote to the seditious and infidel literature so widely disseminated at the time. It made use of historical material in its appeal to British patriotism (R. K. Webb, *The British Working Class Reader, 1790–1848*, London, 1955, pp. 75–6, 95, 159). It is dismissed rather loftily by Patricia Hollis, *The Pauper Press*, London, 1970, p. 137.

[43] In vol. II of *The Plain Englishman* (for 1821) there appeared five articles on the history of the French Revolution. Readers had been informed in vol. I (for 1820) of their approaching publication by a 'prelude to a corrected account of the principal events of the French Revolution' (*ibid.*, vol. I (for 1820), 2nd ed. 1821, p. 283).

would be the infallible consequences of a revolution here. Many mistaken people suppose that a Revolution among Englishmen would be quite another thing; and that, even in the height of the struggle, we should never be guilty of the enormous crimes of the French Jacobins. We would earnestly entreat our countrymen not to delude themselves with this false hope. *Mob* is a monster bearing the same hideous features, the same savage heart, in *all* countries. A walk through Cato-street may help to remind us of this truth. If ever the glorious fabric of the British Constitution should be levelled with the dust—if the King should be hurled from his throne, and the Radicals should be permitted to usurp the government, be assured the streets of London and Liverpool are destined to witness the same dreadful scenes which a few years ago plunged the cities of Paris and Lyons in the deepest despair, while their channels streamed with blood, and the guillotine and the dagger became rivals in massacre.[44]

It is just the same as in France! but as with us the older generation who lived through these disasters is giving way to a new one which only sees the advantages that have resulted from these events. 'The old die off', an Englishman recently told me when we were discussing the opinions of some young aristocrats on the Catholic question.

Another factor which helps to hasten reforms is the weakening of religious feelings. This is very evident, at least in London. In nearly every home prayers are said at meal-times and the head of the family takes everyone to church on Sunday. If, however, you ask their reasons for doing this they say it is customary and they do not want to shock their servants. I asked a very respectable man whether Voltaire was read in England. He said he was not, because his chief merit lay in subverting religion, something which nowadays was already accepted in England. As for the young, I have been able to ascertain for myself that their attitude towards the Church was far from reverential. An Established Church is in great danger when such opinions are about.

You cannot help finding a striking parallel between the events of recent years in England and those which preceded the Revolution in France. The government has been brought to the point where it recognises that reforms are necessary and it is making a start on them. Until now they have been content to proclaim the undeniable excellence of existing institutions and the disadvantages that will

[44] *The Plain Englishman*, vol. 1 (for 1820), 2nd ed., 1821, p. 283.

result from any attempts to change them. Canning, Peel and Huskisson have set off on a new path, and have brought about significant changes in foreign policy, commercial policy and the law. Canning compared himself and his colleagues to Turgot and Malesherbes; it may be noted that they had the same success. They failed in the face of the stubbornness of those with privileges, and a large section of the population failed to appreciate what they had achieved. The frequent changes of government in the last year make the parallel even more striking. These prove that the ministry is not in the national interest and this is always a fatal sign.

Finally, a circumstance which seems to me to be inauspicious for the party of privilege. This is the palpable weakness, the flagrant absurdity of its arguments. The strength of this party consists in being able to claim, 'everything is fine because we find it so', it has to appeal to sentiment rather than reason. But now that the appeal to the 'wisdom of our ancestors' has lost its hold and current ills can no longer be denied, the party is obliged to argue its case and this is its ruin. Thus when it is proved to them that the Catholics have either to be emancipated or to be fought with the sword, they reply that they are not afraid of fighting and that it is better to fight than to give way. If you tell them the usury laws prevent traders raising funds during periods of crisis, they reply, so much the better for them, for their friends make sacrifices to help them. If it is suggested that Parliament should have greater control over the funds in the Civil List they respond that the House should certainly not do so since the moral responsibility of ministers would thereby be reduced. This reminds me of the argument of a member of the Paris *Parlement* who felt that the very wide area of jurisdiction exercised by this body was a great advantage because, he said, parties would settle disputes amicably in order to avoid the expense of travelling to Paris.

These are the reasons which make me think that reform is imminent. Even if the government succeeds in wrenching concessions from those with privilege—which it is not certain that it will—it will still have to tackle the question of parliamentary reform. Once this threshold has been crossed things will move rather quickly. One only has to remember the pace of events that followed the doubling of the number of Third Estate representatives [at the Estates-General]. On the other hand, I realise that not all the middle class in England are in favour of sudden changes and I confess that I still have not managed to understand this.

4 June My indisposition over, we set off with Mr de Schaezler and M. Castellain *fils*[45] at 9 o'clock in the morning to go to Ascot. Adolphe had arrived the previous evening. Unfortunately the weather was frightful and all we could do was to cross the course and then go to W[inkfield] and visit Mr de R[ham], the parson. Mr de R[ham] is one of those fortunate members of the Anglican Church whom pastoral duties do not prevent from living a very pleasant life . . .

5 June We went to the races at Ascot and the weather was fine. The race-course is on the side of a gently sloping hill and most of the time the races are run along a course of about a mile or a mile and a half on the upper part of the slope. The booths and marquees are on the crest of the hill. That particular day the king was there without pomp in his own private tent. We went into the punters' marquee where we saw some twenty booths where roulette and rouge-et-noir were played, each having plenty of patrons. When we came out I quickly noticed a tear as big as a hand above the fob pocket on my trousers. Happily the pickpockets had not had time to complete their work.

The general appearance of the festivities was quite similar to St-Cloud. The only difference was the large number of carriages. We saw some very fine races, generally run at a speed of a mile in two minutes.

12 June I went to lunch with Mr Place[46] who had invited me the previous evening.

[45] H. Castellain, Schaezler & Co. was a firm of City merchants of 3 Copthall Court, London (*Post Office London Directory for 1823*, 24th ed., p. 66).
[46] For Francis Place (1771–1854) see Graham Wallas, *Life of Francis Place*, London, 2nd revised ed., 1918. This was not the first time d'Eichthal had met Place, as he wrote to his father on 30 May, 'As for Mr Place I had already had the pleasure of making his acquaintance in his capacity as a tailor. Brunel had recommended him to me. Since I found him rather expensive and since I was not happy with his work I could not hope for more than to substitute ties of friendship for those which previously existed between us, especially since he seems a very agreeable fellow . . .' (letter from Gustave d'Eichthal to his father, 30 May 1828, Fonds d'Eichthal, *Bibliothèque de l'Arsenal*, 14383, fo. 5).

Mr Place is a former tailor, and is still in partnership with his son; he was only a simple journeyman, unable to read up to the age of twenty-one, and at the outbreak of the French Revolution he became one of those who sought to spread its principles in England. Since then his political activities have never ceased and he has fought for the enfranchisement of the lower classes. He was one of the group which seized the Westminster constituency from the hands of the aristocracy, by persuading the electors to pay the costs of the election themselves and so get representatives who were really men of their own choice. At the beginning of the Revolution he was one of those who organised a Jacobin Society (those were the words he used) among the workers, a society which had thirty thousand members, monthly membership fees and a well-organised system of correspondence, etc.[47] This society did not, it appears, undertake direct political action, but it did much to better the condition of the workers, above all in furthering their education. Children's schools were set up, and clubs for the adults, as well as libraries, both fixed and mobile. 'In order to emancipate the working class, we have made practical politicians of the workers [said Mr Place]; their interests will never be as well looked after as by themselves; they must be made conscious of their social position.' 'If it wasn't for this cursed Established Church,' he continued, 'we would have excellent schools for the people everywhere.' Lancaster and still more his supporters had worked out an excellent system for educating the people.[48] 'But the Established Church has set itself to fight against it everywhere. The Church has built its National Schools, where the children learn only to read the Bible, in opposition to the Lancasterian Schools, where the children learn the basic elements of science. And often when the Church

[47] For this body founded in 1792 (Place joined it in June 1794) see P. A. Brown, *The French Revolution in English History*, London, 1918, *passim*, and H. Collins, 'The London Corresponding Society', in *Democracy and the Labour Movement*, ed. John Saville, 1954, pp. 103–34. Place's figure of thirty thousand was, of course, a gross exaggeration (see E. P. Thompson, *The Making of the English Working Class*, London, 1963, pp. 152–6). Mr Thompson elegantly remarks of Place's later accounts of the L.C.S.: '. . . we cannot fail to be aware that Place was also sitting to James Mill for his own portrait as the white man's Trusty Nigger' (*op. cit.*, p. 155).

[48] Joseph Lancaster (1778–1838) devised the Lancasterian system which used monitors to help teach and keep discipline. Place had been an early supporter of Lancaster's methods and in 1813 had helped to organise the West London Lancasterian Association.

has brought about the closure of the local Lancasterian schools, it closes its own.'

Mr Place told me that *in general* the condition of the workers in England had improved considerably; that drunkenness and depravity were much less common, while education and intelligence were more widespread. He spoke to me about clubs established among different kinds of workers; tailors, shoemakers, printers, etc. for the mutual help among their members, in order to give so much a week to those who are sick or even unemployed, so that the competition of the latter category for work will not bring down the level of wages.

But when I asked him for information about the spinners, after having told me that men of mature years and good workers of this class had made good progress both in education and intelligence, he admitted to me that the condition of a large part of those engaged in spinning was really deplorable. Because children were employed in the cotton manufacture from a very early age, because they worked in a very warm atmosphere, because they never budged from the spot where they worked and because both sexes were together, it appeared that the most frightening and unashamed debauchery often took place between them from the age of twelve years. The openness with which these things take place is unbelievable. Mr Place spoke to me about a worker [named Williams] who had been summoned to London to give evidence before a parliamentary committee. 'You see how puny I am,' said he to Mr Place, 'I shall be weak all my life; I started having intercourse with women at the age of twelve, and so did all my pals.' He then told him that in the mill in which he was employed, which was, I believe, in Stockport, it was the custom to pay the workers in a public house on the pretext of getting small change for the banknotes supplied by the employer.[49] The publican alone was in possession of small change. Mine host used to insist, on every transaction, that each worker should buy a pint of beer. After the first pint a second would follow, and so on until the majority of the workers would get drunk, so that the most frightful disorders broke out. Mr Place asked this worker why the payment of wages did not take place at the mill itself. 'Because', replied Williams, 'a charge of 2 per cent is made for changing banknotes into silver and the master does not want to bear this loss.' 'So,' said Mr Place, 'wouldn't it be

[49] This practice was much denounced by social reformers at the time.

better for you and your workmates to bear this loss yourselves, which will always be cheaper than spending a week's wages in the public house? When you go back home, put your best suit on on Saturday evening, set up a table and with the permission of your employer, undertake the business of paying out the money yourself.' Williams did so, and since that time some of the disorderly conduct has stopped.

The overseers, far from helping in any way to better the condition of the workers, take pride in cohabiting with the largest possible number of young women, and as for the masters, these same workers are objects of indifference or even of active dislike; and sometimes their morality is no better than that of their overseers. Mr Place quoted the example of a young man from London who went on a visit to some of his manufacturer friends in Lancashire. While they were visiting the work rooms, one of his friends asked him which of the girls there he would like to sleep with. The young man thought at first his friend was joking, but on being pressed further, pointed one out. 'Annie,' said the master, 'you will sleep with this gentleman tonight.' 'I'm not in a fit state for that', she said. 'In that case [he replied], go and wash and make yourself tidy.'

I enquired whether this kind of person held any religious opinions. 'A kind of superstition,' Mr Place told me. 'They are Methodists; or belong to some other sect which they have founded. One of the brethren preaches and his exhortation amounts to not much more than saying: "If you do this or that you will be damned; if you don't do this or that you will be damned." ' For this word 'damned' is all the rage among the English. When I remarked that many of the equivalent class of person in France were atheists, he replied that this was true of the more enlightened in England too.

It appears that savings banks do not do well in Lancashire. In bad years the sufferings of these classes are very severe; it is a certain fact that every year several thousand workers die from sheer poverty. They fall ill as the result of an inadequate and unwholesome diet, and die quickly.

The rapid increase of this class of the population is the cause of its poverty; less than thirty or forty years ago the number of spinners was about 20,000, now there are 1,200,000.[50] The workhouses were emptied to provide children for the looms. The

[50] An obvious exaggeration.

modern industrial system, the poor rates and early marriage which
I have mentioned above (for as soon as a girl has a child she is
obliged to get married) combine to bring about this excessive
growth. It is estimated that a [male mule] spinner gets 50s a week
for the same amount of work which earned him 36s formerly.

The first day I saw Mr Place, I talked at length with him on the
subject of the National Debt. I was pleased to find that he shared
my opinion that the existence of the debt had little or no adverse
effect on the British national economy, or indeed on that of any
country which possessed one; that the National Debt was useful
as a place of safe investment, and that before thinking about its
abolition it would be necessary to create a substitute for it in the
shape of a sound banking system.

Mr Place is very much up to date on questions of political
economy. He is a very likeable man, and also much esteemed, full
of the wisdom of experience and possessing a fund of knowledge.
'Judge,' he said to me, 'the prejudices of this country. I really have
many friends and many very influential people regard me with
respect and affection; nevertheless, you will never see me dining
with them. If they were to invite me, it would be a burden on them.
If I were to decide to leave this house and take a pleasant country
villa, my origins would soon be forgotten. But as long as I am a
tradesman I cannot be counted a gentleman. I was consulted about
the establishment of a political economy club; I gave my advice,
my plan; never have my best friends, who themselves are members,
talked about my joining '

At Mr Place's house I once met a scatter-brained fellow who is
busying himself introducing Kant's philosophy to England. I have
never seen such an eccentric.[51]

17 June I mentioned to Mr Place that the prices of bread in
London and Paris seemed to bear no relation to wheat prices; that
at the end of this past winter the price of wheat stood at 22 francs
the hectolitre in both countries, whereas bread cost 16 sous (8d) in

---

[51] It is possible that this unidentified Kantian enthusiast was S. T.
Coleridge, who was about to embark on his visit to the Low Countries and
Germany, 21 June–6 August 1828 (E. L. Griggs, ed., *Collected Letters of
S. T. Coleridge*, vol. VI, 1826–34, Oxford, 1971, p. 747). For Coleridge's
part in introducing a knowledge of Kantian philosophy into England, see
J. Mander, *Our German Cousins: Anglo-German Relations in the 19th and
20th Centuries*, London, 1974, pp. 142–58.

Paris and 10*d* in London; yet I was not at all certain about these figures and finally suggested that the difference might derive from the method of fixing the price of bread in Paris. Mr Place, without being able to give a definite answer to the question I asked, assured me that no monopoly existed in London either in grain or in flour; that there had formerly been such a monopoly when the price of grain was fixed by the Lord Mayor (Assize of Bread), but that he had been one of those who had been instrumental in securing the abolition of this practice, a task which was rendered much more difficult because no one complained about it.[52] He told me that the difference between the price of bread [in London and Paris] might come from the extra charges incurred by the London bakers (transport costs, the cost of credit sales, etc.). He told me that certain master bakers, operating on a large scale, because they sold their bread in the London markets, and thus incurred neither transport costs nor losses through giving credit [because they sold it for ready cash], were able to charge 2*d* less. Their bread is as fresh as it can be and people will only eat that kind of bread (which, indeed, appears to be an economical way of proceeding). But ready money sales, their arrangements with wholesale flour merchants to take large quantities, the advantage of being able to keep their ovens permanently heated (which cuts down fuel consumption) all give them opportunities for lowering the price of bread by an appreciable extent.

As long as the Assize of Bread lasted, it placed the wholesale trade in flour (I don't know how) in the hands of a small number of persons. These people assisted small capitalists to set up as

[52] For the history of the Assize of Bread and Place's part in its abolition in the London area in 1822, see S. and B. Webb, 'The Assize of Bread', *Economic Journal*, vol. XIV, 1904, pp. 196–218. It was not abolished for the rest of England and Wales until 1836. The Assize of Bread, i.e. the fixing of the price of wheaten and other breadstuffs by the J.P.s as laid down by the Act of 1758, entailed not only an assize table in which the price of bread was fixed and the weights of the loaves varied ('assized bread'), but also a price table in which the weights of the loaves were fixed and their prices varied according to the state of the market ('prized bread'). The legislation involved two principles—that in the sale of an article of basic necessity 'the price should be moderate', and that 'all temptation to the seller to deceive the buyer either in its quality or weight should be counteracted as far as possible' (*Annals of Agriculture*, vol. XXI, p. 55, quoted by E. Lipson, *The Economic History of England*, London, vol. II, 2nd revised and enlarged edition, 1943, p. 425. For the 'Assize of Bread' in Scotland, see James Cleland, *Annals of Glasgow*, Glasgow, vol. II, 1816, pp. 497–512.

bakers in a modest way of business, lent them any further funds which they might require, and then proceeded to unload inferior products on them. When such businesses began to go badly, the monopolists foreclosed and, after seizing their property, left them ruined.

A similar system exists today for keepers of public houses, who cannot go into business without first obtaining a licence. Wholesale brewers like Barclay & Perkins have between three and four hundred of these licences which they distribute to their tenants on condition that they sell only Barclay & Perkins beer.[53]

A monopoly also exists in hackney coaches, which have to pay a tax of 18s a week. This monopoly is equally vexatious to the owners, the cabmen and the public, yet no one proposes to do away with it.

Mr Place spoke to me at length about the clearly perceptible improvement among all classes of the population of London, and even among those who seem in the most abject poverty. He told me that even the frightful districts of Petticoat Lane, Drury Lane and St Giles Wapping were now very much better than they had formerly been. He pointed out to me the effect of cheap cottons in improving the clothes of the people and the furnishing of their homes; when they wore woollen and silk garments, these had to last for several years.[54]

We went on to discuss Mr [Robert] Peel's reforms in the law relating to juries. One thing is still lacking—penalties. It had been the intention to get rid of the 'pack-jurors', or paid jurymen, who are all too frequently employed by the magistrates. However, the law goes unobserved, and the former method of selecting juries continues on many occasions. Mr Place himself wishes to exercise his right of being sworn in as a juryman.

20 June In Mr Place's opinion the introduction of machinery has never put a single worker out of a job [and he advanced the following arguments]:

[53] For the growth of the 'tied house' system see Peter Mathias, *The Brewing Industry in England, 1700–1830*, Cambridge, 1959, pp. 130–5. By 1830 Barclay & Perkins had tied 60 per cent of the publicans selling the firm's beer (p. 183).

[54] For similar comments made by Place elsewhere see M. D. George, *London Life in the Eighteenth Century*, London, 1925, pp. 4, 18, 59–61, 103–5, 211, 321–2.

1. New machinery has always been introduced because of a prior increase in demand, which calls for an increase in production.

2. The capital necessary for the building of new machinery only comes into play piecemeal and is usually only forthcoming when the increase in demand has become such that profits seem certain.

3. Improvements in machinery are always gradual and practically never important enough to displace a large body of workers all at once.

4. Finally, [there is always a time-lag caused by] the difficulty of overcoming old habits and substituting new products for the traditional ones.

5. It appears that the time it takes to train a good machine operator is no shorter than that which it takes to train any other handicraftsman, and that likewise the wages of the machine operator are much higher.

Mr Place assured me that after carefully examining all the evidence which had come to his notice he had not been able to find a single example of distress among workers caused by the introduction of machinery, and that in every single instance when it had been claimed that this was so, the distress of the working classes arose from quite different sources. He then quoted a large number of examples in support of his views.

The Thames ropemakers received enormous wages during the war because of the heavy demand for cables for the Royal Navy. A machine was then invented to cope with the demand; which nevertheless had no appreciable effect in lowering the price of cables. At the same time a beginning was made with the use of cables made from iron chains.[55] With the coming of peace, the demand for cables having diminished, wages fell and the ropemakers approached Mr Place with complaints against the machines. Their main complaint was that their wages were not as high as they had been during the war, and since they were unduly high at that

[55] There is possibly a confusion here between the *manufacture* of *wire* ropes, which was started with only moderate success during the War of American Independence, and the *use* of *chains* instead of ropes, which rose steeply in price during the revolutionary and Napoleonic wars as the result of interference with the supply of hemp from the Baltic. For example, Gilbert Gilpin (1766–1827) started a chainmaking business at Coalport and Dawley, Salop, on the basis of this scarcity; his firm was still flourishing in the 1820s (W. H. Chaloner, 'The life of Gilbert Gilpin . . .', *National Library of Wales Journal*, vol. XI, No. 4, winter 1960, pp. 383–4).

period, it was clear that their complaint was quite unfounded. Mr Place went further: he asked them for a statement of the number of persons formerly employed in that branch of industry, and he himself also obtained figures showing the number employed both in the hand-roperies and in those which were operated by machinery. He found that the number of persons employed in the hand-roperies had decreased from 900 to 750; this decrease was largely the result of deaths, but 650 persons were employed in the mechanised roperies and in chainmaking.

The enormous increase in the number of persons employed in the cotton and stocking industries subsequent to the application of machinery is a striking proof that the introduction of machinery does not have the effect of throwing people out of work.

There are certain classes of worker who have always been poverty-stricken and whose lot cannot be worsened by the introduction of machinery. It is very probable that the invention of the machine for making bobbin net has in no way diminished the number of bobbin net workers in Buckinghamshire, but it is highly desirable that machinery should supplant this category of labour, for the workers in it have reached the lowest depths of poverty. They work in their own insanitary dwellings, which are cramped and dark, to earn from 6s to 7s a week.

It is the same with the silk weavers. At present they are protesting vigorously against the introduction of power looms. However, up to a few years ago they had succeeded in preventing the introduction of any improvement. Their machines were nearly the same as those they had brought from France at the time of their emigration [c. 1680–1700]. Yet they had almost always been poverty-stricken. Around 1777 they marched tumultuously to the house of Lord North, in order to force him to propose in the House of Commons that their wages should be fixed by law (the same demand has recently been renewed by the Manchester silk weavers). They also proceeded to the royal palace, where the king was obliged to show himself. Finally between two and three thousand of them made a sortie from Spitalfields and set about plundering passers-by.[56]

[56] For the Spitalfields silk weavers, see M. D. George, *London Life in the Eighteenth Century*, London, 1925, chapter IV, J. L. and B. Hammond, *The Skilled Labourer*, London, 1919, pp. 205–20 and Sir John H. Clapham, 'The Spitalfields Acts', *Economic Journal*, December 1916.

Mr Place considers that the sole reason for the poverty of the weavers is the large number of children they have. He thinks that the nature of their trade, which brings together both sexes in very warm workshops, is very conducive to sexual indulgence. And in addition there is the popular belief among the people that the larger the number of their children, the better it is for them. This was true when a child could earn 7s a week, but now it is a fallacy.

We discussed the necessity of making a clean sweep in order to reform Great Britain. Up to the present, the best-intentioned measures come up against a host of local abuses which make them inoperative (the repeal of the Test Act will be rendered null and void by the local enactments of various municipal corporations). The proposal to allow the county magistrates the power to intervene in granting of licences to publicans has been rejected by the House of Commons as being contrary to the rights of the municipal corporations. The policing of London cannot be improved because the City magistrates are unwilling to give up their rights.

Consequently, it is impossible to foresee a revolution taking place without some more or less violent convulsion, but it is unlikely that it will ever be accompanied by the same kind of disorder as the French Revolution. Here people are in the habit of participating in the political process. In some cases they enjoy the franchise, as I took the trouble to check by means of certain clubs which are accustomed to debate and to act collectively. 'Such,' Mr Place told me, 'was the great aim of our London Corresponding Society. Our purpose was not to foment revolution; we knew that that was impossible, and in any case it would have been dangerous at such a time. But we wanted to get the lower orders into the habit of acting together. We had our representative assembly and also our executive committee which kept up a correspondence with the committees in the various towns in the Kingdom.

'This attempt was not a complete failure. Since then, the whole of the working class has remained organised or ripe for organisation. You have heard much talk of the Luddites, who broke machinery in 1812. I found myself one day in the company of a number of M.P.s, among them Mr [George] Rose, who were loud in their complaints about the Luddite outrages. I pointed out to them that in the course of these so-called risings not a single man had been killed. "These men," I told them, "whom you believe are acting from blind fury, obey the orders of their committee; they do as much as, but no more than, the committee directs them to do. Explain to the committee, demonstrate to them that they will gain nothing by breaking the machines, and the violence will stop." Indeed, I wrote to King Ludd (a man named Henson)[57] and he then wrote to Mr [George] Rose,[58] offering to come and meet him in London if he would promise not to have him arrested. Mr Rose gave the required promise, had a meeting with Henson, and the disorders stopped. Since then, the committees have declared that the machinery will never be broken in future. In 1826 a few power looms were broken. But the disorder in this case was caused, by government *agents provocateurs*. I had had been warned of this a few days before. I informed Mr Peel and some M.P.s. In spite of this, there was no time to prevent the outbreak. Some power looms were broken, and the troops called in, but there was no struggle.'

Mr Place told me of several articles he himself had published in the *Manchester Journal*[59] with the aim of convincing the workers that machines would bring them no harm.

In a subsequent conversation Mr Place came to the conclusion that the standard of life of the manufacturing population is lowered not so much by the great number of children with which it is burdened but by the competition which it faces from women and

[57] This statement by Place made sixteen years after the event, and described by Church and Chapman as 'the popular view', is repeated in the Place MSS (B.M. Add. MSS, 27,809, 1876), but most of the trustworthy contemporary evidence points the other way. Gravener Henson (1785–1852) of Nottingham was the organiser of the United Committee (or Union Society) of Framework Knitters, which in 1812 sponsored the introduction of a bill into the House of Commons to prevent indirect abatements of the knitters' earnings. It was eventually thrown out in the Lords. His activities during the Luddite incidents of 1811–12 in the East Midlands are not well documented (R. A. Church and S. D. Chapman, 'Gravener Henson and the making of the English working class' in *Land, Labour and Population in the Industrial Revolution*, ed. E. L. Jones and G. E. Mingay, London, 1967, pp. 137–40; and G. Henson, *History of the Framework Knitters*, 2nd ed., with introduction by S. D. Chapman, Newton Abbot, 1970, pp. ix–xx; M. I. Thomis, *The Luddites*, Newton Abbot, 1970.

[58] This was George Rose, M.P. (1744–1818), vice-president of the Board of Trade and Treasurer of the Navy, 1807–12 (*Dictionary of National Biography*).

[59] D'Eichthal means 'a Manchester journal' for there was no paper of this name. In 1825 Place wrote a letter to the *Manchester Gazette* defending his and Mill's views on the effect of machinery on wage rates (*Manchester Gazette*, 19 February 1825).

children, and not only from its own children but also from the children of all other classes. Formerly, practically all the children received into the workhouses died there. Today fewer than one in *eight* die. At the same time the number of infants abandoned has decreased enormously. In the parish of St Clement's, Westminster, where previously a large number of infants were abandoned, only one has been abandoned during the past ten years.

28 June We left London at midday. Our stagecoach was more loaded with baggage than any French coach could be. It is put on top and in chests underneath the front and back seats and is sometimes slung underneath the vehicle itself. Fully loaded our coach weighed at least 2,000 kg. Despite this and despite the heat we covered 15 leagues in five hours, which is very good indeed in view of the number of times we stopped. There is competition between different companies on this route and this is the reason for the great speed. Sometimes we went at full speed and you can imagine what full speed is with English horses. One is in no danger because the roads are so good. The critical reason for the good condition of the roads seems to me to be the absence of goods transport; I do not think that the turnpike system is a factor, and this is why it is currently being proposed to remove tollgates around London and to replace them by a property tax of no more than 2 per cent of its value. At every place that the coach stopped we were pestered by strawberry sellers. They hardly have any variety here apart from the pineapple type; these are very common and a basket, enough for a good plateful, sells for 12 sous.

I left London with an elderly blind general for a companion and we were joined en route by a young man, a very handsome fellow whom I took to be a soldier but whom I met again two days later during the episcopal visitation at Newbury, when he was dressed in clerical garb.

The Berkshire countryside is magnificent. It is open country or, to be more exact, wide valleys, for the terrain is not at all flat. It closely resembles the most beautiful parts of Normandy, but the green of the vegetation is still more beautiful if that is possible. The tenant farmers and artisans seem to live very well here but the agricultural labourers are in the same wretched conditions they are in throughout England. The parish of Bucklebury, with a population of 1,200, pays £1,200 in poor rates. Large-scale agriculture, which has deprived the labourer of the advantage of living-in, and the Poor Laws themselves seem to be the causes of this pauperism. The dress of this class of agricultural labourers and their condition in general are certainly no better than those of their counterparts in France and I would say that they are worse. The appearance of the countryside is not improved either by the bands of ragged Irishmen who land in Bristol and move about the area looking for work or by the gangs of gypsies who wander from one end of England to the other living on what they can scrounge and pilfer without any steps being taken to put an end to their vagrancy.

I now come to a description of my residence. It is a small house, a cottage as it is called, set on its own, as are all the houses, some four leagues from Reading and roughly the same distance from Newbury. It has the usual flower-bed in front of the house and kitchen garden with strawberries, gooseberries and vegetables at the back. My landlord is the curate of the parish of Bucklebury,[60] in other words he receives £150 a year from the incumbent for carrying out his duties. The incumbent is a fellow who has an income of 150,000 francs a year from property he owns in the parish.[61] His benefice also brings him £800 a year, out of which he pays his curate. This benefice is hereditary in his family; if someone inherits a benefice and does not want to take it up, he sells the usufruct. Many benefices are the private property of families in this way. There is a minister in this area who has held a benefice for twenty-seven years and is about to have it taken away from him because a member of the family which owns the benefice has proved that the present holder bought it from a vendor who did not have the right to sell it. This is what the Established Church is like! But if I do not care for the Church I like churchmen very much, or at least the minor clergy. Until now I have made the acquaintance of three of these who were as easy-going as it is possible to be and the only Englishmen I know who appreciate pleasantries.

Mr Hemus, who is my landlord at the moment, was originally destined for the bar but his father, who had two benefices from

[60] This was the Rev. J. E. Hemus who died in 1836 (letter from Mary Hemus to Gustave d'Eichthal, 15 November 1847, Fonds d'Eichthal, *Bibliothèque de l'Arsenal*, 13751, fo. 49).

[61] The patronage of the Bucklebury vicarage was in the hands of the Rev. W. H. H. Hartley (S. Lewis. *Topographical Dictionary of England*, London, 1831, vol. I, p. 297).

Lord Eldon, found a way of securing one for his son, and Mr Hemus wisely chose a career in the Church. He is an extraordinarily lively and gay young man who always has a joke to tell or play. He is also intelligent and genuinely thinks himself very orthodox. I am sure he is liked in his parish. He allows his parishioners to play cricket on Sundays, which offends the zeal of several of his fellow clergymen and even of some of his flock. His wife is about thirty years old, seems to be an intelligent woman and has a pretty turn of conversation. Since they have no children and since Mr H[emus]'s spiritual family is not too preoccupying, they have plenty of time to devote to entertaining foreigners, and they even take in paying guests, more as a distraction than as a means of making money. I have been with them a week and have greatly enjoyed it, apart from a few calls on their neighbours. The household consists of a carriage horse and a pony, which are felt to be indispensable for the country, a cat, a pet dog and two hunting dogs, a manservant, a maid and a stout cook.

In Berkshire farms are normally held on three- or seven-year leases, [but] sometimes on a yearly basis . . .

A family [in Bucklebury] was mentioned to me in which husband, wife and five children live on 10s a week.

A day-labourer earns 7s, 8s or 9s in summer and 6s in winter; they live on bread and water. The rent of a cottage ranges from 50s down to 10s a year.

Mr Hemus assured me that day-labourers worked for 4s a week. He had one at home whom he paid at this rate, but he also provided his food. When the day-labourers have no work the parish allows them the price of two loaves of bread a week, a sum which varies from 2s 6d to 3s (when there are children, one loaf of bread per child is given). Such unemployed labour is set to work repairing the roads. The parish of Bucklebury has spent £100 during the past year on work on Chapel Row, for which there was no real need. In some circumstances the sick and the aged get extra allowances in kind which supplement their normal weekly dole.

As one may well imagine, after looking at the level of wages, many people live mainly on bread and water; bacon is the principal foodstuff apart from bread.

It appears that the villagers are no longer ashamed to receive parish relief: they come to ask for it with the words: 'Sir, give me money!'

A bricklayer at Bucklebury can earn 18*s* or a guinea a week, but only in the summer-time.

Mr H[emus] told me that a gentleman and his lady (without children) cannot live decently in the country on less than £500 a year. A female servant must be paid £12 per annum, a male servant twice that. It is claimed that the wheat-threshing machine is one of the causes of rural poverty, because it has deprived the labourers of the only work of which they could be certain during the winter.[62] Here as elsewhere, girls are often pregnant before marriage.

1 July This was the day of the pastoral visitation to Newbury, a visitation not by the bishop but by the archdeacon. Mr H[emus] had to go, and I went in the trap with Mrs Hemus. On the way we met several of his colleagues, as well as parties of churchwardens, all going to Newbury on horseback or in carriages. As my companion knows how to take a joke I told him that in France we called these men in black, rooks, and he replied that this was their nickname in England too. When we arrived at Newbury we went straight to the church where the clergy were gathered. We listened to a clergyman give a very poor sermon on the qualities of the Holy Ghost, for dogmas and mysteries are always the favourite themes of those who give sermons. Afterwards we had a talk from the archdeacon which was generally well received. Leaving aside the religious aspect of a clergyman's duties, he surveyed all the difficulties he had to surmount in his civil functions, for the clergy has in fact a powerful say in local administration. He has constantly to struggle with tenant-farmers and landowners for payment of his tithes and the poor rates and he is often at cross purposes with Dissenters in the vestries or municipal corporations. The archdeacon's speech, which dealt with sensitive issues, was certainly written with great tact and intelligence but the enthusiasm it generated proved to me that such speeches were rare. I should add that his speech was written, though he did not seem to need this precaution at all. It is however a practice which is imperative for members of the Anglican Church, to differentiate them from Dissenters who affect to be inspired from above in their sermons.

[62] On the threshing machine and its effects on the agrarian economy in general and on the 'Captain Swing' riots of 1830 in particular see E. J. Hobsbawm and G. Rudé, *Captain Swing*, London, 1969, *passim*, but especially pp. 359–63.

We returned to Bucklebury for dinner and when we had reached the dessert we saw a tenant farmer from the neighbourhood arriving on a pony. He was what is called the overseer of the poor and had come to collect Mr Hemus's poor rate. At my request he was invited in and offered a glass of beer—by inviting him in his vicar did him a signal honour. He was only ever addressed as 'farmer', never by his name. There is one vicar who will not raise his hat to his parishioners. However, their power is based in no way on their moral influence but on the independence that their benefices give them.

4 July I returned to Bucklebury on my horse, which had nothing marvellous, I might even say good, about it except for its trot. Perhaps I might get a better one in a few days. I pay four guineas for the hire of the horse and four guineas for its upkeep, which is certainly not very expensive. We went to dinner with the vicar of Newbury who has a son and a daughter, both of whom were very amiable. When I asked what the son did I was told that he was an officer on half pay. I remarked that he seemed very young to have served in the army and I was told that he had not served in the army but in the militia. In fact this militia is about as effective as our National Guard—not even that, because they never muster. Despite this, the officers are paid and this creates sinecures for the sons of clergymen and the county gentry. This year there was a discussion in Parliament on this question and it was shown that the militia and volunteers cost the Exchequer £500,000 a year. . . .

20 July Mr H[emus] was asked to read prayers for the infirm to a poor wretch aged eighty who suffers from the stone and who lives nearby, and I went along with him. Although these were poor people their thatched cottage was kept very clean. I was told, however, that the dwellings of the poor do not all have the same pleasing appearance. I listened most devoutly to the prayer-reading, but when having finished the prayers Mr Hemus asked the poor invalid whether he had been comforted by the prayers I had some difficulty keeping a straight face. True he quickly added that he would send him some left-overs for his dinner, a promise which contributed just as much as the prayers to comforting the poor fellow.

21 July I had arranged to meet John [Stuart] Mill who was to come to Reading that day with some of his friends. I met him in the afternoon, went a walk with him and his friends, and then we had dinner together. He has a position in the [East India] Company where his father also has a rather important post, but he spends his time in literary and scientific pursuits. Like his father, he is one of the principal contributors to the *Westminster Review*. Both therefore belong to the ranks of the Reformers. Mill is extraordinarily well-educated, shrewd and intelligent for his age, for he is only twenty-two years old. He is very well informed on the history of the French Revolution and we talked at length about recent events in France whose importance for their own cause the English liberals are well aware of. My table companions were extremely surprised when I told them that M. Corbière's[63] two sons had resigned from the Rennes bar while their father had been a minister, and that M. de Villèle's [64] son had, in similar circumstances, given up the *Cour royale* in Paris and retired to Toulouse. They saw in this important evidence of the superiority of our public morality over theirs and this is not the only reason why I share their opinion. A walk as far as the outskirts of Reading was suggested and I accompanied them part of the way and then took leave of Mill with whom I hope to form a lasting friendship.

28 July We had the privilege of attending the 'Revel' at Bucklebury. The lord of the manor, Mr Hartley, used to give a prize for single-stick fighting; but since a man had once been killed he now donates a cup to the value of £5 for a pony race (the law does not permit the holding of horse races unless there is a stake of at least £50, in order to limit the number of them; but this requisition is not strictly observed). Two days before this fair, the gypsies began to arrive; they are a kind of nomadic people. They travel in wagons of very pleasing appearance, and when they wish to settle anywhere they set up a few miserable-looking tents. They have preserved unchanged the physiognomy of their ancestors; the women and children go about dressed in rags, and taken by and large their general appearance is disgusting, although one can pick a number

[63] J.-J.-G.-F.-P. Corbière (1766–1853), right-wing politician and close friend of Villèle, was minister of the interior, 1821–8. His two sons were Ernest and Eugène-Marie (see *Dictionnaire de biographie française*).

[64] J.-B. G. J. de Villèle (1773–1854) held power from 1821 to 1828.

of handsome specimens. They get a living by peddling in the countryside, and above all by pilfering. The fair has been on the decline for the past few years, and I was told that this year it was worse than ever. Nevertheless several carriages were there, and a goodly number of gigs and men on horseback. But I was told that in general they did not belong to the more respectable part of the community. I saw there a number of horse-fanciers, some of them quite rich, but ruffians for all that. In the course of the day and evening five or six cottages and one bedroom at the inn were wrecked. Pitched battles took place: a constable and his deputies, sent to arrest a woman, were set upon by her gang and left for dead on the scene of the riot. Next morning at nine o'clock I went down to the inn, where I found the gypsies drinking and dancing to the music of a fiddle. I also saw a recruiting sergeant and his recruits come in, all somewhat tipsy.

2 VISIT TO THE NORTH OF ENGLAND AND SCOTLAND, 1 SEPTEMBER TO 1 NOVEMBER

On Monday 1 September we took our seats in the coach for York, which is two hundred miles from London, and we left at 8 o'clock. I reckon that the average cost of an outside seat on a stage coach is:

9s for 50 miles
3s for the driver and coachman
———
12s total

It costs half as much again for a seat inside: 18s altogether.

The difference in price means that nearly everyone travels outside. Each coach usually carries eight passengers outside and only four inside, not counting the coachman and the driver. When there are no packets to be carried on top they can take two extra passengers. Most of the luggage is put in two enormous chests beneath the seats of the outside passengers, and on top of the coach. We have never had to pay for the luggage we have taken with us.

When like everyone in England you take the precaution of equipping yourself with two or three overcoats or riding coats and kerchiefs to wrap around your face, there is no hardship in travelling outside. At night it is advisable to face the back to avoid draughts.

We went from London to York in twenty-five hours, an average of 8 miles an hour, a very good speed, one only reached on good roads, although mail-coaches and a few coaches reach 10 miles an hour. To travel at these speeds you need English roads. If the roads were not paved, outside passengers would not stay in their seats for long. A good set of harness and good horses are necessary, for without them such speeds would be dangerous. Besides, the driver has to have had experience not to be afraid when he starts his team off at full gallop, perched as he is on top of this towering structure. Between London and York we only stopped half an hour for dinner and half an hour for lunch.

The usual cost of a dinner (without wine) is	3s
The usual cost of a lunch and tea is	2s
The cost of a hotel bed per day	2s
waiter	1s
maid	6d
manager	3d
food and lodging per day	9s (at minimum)

You should not expect to pay much less than this or much more. Travelling expenses are steady and can be calculated in advance. It must be said that a foreigner is treated in exactly the same way as an Englishman would be and that no attempt is made to profit from his inexperience. I was assured of this when I arrived and have always found it to be true.

In the inns we have seen the bedrooms are usually poorly furnished. The rooms are dirty and the staff, both male and female, are dirtier still. Beds consist of a feather mattress on top of a palliasse and there is usually a woollen blanket under the sheets. Everywhere you stop you are sure to find one or more portions of good meat, potatoes, some vegetables and a good wedge of cheese. This is the best feature of English inns.

The London to Edinburgh road skirts the east coast of England. We passed through nine counties, namely, Middlesex, Hertford, Cambridge, Huntingdon, Northampton, Rutland, Lincoln, Nottingham and York. To get to Scotland we have still to go through Durham and Northumberland. . . . There is hardly a single mill along the way. The terrain is flat and chiefly agricultural. On this side of England there is not one industrial town; there are several pretty little towns along the way but it should not be supposed that they are very different from òur small towns. They are better kept and that is their principal merit.

York, 1 September While commercial towns in England have grown enormously in recent years, market towns in agricultural areas have remained unchanged or even been reduced in size. York, which was once the second largest city in England, now has only twenty thousand inhabitants and has not grown at all. The cathedral is the only historic building of note. It is a Gothic building, chiefly noteworthy for its size and simple lines. Descriptions of churches are not usually very interesting, and I will restrict myself to a few observations on the English cathedrals I have seen so far: (i) the care, the great expense and the good taste with which they have recently been restored; (ii) the admirable finish on the stonework. The joining you frequently see in one building of Norman architecture with the more modern Gothic style.

We also visited the prison at York. I think this prison has the same defect as all English prisons: the convicts are too comfortable. However, it is always a distressing sight when you enter the yard of an English prison and see walking up and down poor workmen or small traders who have been imprisoned for debt. English law allows debtors to be imprisoned and even to be arrested for a short period without the creditors having to pay anything for their up-keep, and frequent use is made of this right. Under a recent law, however, a debtor can secure his release after a few months by assigning his property to his creditors.

A very high wall, flanked by towers, is being built around York prison so that it looks like an ancient citadel. This is the taste in England and today they are building only Gothic churches. The circumvallation of York prison will be a magnificent sight but it is money ill-spent. It is another example of municipal government by magistrates who are neither elected nor accountable.

We found York Minster cluttered up with the preparations for a music festival which is to take place on 15 September. There is seating for seven thousand people, and there will be three hundred choristers, four hundred musicians and Mme Catalini. The arch-bishop is patron of the festival. Such periodical music festivals have become very fashionable in every town in England. They are lavish affairs which foster the art of music.

In York we found our bedrooms provided with bibles from the Bible Society of the town and the same thing happened at Durham later. Be converted!

We found good peaches in York and later at Newcastle for 6 sous each. They are not very expensive and I think they are greenhouse-grown. There are grapes, too, passable if tasteless Muscats. We bathed in the Ouse.

2 September We left York and arrived at Durham, some sixty miles away, at three o'clock in the morning. On the way we had a light supper. One of our table companions had a piece of chicken. 'I am holding the parson's nose,' he said. 'Then squeeze it,' said another, 'they need squeezing.' In Durham we were put up very comfortably at a little hotel run single-handed by a Quaker. It was the best we have had on our journey and we paid 1s for the room and 2s 6d for dinner. His wife, too, was very respectable and she told me she had recently had news of her son from Java. He is a sailor and his ship was returning from Australia via Java and Madras. I think there is hardly a family in England which does not have someone overseas.

The bishopric of Durham is the richest see in England; most of the houses in the town and in the country round about belong to it.[65] The town therefore resembles the England of yesteryear. The tenants of these houses do nothing to improve property they will never own. It seems that the bishop's annual income amounts to £60,000 and that of all the other clergy in the see to £200,000.

The Wear, on which Durham is situated, runs through a deep ravine and at a bend in the river are Durham Cathedral and Durham Castle, standing well above the river level amidst the trees that cover the sides of the ravine. Two extremely high bridges join the two banks of the river and look very picturesque. Adolphe and I regret we do not know how to sketch when we find such views; I would rather draw them than describe them.

Durham Cathedral is very interesting because its architecture is pure Norman which, apart from the general lay-out of the church,

[65] For the wealth of the Bishopric of Durham see Edward Hughes, *North Country Life in the Eighteenth Century: The North-East 1700–1750*, London, 1952, chapter VII.

is very different from the Gothic. It is clearly derived from the Roman style, with its straight lines, massive columns and rounded arches. It resembles an ancient temple. A superb Gothic chapel has been added at the end of the nave. Seeing the two styles together makes you aware of the differences between the two, with the Gothic making use of curves that intersect and never end. The cathedral was founded in the eleventh century, as were all buildings in this style and as was Notre Dame in Paris.

It was also a pleasure to see the great halls of the castle, which is nowadays the bishop's residence. We particularly admired a Saxon archway discovered by chance in the wall about twenty years ago. The fineness and tastefulness of the stonework make it a most remarkable and original piece of work. A collection of pictures of churches in England, France and Germany by the best water-colourists in England is being published at present in London.

3 September At six o'clock we left the mean streets of Durham to go to Newcastle, 15 miles away, and we arrived at 8.30. It is here that the mountainous terrain begins. When we neared Newcastle we found the sky darkened by smoke from the steam-engines and the coal dust burned at the pit-head to get rid of it. Since they do not want to keep the coal dust, the export duty on it has been reduced to one third of that on coal itself, and this is the coal dust we get in France. When it has been exposed to the air for a long period it is no longer worth anything and it is with such coal that Newcastle merchants sometimes trick their customers. London merchants also mix their coal in this way as they do in Paris. On our journey we saw railways everywhere. They are found to be so useful that they are employed even on temporary works, as for instance in constructing the new London Docks. Moreover, they take up very little space and need no more than a couple of rails that run along or cross a path.

We stayed at the Turf Hotel, the first English hotel I have come across where the service was good.

The banks of the Tyne are no less steep than those along the Wear, and Newcastle stands on its steep slopes. I confess that like a typical Parisian I had thought of all English towns as so many jewels. This is true of some, those that have been built recently and are usually inhabited by rentiers, but it hardly applies to Newcastle or to the other seaports like Shields at the mouth of the Tyne, Sunderland on the Wear, Dover or Portsmouth. These towns still smack of the time when they were built, and Newcastle, particularly in its lower part, is a veritable slum.

4 September We decided to go down the Tyne to Shields. The rocks that line both sides of the river stretch as far as the sea and remain close. As a result the water is as smooth as a lake even near to its mouth and you realise what an advantage such a river must have been for Newcastle.

Along the 10 miles that separate Newcastle from Shields the river calls to mind the theatre of M. Pierre. Along the steep slopes of the banks of the river is an unbroken succession of glassworks, pottery works, foundries, lime kilns, rope works, shipyards, paper mills, etc. Fifty steamboats are in service on the river, used either as tugs for the ships or to carry passengers. The journey costs 6*d*. Since a boat with a 7 or 8 horsepower engine only costs £500, entrepreneurs can still get a good profit. Last year the master of the boat we were on, an ex-seaman, managed to save £100 when all his expenses had been paid. A large number of spouts on staiths are to be seen along the river. These are large balances connected to the mines by railways, which are used to load coal on to the ships. These spouts have made superfluous a large number of the keels or boats which used to carry the coal to the waiting ships. The keelmen therefore did all they could to prevent the building of the spouts. They even brought the mine-owners to court on the grounds that the spouts were blocking the river but their case was dismissed.[66] I am told that the rails cost 3*s* 6*d* a metre.

Almost the only ships to be seen on the river apart from the English are from the Baltic and bring grainstuffs, timber and old bones. Sometimes ships from Normandy are to be seen bringing apples. Since the ships that come to Newcastle usually arrive in ballast, the ballast has accumulated and forms the huge hills that are to be seen at different places along the Tyne.

I had a letter for a sailor from South Shields called Henry

[66] The keelmen went much further than this. They went on strike in 1819 and one man was killed in demonstrations. In 1822 they staged their last strike (see D. J. Rowe, 'The decline of the Tyneside keelmen in the nineteenth century', *Northern History*, Leeds, vol. IV, 1969, pp. 111–31 and 'The strikes of the Tyneside keelmen in 1809 and 1819', *International Review of Social History*, vol. XIII, Amsterdam, 1968, pp. 58–75).

Woodroffe who is president of the Tyne Sailors' Club.[67] I called on him but, as he was busy, put off seeing him till the evening and we went to Sunderland, which is also a coaling port and is situated at the mouth of the Wear. The town closely resembles Shields and Newcastle. On our way we had three young women as fellow passengers in the coach. They were wives of sailors who had left for Portsmouth that morning, whom our driver had probably charged a reduced fare. It would be difficult to think them pretty for they were extremely dirty, a common defect among lower-class women in England. They were very worried about the war between the Greeks and the Turks because they were afraid their husbands might be sent to intervene. . . .

In the hotel dining-room I found myself in conversation with an eccentric retired army officer who told me, among other interesting things, that potatoes were becoming a common foodstuff in India, from which country he had just returned. He had also been with the army in France in 1815. It is incredible how many Englishmen have been to France, you hardly find a single gentleman who has not been.

5 September   After leaving Mr Woodroffe I returned to Newcastle and rejoined Adolphe. We had letters of introduction to Mr Chapman, a Newcastle banker[68] and to Mr Carr, manager of the Newcastle branch[69] of the Bank of England.

English bankers are not markedly different from our provincial bankers except that they issue bank-notes and that their business is on a larger scale. They get their funds from merchants, farmers, and even from private individuals. They give $2\frac{1}{2}$ per cent interest on deposits and have recently had to lower their discount rates from

[67] Henry Woodroffe was chairman of the Loyal Standard Seamen's Association, Masons' Arms, Waterloo Place, South Shields. D'Eichthal had an introduction from Place. Woodroffe had defended unions before the 1825 Select Committee on Combinations and had published a pamphlet on the appalling conditions in the merchant navy which was to be submitted to the committee. There are a number of letters between Woodroffe and Place in the Place Papers (B.M. Add. MSS, 27,803 and 37,949).

[68] Little seems to be known about the banking partnership of Chapman & Co., of which William Chapman was the head. He had a brother Henry, also a banker in London.

[69] Opened in Grey Street in 1829 (S. Middlebrook, *Newcastle upon Tyne*, Newcastle, 1950, p. 259). It appears from d'Eichthal's notes that Carr had previously been a merchant in St Petersburg.

5 to 4 per cent. They give credit to their customers, and the interest they charge varies according to individual circumstances. Once a week bankers in the town exchange their banknotes, and the balance is paid in bills on London banks. Banks in Scotland have the same system. This weekly exchange has, as you will quickly discern, a peculiar consequence: once their banknotes are returned to them by the other bankers, the bank's profit from the interest on the notes they issue is lost since they then have to pay an interest to the other bankers and thus the advantage they possess in having customers who have a large number of transactions on their current account which brings them the notes issued by other banks (when they make a remittance) and leads them to issue their own notes (when they draw). A customer who works with funds advanced to him without making any remittances does not suit them because the notes they have issued to him come back in a very short while and they have to pay interest on them to other bankers. Clearly, this exchange of notes acts as a check on bankers' note-issuing.

Following the 1825 crisis the Bank of England set up branches with the ostensible purpose of extending circulation. Up to now they have not managed to overcome the influence of local banks, and when you remember that the operations of the Bank of England are not submitted to any public scrutiny, and when you remember the harm already done by several blunders by its directors, you can hardly hope to see the trade of the provinces also fall into their hands.

With Messrs Chapman and Carr we visited various institutions. The Newcastle Literary and Philosophical Society occupies a magnificent building, erected two years ago at a cost of £10,000. It was built by means of private subscriptions and the building belongs to the members of the Society. The same is true of the Assembly Rooms which are very fine. It is also true of the Infirmary where each subscriber who pays 2 guineas is entitled to have one in-patient and one out-patient treated. In some respects this 'esprit d'association' cannot be too greatly admired, a spirit that results from the political history of the country and which cannot be found to the same degree anywhere else.[70] In front of me I have

[70] Other French observers also praised the British 'esprit d'association'. Blanqui, the economist, who visited Britain in 1823 compared French *étatisme* with the private initiative that had built schools and hospitals

the account of a recently formed society to treat eye diseases, which already has 150 guineas in subscriptions. I also have before me the account of the [Newcastle] Savings Bank (for nowadays there is one of these in every little corner of England). Total deposits amount to £200,000, a modest rather than a considerable sum, and 132 friendly societies account for £35,000 of this. These are just a few examples among thousands. All too frequently, however, an 'esprit de coalition' takes the place of the 'esprit d'association'. This town, for instance, is one of those which are fortunate enough to have what is called a corporation, a kind of self-appointing municipal body which is responsible to no one. It draws a very large revenue from certain tolls on ships and a duty on goods. The mayor is chosen by the aldermen and receives an allowance of £2,000—or so at least one of the leading citizens of the town told me. He believed this was so, though he was not sure about it: such are the relations between the corporation and the townspeople. Like many corporations it has some power over the citizens and like the system in general it shrouds its revenues and its operations in mystery.

At the Infirmary we met the hospital surgeon, a very knowledgeable young man who is enamoured of French medicine like all young doctors in England. A mass of prejudices still hinders the exercise of this profession here. Dissecting is difficult because only stolen bodies or the corpses of those who have been hanged can be dissected. A parliamentary committee has recently drawn up a report on this, recommending that unclaimed bodies in hospitals should be handed over to anatomists. But they felt it necessary to add that surgeons should ensure a Christian burial of the bodies once they have finished with them.[71] Amongst other hindrances there is still a distinction between surgeon and apothecary. A surgeon who makes out a prescription dare not sign it. A doctor cannot accept less than a guinea for a call, a rule which the old stagers insist on, and all that a young doctor can do is not to accept any payment for a second visit. Since a guinea per visit is rather expensive, people fall back on apothecaries, and these charge for

---

in Britain, while Horace Say saw in the 'esprit d'association' the 'grand levier' of British industry (see Ethel Jones, *op. cit.*, pp. 132–3).

[71] *Select Committee on Medical Education and Schools of Anatomy*, 1828. It was not until 1832 that the Anatomy Act was passed. This act abolished the dissection of the bodies of convicted murderers and thus removed the stigma attached to it. It also insisted on proper death certificates and a decent burial afterwards.

their calls through the medicines they prescribe—which is why so many medicines, pills and potions are taken in England. The young surgeon confirmed what I had already been told about the large number of consumption cases in England, which are apparently the result of the changes in temperature.

7 September   In the morning Adolphe left to visit Alnwick Castle, which belongs to the Duke of Northumberland and which is on the road to Edinburgh, and I am to pick him up tomorrow. I went to a camp meeting, an open-air meeting held by the Independent Methodists, by the river a couple of miles outside town. When I got there a little after the stated time I saw four or five individuals on a cart with a flute and a bass player by the side of it. There was barely a score of people there and most of these were street-urchins. Gradually the numbers increased, though the number of enthusiasts seemed to me to be very small, and the majority were just curious. In the end a good five hundred people were there. You would not believe the grimaces and intonations made by those creatures, especially when they were praying, at which times they closed their eyes and spoke so quickly they lost their breath. The first preacher looked demented and was infatuated with the prospect of Hell. He lamented the large number of unbelievers who shrugged their shoulders at his sermons—this was the only part of his speech that was well received. He railed against reading stories and novels. The second preacher looked like a rather mangy dog. He complained a great deal about some of the adults in the crowd who were not behaving as well as they might and said that at Sunderland they had held a camp meeting attended by seven thousand people where everyone had behaved very well. He then said prayers in such a rush that he lost his voice. The third preacher seemed a better sort of fellow than his predecessors, a respectable numskull. But as they were to go on until four o'clock and since I had already been there from ten to twelve, I took my leave of them.

In England nearly all the lower class are Methodists[72] and at South Shields, a town with a population of twenty thousand, there

---

[72] This is, of course, an exaggeration. For the *embourgeoisement* of Methodism and for the decline in working-class religious observance in the cities see K. S. Inglis, *Churches and the Working Classes in Victorian England*, London, 1962, *passim*.

is but one Anglican church. Since they are accustomed to join together for every kind of purpose they like the same independence in their worship, and since they feel just as capable as their priests of discussing Heaven and Hell and interpreting the prophecies, they give themselves the satisfaction of discoursing rather than hearing someone else doing it.

I am about to take my leave of Newcastle. The stone buildings and the layout of the streets give the town a certain similarity with French towns.[73] The wide distribution of wealth and the thrift of its citizens make for a further similarity with the citizens of a French town. Enormous fortunes have been made and lost in the coalmines; people talk about the former and forget the latter. A certain Russell has a revenue of £50,000 or £60,000 from a coalmine.[74]

As the parliamentary session has ended, English newspapers give a large number of extracts from French papers. We are given everything: details on the Morea expedition,[75] the bishops' remonstrance and M. Broussais' funeral orations,[76] the epistle of the Abbé Grégoire[77] and reports from the police courts. Each paper cites extracts according to its political leanings.

8 September   I left Newcastle at six o'clock in the morning and set out for Edinburgh via Alnwick, Berwick and Dunbar. The soil of Northumberland is not very fertile, and they grow crops by marling the soil. It is a grain-producing area, very bare, with some

[73] For the 'first big scheme of deliberate town planning' in Newcastle, carried out from the 1780s until the 1820s, see S. Middlebrook, *op. cit.*, pp. 144–50. The rebuilding and extension of the town were carried out chiefly according to the plans of the architects David Stephenson, John Dobson and Richard Grainger (L. Wilkes and G. Dodds, *Tyneside Classical*, London, 1964).

[74] A Mr Russell was owner of the deep newly-sunk Wallsend colliery in the early 1790s (R. L. Galloway, *A History of Coal Mining in Great Britain*, London, 1882, p. 128).

[75] Marshal Maison's expedition of 1828 which forced out the Turks and handed Morea over to the Greeks.

[76] F.-J. V. Broussais (1772–1838), professor of medicine at the University of Paris, achieved considerable renown in the 1820s because of his eccentric medical theories, his interest in phrenology and his oratorical powers. In 1828 he published his *De l'irritation et de la folie* which was widely discussed (see *Dictionnaire de biographie française*).

[77] The Abbé Grégoire (1750–1831) had been a prominent member of the National Convention and under the Restoration became a liberal opponent of the régime.

resemblance to the Champagne district. The Duke of Northumberland's castle at Alnwick is an old Gothic edifice, in no way remarkable, nor is the park. Near to the castle is a memorial erected to the last Duke by his tenants in recognition of his kindness in remitting arrears in bad years.[78] I rejoined Adolphe at Alnwick and he told me that the present Duke has adopted the practice of granting only yearly leases and of insisting on a surety from tenants. It seems that this is only a precaution, that he never changes the leases and that he is generally liked in the area. It is also common practice in Berkshire to grant only leases of one or three years and it seems that landowners in England are trying to reduce the length of lease.[79]

Between Alnwick and Edinburgh the road hugs the coast practically all the way. The coast is dotted with islands and deep coves which are very picturesque but make coastal navigation very dangerous. There are large salmon fisheries at the mouths of the rivers. This fish is so common in Scotland that it is claimed that domestic servants stipulate that they are to be given it only three times a week.

When you near the Tweed the appearance of the country and the people changes completely and you have to arrive from England really to appreciate this. Doubtless most of England's advantages stem from the nature of the terrain. From Wales to the eastern counties and from Northumberland to the south is but one vast plateau without mountains, not very wide, rising very little above sea level and endowed with a magnificent vegetation. As a result communications from one end of England to the other are easy. These are things nature alone can give. When you get to Scotland the people change. People are not as tall and no longer have that fine complexion, the men are smaller and thicker-set. There is, though, a greater ease and familiarity in relationships, people are not afraid of exchanging a few pleasantries and in this respect Scotland is rather like France.

It seems that the approaches to Edinburgh are very beautiful, but it was dark when we arrived. The city is built very much in the

[78] This was the Percy Tenantry Column erected in 1816. See *A Descriptive and Historical View of Alnwick, the County Town of Northumberland, and of Alnwick Castle . . .*, 2nd ed., Alnwick, 1822, pp. 295–8.

[79] This provides additional evidence that the short lease was increasingly preferred by landlords in the early nineteenth century (J. D. Chambers and G. E. Mingay, *The Agricultural Revolution, 1750–1880*, London, 1966, pp. 46–8).

French manner and New Town is magnificent. When we got out of the coach we again met the street-porters that are not to be found in England. One of them took all our baggage on his back, tying it very artistically with a rope and we went to our hotel where we have been treated with a solicitude we have grown unaccustomed to in England.

Edinburgh, 16 September   We have now been in Edinburgh for eight days and the time has passed very quickly. It is certainly one of the most beautiful cities in the world, the most beautiful if you except Naples which it is hard to better. Imagine a city girded to the north and east by the Firth of Forth, that backs onto a mountain at least eight hundred feet high whose crest is frequently hidden by clouds and on whose slopes, extending south and westwards, the city is built.

. . . Everything here is stone-work, so fine and so cheap is the raw material in Edinburgh. Public buildings and private houses are built with perfect taste. They have been careful to erect only buildings in the Gothic (?) style to ensure that they harmonise with those that have been there a long time. They make much less use than we do of Corinthian columns, which require much more elaborate ornamentation and have the added disadvantage of making columns of badly chosen proportions appear more squat. The style of architecture here is very simple, even austere and yet new and imposing. I will never forget the new university buildings, St Paul's church, or above all, the temple-like building that the Society of Arts has had constructed by North Loch.

The magnificent stone quarries close at hand and the picturesque setting of Edinburgh greatly enhance the appearance of the new buildings, and the citizens of Edinburgh, realising the importance of such a situation, have always watched over extensions and improvements to the city and ensured that it remained worthy of the surrounding countryside.

There is, however, another factor which above all has helped make Edinburgh so splendid, and this is the way in which public works are managed. Public works in Britain, main roads, canals, bridges, prisons, schools, churches, improvements in towns, etc. are in no way under government control, nor are they, as is commonly thought in France, under the control of municipal authorities. Some are founded by charitable organisations and paid for by private subscriptions, in which case they are operated by a committee of subscribers. This frequently happens with hospitals, schools and various other charitable institutions. But when the cost of the undertaking has to be paid for by public taxes, either by a toll or by taxes levied by towns, parliamentary approval is needed and, whether the work is undertaken by the government or by private individuals, in this case too control over the works is given to a special commission, nominated either by shareholders, or by Parliament when the government itself provides the capital, in which case the commissioners are unpaid. When work on improving Edinburgh began in 1757 it was initiated neither by the Home Secretary nor by the municipal authorities. The Act of Parliament that gave authorisation for the improvements laid down the establishment of a board to direct operations. This board called for plans from the leading architects of the time and the numerous plans were publicly discussed, attacked and defended by the government, the municipal authorities and the citizens. A plan was finally adopted which seemed to embody all the best points and which in fact has made Edinburgh arguably the most beautiful city in Europe.[80] Each public building in the city has since been erected in the same way either by a board or by a parliamentary commission when the capital was provided by the general public. In this system everyone's pride is involved and they therefore do everything they can to ensure that the work is done as well and as quickly as possible. I know of only one institution in France that corresponds to these trusts or commissions in Britain, and this is the administration of Paris hospitals. If every public building in our capital had been entrusted to a special, unpaid commission chosen from among Parisians, some of them would probably be completed today.

Since people are the same everywhere, in the small number of instances where the French practice has been adopted in England, i.e. in works built out of the Civil List and operated by government ministers, the waste and blunders are ten times worse than they are with us. So much so that they are forced to begin again once works have been completed.

[80] The Edinburgh town council held the competition for the plan of a New Town in 1766. It was won in 1767 by James Craig, the young nephew of the best-selling poet James Thomson (A. J. Youngson, *The Making of Classical Edinburgh, 1750–1840*, Edinburgh, 1966).

Edinburgh is in latitude 56° north and therefore very northerly. Its climate is wet and not very warm, and if they manage to harvest their crops they call it a good season. The only peaches and melons there are hot-house grown but you can buy a good peach for 6 sous and an average-size melon for 50 sous. Although the prevailing temperature is low in these latitudes, proximity to the sea prevents severe cold and frosts are rare and short-lived.

The population in the lowlands is of Germanic origin and speaks an Anglo-German dialect. Highlanders are Celts and their chieftains speak Gaelic themselves and raise their children in the glens so they too can learn the language. Thanks to the Highland Society a Gaelic dictionary has just been published in two enormous volumes,[81] and will be of great interest to English, French and German scholars.

The character of the Scots is quite different from that of the English. They are not at all starchy, formal and fastidious like their neighbours, whose lack of free-and-easiness often makes them very tedious. Here you are allowed to have the knot of your tie awry, to wear grey instead of black trousers, to wash your hands only when you need to rather than ten times a day, and, finally, to talk and laugh simply for the pleasure of it, to express your opinions without having to dress them up in diplomatic language. In after-dinner discussions a Frenchman is reminded of home, and if the conversation is less formal it is no less instructive. We had letters of introduction to the famous Mr McCulloch, to Mr Scarth Williamson, a merchant at Leith, to Mr Borthwick, Mr Blackwood, a silk merchant etc. They have all been so hospitable that we have not dined once at the hotel and only once had lunch there in the past eight days. Mr Scarth's brother, who is a young lawyer only recently married, made his wife go to church alone on Sunday in order to show me the churches of the city. A young man we met at Borthwick's house invited us to lunch with his parents the next day and spent the whole day showing us round the city.

There is no denying, though, that Edinburgh, despite its population of 150,000, its wealth, its splendour, is really a small town. Everyone knows everyone else and is treated on an equal footing. I was surprised to find how little even well-informed men knew about France. In London you could imagine you were at the gates

[81] John Jamieson published his *Etymological Dictionary of the Scottish Language* in 1808 and a supplement in 1825.

of Paris, for everyone knows all about happenings on the other side of the Channel. But here they know no more about us than they would if France was in the depths of Poland. I have found this even with men of letters like Mr McCulloch or Mr Blackwood, the bookseller, or at least these gentlemen were much less well informed than people are in London. You rarely see French newspapers here. However, the close links between the two countries have left their impression. Many of Scotland's political institutions and much of its legal system are taken from France, and a good many words and customs have a similar origin. Unfortunately, commerce between the two countries is mostly confined to the wine trade. I was told that £500,000-worth is imported each year through Leith, and much more would be imported if the duty were lowered. Our brandies pay nearly 4s a bottle and wine about 1s 6d.

A few days before we arrived a company of French actors were here and they were very well received although they were hardly understood. The actresses were especially appreciated even though they were no longer young.[82] However, they knew how to dress, an art they are only just beginning to learn here.

I did not find Scottish education at all what I had expected. I thought that standards in this home of Hume, Adam Smith, Dugald Stewart and Fergusson would be on a par with those of these great men but I fear I was mistaken. The only important periodicals published in Edinburgh are, I think, the [Edinburgh] Review and Blackwood's Magazine. Popular education is confined, as it is in every other Protestant country, to reading, writing and arithmetic for the lower classes, with Latin and a little Greek and Hebrew for the middle classes. Middle-class children early abandon their studies to take up a profession. Mathematics and the exact sciences are only just being introduced into education. Courses at the university are attended by a very few young men who intend to follow a liberal profession; the exact sciences have been rather well taught at the university for some time.

Religious beliefs and even religious practices appear to have retained much of their strength in Scotland. No one ever forgets to say grace before dinner even when only men are present. People go to church twice on a Sunday and on that day public conveyances do not operate and any obligation undertaken on that day is void.

[82] 'de vieux plâtres' in the text.

There is great interest in Mr Irving's prophecies about the end of the world and similar things, and people are very interested in the dispute between Dr Thomson and Dr Grey—or rather Dr Grey's wife—who are at loggerheads over the question as to whether or not the Song of Songs and the Book of Mordecai are authentic: and even though the Synod has judged the one insolent and the other a liar they are again rushing for edification to their sermons.[83] One powerful factor strengthening religious observance is the cautious behaviour of the upper classes who, having learned a lesson from the fate of the French nobility, act with the greatest circumspection. An elderly lady was telling me the other day what she termed a charming story about the Duke of Buccleuch. [84] The Duke is a young man of twenty-two, who has the considerable income of four million francs a year, and was honest enough to pay off his grandfather's debts when he took possession of his estate. He is a first-rate fellow who spends a large part of his time in the saddle, fox-hunting. It is said that he has the kind of horses one rarely sees, horses on which he can jump across ditches that are thirty feet deep and seventeen feet wide. Now, this good lady told me, the Duke was spending one Sunday steeplechasing and tried to jump a hedge that was a little too high and fell off his horse. 'Oh!' he said to his man-servant who had come to help him to his feet, 'I deserved this!' And from that day on, said the good lady, he has never gone steeplechasing on a Sunday.

From the information I have gathered both in England and in Scotland I am convinced that religious observance has shown a marked increase among all classes in the last ten years.[85] Certainly, there are many in respectable society who are persuaded by local Tories or their priests that the French are werewolves, an accursed people who have neither faith nor law. . . . I have found the following rather strange passage in a description of Edinburgh:

[83] Andrew Thomson (1779–1831) and Henry Grey (1778–1859) were not only both ministers and eloquent and fashionable preachers but personal friends before they disagreed in the famous Apocrypha controversy that began in 1827.

[84] Walter Francis Scott, fifth Duke of Buccleuch (1806–84) succeeded his father at the age of thirteen.

[85] Others also found an increase in religious observance. Henry Cockburn observed of Edinburgh in 1832: 'Religion is certainly more the fashion than it used to be. There is more said about it; there has been a great rise, and consequently a great competition of sects; and the general mass of the religious public has been enlarged.'

The revolutionary and levelling principles inspired by the French Revolution gave rise in Edinburgh as in other parts of the Kingdom to many disorders which led to the trial and conviction of several persons who had too great a hold on popular opinions. But these idealistic notions of freedom have long since given way to that real freedom guaranteed by the British Constitution and through a long war the citizens of Edinburgh showed by their zeal and their efforts their devotion to the laws handed down to them by their ancestors.

There are many in Great Britain who are paid to foster a distaste for 'revolutionary and levelling principles' among their fellow citizens. In Scotland their task is easy. People are generally quite content. There are no complaints about the aristocracy, and the Church is not too costly. It would be a mistake, though, to suppose that there exists a fervour here equal to the respect publicly shown towards religion. I have irrefutable proof that the contrary is true. Different people, merchants, lawyers, etc. confessed to me their real feelings, feelings they are forced to hide, for if they did not go to church they would be the butts of all the local gossips and they might later have to face the unfortunate consequences of this. On occasions public opinion shows itself in a different light. In 1815 it was proposed that a church be built on Calton Hill as a memorial to the feats of the British army. Few people found this idea attractive but when the erection of a church modelled on the Parthenon was suggested, subscriptions immediately doubled.[86] Some fifteen years ago Mr Leslie, a very famous physicist[87] who was strongly suspected of irreligious ideas, was proposed for the chair of physics at the university here. Appointments to chairs must be approved by the city council which has to take advice of the Edinburgh Presbytery. This question led to a violent storm in the Presbytery when the ultra-religious party strongly opposed the appointment of Mr Leslie on the grounds that since theology students were obliged to attend physics courses it was not seemly to give them for professor a man whose beliefs were so much at variance with those they

[86] In 1816 the Highland Society of Scotland launched a scheme for a memorial to the Scottish soldiers who had fallen at Waterloo. The monument, which was to be a replica of the Parthenon, was never finished.

[87] Sir John Leslie (1766–1832), a physicist who played an important part in developing the physics of heat and cold, was the first man to make ice artificially and in 1804 had published *An Experimental Enquiry into the Nature and Properties of Radiant Heat*.

would have to preach one day. Nevertheless, when it came to the vote a majority of the members voted in favour of his appointment.[88]

My only purpose in making these observations has been to show the true state of affairs. Furthermore, there are here, as there are in France, people who on their death beds close their doors to priests. But whatever might be the feelings of some, I might even say of the majority of the enlightened and especially of the young, there can be no doubt at all that public opinion is strongly in favour of the established religion which has certainly proved propitious to national prosperity in the last two centuries, and when someone has different views it is prudent for him to hide them with as much care as if he were in Spain.

There is one institution which in time will produce a complete revolution in opinions in the country: Mechanics' Institutes, a kind of school and meeting-place for workers where they are taught the rudiments of the sciences and where they can read the various periodicals. Each town in Great Britain now has one of these schools. There is a very good one in Edinburgh and another one in Leith founded by merchants, one of whom is Mr Scarth. They will take the lower classes away from their bibles and out from under the iron rule of the sermonisers.

The very widespread interest in phrenology is in strange contrast to religious beliefs. Ministers of religion who take an interest in people's appearance also take an interest in phrenology, and since they find this study is consistent in every particular with Christian dogma they think there is no harm in it.[89]

The Scots have long had a well-deserved reputation for thrift and for astuteness in business. Their banking system is a truly national one and nowhere else is there such a developed network. They are true savings banks, with this characteristic: that they put their funds in banks who give them 5 per cent interest and they then give 4 per cent to their own members. There are today more

[88] In his 1804 work Leslie had praised Hume's discussion of causation, and the cry of atheism was thus raised. The issue came before the Edinburgh Presbytery in 1805. The synod referred the case to the General Assembly; the Assembly discussed the matter for two days and then found in favour of Leslie.

[89] D'Eichthal had read in the *Edinburgh Gazette* that a minister had declared that after careful consideration he had found phrenology quite consistent with Christian teachings.

than thirty such banks in Scotland, and they are successful. In nearly all of them members are jointly liable for all the debts of the company and yet there is not a single instance of a bank failing. The Bank of Fife collapsed in 1825 because of embezzlement by the manager, but the public lost nothing. Banks have now lowered their rate of interest on deposit accounts to $2\frac{1}{2}$ per cent and their discount rate to 4 per cent. The circumstances which have favoured the setting up of these banks seem to me to be the industrious habits of the people and even the small size of the country and above all an excellent mortgage system, for in this respect Scotland has been ahead of France for two hundred years.[90]

As far as I can tell from necessarily imprecise information, the nobility are nothing like as rich as they are in England. There are a great many impoverished nobles, ruined by extravagant living. The entails which exist in full force here greatly add to their troubles and there is talk of drawing up a bill which would introduce English law, which allows the owner of an entailed property to sell it with the consent of the immediate heir. The Duke of Buccleuch has the enormous income of £160,000 a year but no one else has as much as that. On the other hand, a number of commoners or middle class have considerable fortunes and there are many so-called small landowners who have between two hundred and one thousand acres. Farms generally vary in size between five hundred and one thousand acres and income from an acre of good land varies between £3 and £5. I was told about one tenant farmer who pays £14,000 a year for his lease. Farmers follow the practice of having their labourers living in and of paying them partly in kind. In England agricultural labourers are treated in the same way as factory workers and this has had a deleterious effect on their character. Leases are usually for nineteen years; farmers would not accept shorter leases but they are not usually given longer ones. In recent years there have been too many instances of landlords treating their tenants unfairly, and the tenant farmers have complained loudly.[91] There is, however, no general ill-feeling towards landlords. They take great care to avoid doing anything which might offend the people, and since only heads of the family bear

[90] D'Eichthal discussed banking problems with McCulloch and on 15 September had lunch with the manager of the Leith branch of the National Bank.

[91] D'Eichthal discussed Scottish agriculture with McCulloch.

titles here, distant relations gradually become commoners. Besides, whatever privileges their rank confers on them the general public is not offended when the nobility make a show of their superiority, and this is an essential factor making for social harmony. The middle class, moreover, also have their aristocratic pretensions; they all buy their coats-of-arms. Thus at least in Edinburgh—for I cannot say that the same is true in Glasgow—all is for the best.

The administration of Edinburgh, as of the other Scottish burghs, is still in the hands of the town council and, though this is better than the very similar system in English towns, there is the same absence of free elections and the magistrates are still not accountable for their actions. Leith is or at least used to be under the jurisdiction of Edinburgh corporation. For some time the citizens of Leith have sought to free themselves from this control and have succeeded in gaining a much greater say in the choice of their magistrates, who were previously chosen by the Edinburgh magistrates, and they are currently disputing the right of Edinburgh corporation to levy certain duties at the port. They have already spent £15,000 on this dispute.

Leith is fortunate in being administered by the Grand Admiral of Scotland. As you may imagine the Grand Admiral does not act himself but nominates deputies who are assisted by a clerk from Edinburgh who reads out all their decisions. Nearly every large port in England has been able to make good the lack of local government institutions by setting up special bodies.

The corporations have retained their power in Edinburgh as they have in other towns. No one is allowed to set up shop within the confines of the city without buying a licence, which costs, I believe, £25–£50.

Yesterday we visited the Bridewell, or prison, built along the lines of Bentham's panopticon. Imagine being in a position to see men in their cells on all sides and above and below. I have never seen such a disgusting sight; it made me think of the hyenas in the botanical gardens.[92]

Holyrood and its neighbourhood are still a place of refuge for debtors. Houses are very expensive to rent. On Sundays debtors can go outdoors without being molested, except if it is suspected

[92] Whilst in Edinburgh d'Eichthal visited the botanical gardens founded by Dr Jamieson.

that they plan to leave the country, when a warrant for their arrest can be obtained. This is the only instance of a writ that can be served on this holy day.

Before I leave Edinburgh I must not fail to mention the number of houses here that are for sale or for rent. This is the case with at least a quarter of the newly-built areas. In 1825 a building mania gripped everyone here, and since the law allows ownership of a floor of a house as opposed to the whole building, many petty capitalists joined together to build houses. However, the increase in population has been so rapid in Edinburgh (it has doubled in the last fifty years) that these houses will soon be occupied.

We left Edinburgh delighted with beauty of the city and the character of its citizens.

Glasgow, 21 September After just managing to pack our bags and send them to Glasgow we boarded the steamboat at twelve o'clock on 17 September to go up the Forth to Stirling. . . . The distance between Edinburgh and Stirling as the crow flies is 30 miles and by water is 50 miles because of the meandering of the Forth. The journey by steamboat cost 7*s*. Though speedy and convenient, this mode of transport is not very pleasant: the engine's vibrations gave the boat a very unpleasant motion and though the river was very calm and smooth as glass, the throbbing and the smoke made several poor ladies very ill. . . .[93]

The workers: hours of labour: combinations. The normal working day is twelve hours, from 5 a.m. to 5 p.m., with three-quarters of an hour allowed for lunch and the same for dinner. In certain cases additional hours are worked.

A few years ago the number of hours worked was much higher; in 1824 the spinners sent a deputation to Parliament and by getting

[93] D'Eichthal visited Stirling and made a short trip to the Highlands. He arrived in Glasgow on 21 September, visited the University, the Mechanics' Institute and several factories, including Owen's at New Lanark. He left Glasgow on 27 September.
The discussion of the Glasgow cotton industry that follows is based on talks he had with the Thomsons (Robert, John and Robert junior) of the Adelphi Mills, 3 Adelphi Place (see *Glasgow Directory*, 1828), and with Peter McDougal and William Smith who managed the cotton-spinning factory of Graham & Co. D'Eichthal had introductions to McDougal and Smith from Francis Place. Place had met them when they had given evidence to the 1824 Select Committee on the Combination Laws. He described them as 'two very respectable serious men' (Place Papers, vol. XIII, B.M. Add. MSS, 27,801).

the repeal of the Combination Acts, succeeded in getting a reduction of the hours of labour from fourteen and sixteen to twelve.[94]

Since 1824–5 the workers' associations have been kept in existence so effectively that the hours of labour have not been lengthened and wages have not been reduced in nominal terms. The spinners preferred, with good reason, to work only half a day rather than see their wages reduced. 'No doubt', said Mr McDougal, 'Wages should fall with the fall in the demand [for goods]. But then the master cotton spinners would have to raise them when demand picks up again. As they do not fall, we are forced to keep them at a constant level as long as we can. The masters themselves are very satisfied with this agreement between the workers, because it has put an end to all disputes, and provided the master know that they are all paying the same rates of wages, the actual rate of wages means rather less to them.'[95]

[94] About this time Parliament passed an Act prohibiting [the employment of] children in factories. Then the spinners demanded that the hours of work of adult males should be regulated as well. The reply to this was: 'Society has a duty to protect children, but you are grown men. It's up to you to look after your own interests.' Since this episode the hours of work on Saturdays have been reduced. Work now stops at 3.45 p.m. The act forbids the employment of children for more than nine hours on that day, but once the children have quitted the mill, the adults cannot carry on working. It is an excellent regulation. The pleasurable prospect of being free on Saturday evening buoys up the children's spirits during the two previous days. They get up earlier on Saturday morning than on any other day of the week. They have time to get everything ready for Sunday [d'Eichthal's footnote].

[95] The people I questioned told me that this arrangement was not a just one, in that it deprives newly-established mills of the advantage arising from the superiority of their up-to-date machinery. But the owners of old-fashioned machinery, being in a majority, agreed to the legislation. In this way all the profits from improved machinery are channelled to the workers. They told me that in England prices are regulated so that profits are divided in fixed proportions between workers and masters. Formerly in Glasgow the worker got no share in the profits of increased productivity, and his wages actually diminished in proportion to the increase in the size of the mule-frame. At present, however, the pendulum has swung to the opposite extreme. They even consider that anyone operating a big mule-frame at the same wages as the spinner on a small one is at a disadvantage, because of its greater weight and the consequent greater difficulty in handling it. The difference is particularly noticeable with fine counts. Smith and McDougal told me that in general there were few complaints against the master cotton-spinners, that, by and large, their business having prospered, the masters had had little reason to engage in disputes with their workers and that when disputes had occurred these had almost always been caused by the malevolence of two or three individuals. In Scotland there are far fewer combinations than in England, both among

It appears that the masters for the most part approved the setting up of a uniform wage for spinners, whatever the size of the mule-frame. It is clear that this is a means of restoring the balance between manufacturers that differences in machinery tend to upset.

Wages. In order to produce fine counts, cotton must undergo four processes: (i) carding; (ii) spindle fly frame; (iii) stretching frames; (iv) . . . [omitted in original].

The spinner is paid on a piecework basis: his output obviously depends on the size and quality of his machine. Nevertheless, by a recent agreement, the price paid to all spinners is the same. After deducting what he has to pay to his piecers, a spinner can earn between 30s and 35s a week, depending on the size of his machine. But since plenty of frames contain between three hundred and four hundred spindles, a spinner's weekly wage can be assumed to be between 21s and 23s per week. This is 15 per cent less than it was a few years ago, up to 1826, when the masters succeeded in cutting the standard rate. An overseer gets £1 per week.[96]

It is the general rule to employ women on stretching frames; they are capable of performing the job. The frames call for less attention and are lighter. Besides, women's labour is cheaper. They earn from 8s to 10s a week. On the spindle fly frame women and young girls are employed. They earn between 6s and 8s a week. There are different grades among piecers: a sweeper earns 2s 6d, a little piecer 4s, a piecer 7s. In general the little piecer and the spinner look after one half of the frame, the other piecer takes care of the rest.

---

the masters and among the men (Mr Thomson wishes to reduce the working day to ten hours). I told these gentlemen that I considered such trade combinations very useful provided they were properly organised, particularly for unemployment relief. They would prevent the unemployed from lowering the normal rate of wages by offering their services at a lower figure. But this same system of fixed wages carried to extremes could have unfortunate results for the workers by rendering their masters' goods unsaleable owing to the high cost of production. They are fully aware of the awkward position they are in and complain a good deal about the type of person on both sides who is never satisfied [d'Eichthal's footnote].

[96] In spite of the nominal lowering of wages, a good spinner gets as much today as he ever did. The reduction [of 1826] has been compensated for by an increase in the speed of the machines and other improvements. Twenty years ago a spinner received 1s per pound of yarn, which today brings him in 3·1d only; nevertheless he earns just as much. . . . When the reduction took place the masters promised that it would be cancelled out by an increase in speed, etc. [d'Eichthal's footnote].

Weavers. Their wages are very low. Women are generally employed on power looms (Messrs Moir, Brown & Co., Glasgow). One woman looks after two looms at the same time and earns between 8s and 10s. On the hand loom, a weaver does not earn more than 6s to 8s. A silk weaver earns 15s to 18s a week.

Standard of living. In general a first-class spinner has a kitchen and a bedroom. This accommodation costs him £5 [per annum] and £1 in local rates. I was told of a flat of three rooms which costs £8 and £2 in rates. A single bedroom costs 2s a week. Breakfast (?) consists of oatmeal porridge or tea or coffee; for dinner, soup and meat; for supper, tea.

The price of bread is now 9d per quarter loaf (4 lb 4 oz); normally it is 10d.

The price of a bottle of beer is 4d; water is also usually drunk.

A man can feed himself well by paying out 5s to 6s a week. He can live very respectably (laundry, board and lodging, etc.) for between 8s to 10s a week.

A complete suit of clothing can be bought for £4 10s.

The price of meat in September 1828 was from 3d to 7d a pound for beef and mutton.

The price of ordinary whisky is 6s a gallon, or so I was told, or 1s a bottle.

Condition of the spinners. In general, spinners of all types are poverty-stricken.

There are a number of reasons for this, some of which are peculiar to Britain. [First of all] there is Irish immigration; according to a moderate estimate there are between thirty thousand and forty thousand in Glasgow. They displace the native workers, who emigrate to America. Some idea of the ease with which the Irish can get to Scotland may be gained from the fact that on 24 September 1827 the steerage fare by steam packet was 6d.

At least half the male spinners and almost all the female spinners are Irish.

At the present moment, when full time is being worked in all the mills there are at least two hundred spinners unemployed. If a man is laid off from a mill, it is sometimes several months before he can find a fresh job. His debts pile up, and he is in no condition to recover financially for some time.

The other causes of poverty are rooted in the very nature of the trade:

1. Periods of short-time working are frequent. The last one continued with various degrees of severity from 1825 to 1828.

2. The number of children employed in this trade is much greater than in any other, and they begin to compete with adults much sooner. At the age of sixteen a piecer feels he ought to be upgraded, 'to expect a pair of wheels'; there are two piecers for every spinner. At the age of forty or forty-five a spinner is redundant; he must seek work of another kind. Young men could well continue to follow the trade of piecer, but they need higher wages than children; in addition, the employers prefer children.

3. Generally speaking, because the wife of a spinner stays at home, he must earn enough to keep both of them. It is quite true that they all too frequently send their young children to work in the mills.

4. The spinner, shut up all day in a warm atmosphere laden with cotton fluff, is very prone to indulge in strong drink. In the evenings he goes to the public house and stays there longer than he originally intended. This is the source of much disorderly behaviour, for after fourteen hours in the factory he looks for company rather than going straight home.

Parents neglect their children, and moreover, many of these children do not live with their parents and have been completely abandoned by them. 'I don't know anything more distressing', Mr McDougal told me, 'than the abrupt change in the style of living of the little piecer when he becomes a spinner at the age of sixteen or seventeen. A wage of a guinea a week seems so enormous to him that the desire to spend it leads him into all sorts of extravagance.'

Debauchery is rife in the extreme among spinners, particularly of the lower grades and above all among the Irish. They sleep twelve or fifteen to a room—men, women and children all higgledy-piggledy. The kind of talk among the women can well be imagined.

Habits of thrift are unknown to them. Perhaps not a quarter of the most skilled spinners have money in the savings banks, and practically none of the other grades.

Weavers. Their state is perhaps even worse than that of the spinners. The latter soften the worst effects of competition because they allow only those brought up in the trade to enter it. Besides there is such a great body of spinners that there is little room for newcomers.

As for the cotton weavers, the superabundance of hands is very considerable. A few years ago the trade was so profitable that people rushed into hand loom weaving and apprenticed their children to it. For this reason the trade is overstocked. The Irish weavers, who are very numerous, raise the numbers a good deal.

Finally, the spread of power looms has undoubtedly hit the hand loom weavers. One weaver is still needed for every two [power] looms, but the workforce consists entirely of women and girls, and ex-hand loom weavers are never employed. Power looms for silk weaving have come in very slowly, because the cost of weaving is a very small element in the cost of the finished article. (Perhaps also there would not be the same possibility of employing an inferior kind of worker as in the cotton industry.)

At ten o'clock in the evening on our return from the village of Langside, near Glasgow, we could still hear the weavers at work. Their dwellings look poverty-stricken.

Education. The education provided for children who work fourteen hours in the mill cannot be very elaborate. Nevertheless some of them go to school on coming out of the mill, and practically all of them go to the numerous free Sunday schools.

As for the men, in return for an annual subscription of 10s, they can go and hear lectures on mechanics and the natural sciences at the Andersonian Institution, founded in 1795 by Professor Anderson, or at the Mechanics' Institution, founded in 1823 by the workers, in opposition to it. They complained that Dr Ure,[97] professor of chemistry and mechanics, could not always be understood and refused to explain difficulties when asked. The new Mechanics Institution has had as many as six hundred subscribers; the difficulties of the last few years have checked the flow of subscriptions, but not the desire for learning. Nevertheless the new institution has not found it easy to struggle against the older one. Dr Birkbeck[98] is a product of the Andersonian, and Glasgow bears the honour of being the first in the field with an institution of such a kind. There are libraries attached to both institutions, and strenuous attempts are being made to found similar ones all over Scotland. I read today in the *Glasgow Free Press* an article criticising the inhabitants of Renfrewshire for being slow to welcome them and

[97] For Ure see W. S. C. Copeman, 'Andrew Ure ... (1778–1857)', *Proceedings of the Royal Society of Medicine*, vol. XLIV, No. 8, August 1951, pp. 655–62.

[98] For Birkbeck see Thomas Kelly, *George Birkbeck, Pioneer of Education*, Liverpool, 1957.

the local magistrates for not doing everything in their power to encourage them. Much praise is given to the education given to the children in the New Lanark establishment and also to the way in which the workers there are treated. But their money wages are too meagre and they find it impossible to save and to become self-reliant.[99]

Religious opinions. Religious opinions appear to be almost extinct among the Irish population. They still seem to exist among the native Scots families. At least, Mr [William] Smith told me, Sunday churchgoing is a mechanical observance, and anyone who stayed away would be frowned upon. I told him that in France the country people still attend church in this way, but more in order to transact business than for any other reason. 'It's about the same here,' he added!

I asked Mr McDougal whether he believed that a sermon was ever of any use. 'No,' he told me, 'no, but pastoral visiting is often very useful.' This is the custom here, above all among Nonconformist pastors, often with the best effects.

Freemasonry is much practised in Glasgow; lodges are numerous. The burial of a freemason forced Mr Thomson to close his factory for two hours.

Politics. There is little interest in politics, except on the subject of Catholic Emancipation. The opinion of all the enlightened operatives and indeed of the majority of the workers is in favour of it.

I gave my own views on the significance of what was happening in Ireland. I was annoyed to see Daniel O'Connell in alliance with Henry Hunt. 'We were shocked by that too,' said Mr McDougal.

Nevertheless he assured me that William Cobbett did not lack admirers in Glasgow. Several former Glasgow operatives are now rich men. There is Mr Done [*sic*], a former blacksmith,[100] today

[99] It is not unusual at Glasgow to see poor young men working as spinners during the summer and using their savings to attend lectures at the university during the winter. Several persons who were planning to do this during the coming winter [1828–9] were brought to my notice. Such students usually take up medicine; there are now two or three surgeons in Glasgow who got their training in this way. Glasgow University is not considered a *fashionable* one. Young men of good family go to Edinburgh. The fee for the lectures is 2 guineas a session. Medical students must attend for three sessions; and so these poor students have to save up 6 guineas [d'Eichthal's footnote].

[100] This was William Dunn (1770–1849) who owned the Dalnotter

worth £300,000. Also Mr [John] Houldsworth[101] and Mr Girdwood.[102] It is said that Arkwright's son, still a manufacturer, has an income of £300,000.

25 September   Mr Robert Owen's establishment at New Lanark. The spinning mill is nothing out of the ordinary; the machinery is old, but very well maintained. As the mill produces low counts, it is not necessary to maintain such high temperature in the workrooms. The women look respectable.

The length of the working day is eleven hours, while it is twelve elsewhere. Wages are paid in coin and only at monthly intervals.

The school for children.[103] This school is intended for the children of employees, and anyone else who wishes to be admitted. Children are taken in at two-and-a-half or three years of age, as soon as they can walk properly; for a while all they do is to play in the courtyard under the supervision of a female; at the end of a certain time, they start to learn the alphabet, geography and natural history.

Class I: About the age of four to five years, they enter the school proper; they continue with reading, geography and natural history. They start on writing and arithmetic.

Class II: They enter this class at about eight years; they must by this time be able to read and write and know the elements of geography and of natural history, and the four rules [of arithmetic]. These branches of learning are continued and a little botany and astronomy are added. At the same time they receive instruction in dancing and music; the boys learn drawing and the girls dressmaking.

After the age of ten years, the children are usually set to work in the mill. The management will not employ them under the age of ten; from that age onwards they continue to attend school in the evening, and they are taught reading, writing and arithmetic; an attempt is made to keep up with what they have learnt in the exact

---

ironworks (1813) and built cotton-spinning works at Duntochter (*DNB*).

[101] John Houldsworth (1807–59). See J. Butt and J. T. Ward, eds., *Scottish Themes*, Edinburgh, 1976, pp. 76, 184.

[102] For Claud Girdwood, who ran C. Girdwood & Co., founders and machine-makers in Govan Street, see *Glasgow Directory*, 1828.

[103] The most recent study of Owen's schools is by Margery Browning, 'Owen as an educator', in *Robert Owen, Prince of Cotton Spinners*, ed. John Butt, Newton Abbot, 1971, pp. 52–75.

sciences. But time is not sufficient to break any fresh ground. That would be possible if the teachers had them on Sunday, but on that day they are obliged to accompany their parents to church, and they are brought together only at 4 p.m. for an hour's psalm singing. We were present during a reading test for Class II. It consisted of making the children spell out from memory words read out to them from a printed list, made up of all the irregular words in the language. The children replied with the greatest accuracy and rapidity.

They were made to read aloud from an anthology of select passages; there are excellent large coloured pictures for geography, astronomy, natural history and botany. The master questioned one of the boys in my presence (it is true that he was one of the better pupils) about the elements, or at any rate the general principles, of the various sciences mentioned above, and even a little about the history of astronomy. I satisfied myself that he understood it all well enough. In the room where the pictures were prepared I saw one which had just been started. Its object was to show the progress of humanity by a series of paintings illustrating the principal events of each epoch. The idea is a very good one but some general philosophic outlook is necessary in order to make it work. The artist had got the Babylonians, Assyrians, Greeks, Romans, etc. marching together in the same epoch. He had not yet tackled the Middle Ages. The task is probably too difficult; if he had some idea of the unity of all history, his job would have been easier.[104]

In all the memory tests, it is found that the little girls are at least equal to the little boys; in geography for example. But in all things which require logical thought the girls are decidedly inferior. The schoolmasters teach phrenology; everybody dabbles in it; they feel the bumps of the children's heads.

There are always at least two teachers in each classroom. This is a very good thing because they are more careful. It appears to me that the only punishment inflicted on the children is to keep them in a special place just behind the master. When their attention flags, they are sent out to play.

While we were there, some prizes were distributed among the best readers. These consisted of household utensils, arithmetic books and copies of the New Testament. The children seemed to prefer the Testaments, but the masters did not. It is true that they

[104] D'Eichthal is writing as a disciple of the historicist Comte.

were better bound but this was no doubt also a reflection on the preferences of the parents.

Religion in Scotland. Sermons by the Rev. Dr [Thomas] Chalmers on astronomy. He demonstrates that it does not conflict with religion.

Posters in the Glasgow streets announce that Mr Edmunds of London, of the congregation of Universalists (those who believe in universal redemption), will preach a sermon on the universality of the evangelical doctrine, followed by a lecture on astronomy.

Manchester, Bolton and Liverpool, 30 September – 16 October. Conversations with Mr Smith, editor of the Bolton Chronicle,[105] *formerly an operative [mule] spinner.*

Manners and habits of the workers in general. In Bolton (and unfortunately practically everywhere else), the public house is the road to ruin for the workers. All their spare cash goes in strong drink, and this leads on to heated discussions, quarrels and fights.

The journeyman boot- and shoemakers and tailors are just as disorderly as the textile workers. The weavers are now pretty sober because their wages are very low; but when wages were high, their conduct was worse than that of all the others; working in their own homes, on piece-work, they are not under any outside discipline. The operatives who work in cotton mills are extremely debauched: this state of affairs is widespread throughout the countryside. It is not unusual for a young man to have three or four illegitimate children by different women, for whom he pays 1s 6d a week each, but nevertheless remaining single.

Women generally work as piecers for the spinners, and practically every spinner seduces his piecer. The boys and girls, toiling in a warm atmosphere, work practically naked in summer. The girls, as a result of the high temperature, are ready for marriage very

[105] William Smith had been in correspondence with Place for some time. In 1826 he had supported Place's family planning campaign (B.M. Place Collection, vol. LXI, part II, p. 60, letter of 18 March 1826). The *Bolton Chronicle*, which first appeared on 9 October 1824, was owned by Thomas Crapp and was at first a Radical paper supporting working-class causes, though it had become more moderate by the early 1830s. The paper supported Doherty's Association for the Protection of Children Employed in Cotton Factories and in January 1829 Smith became secretary of its Bolton branch (B.M. Place Collection, vol. XVI, part II, p. 95).

early, often at twelve years of age.[106] Even the lowest-paid worker contrives to save something on which to get drunk on Saturday evening, and this holds true for the whole of Lancashire. There are really very few respectable men in this class of society.

As a result of the feelings aroused by the dinner to Mr Peel the previous day, the town was full of drunks.[107]

In all probability, drink is a necessity for the spinners; it is the only thing that keeps them going.

State of education. People generally assume that English workers are far better educated than they really are. The more intelligent of them are sent up to London in deputations and people imagine that the rest are of the same calibre, which is quite untrue.

A Mechanics' Institution has been established at Bolton;[108] good lectures are given and it has a good library of one thousand volumes; the rate of subscription is 10s [per annum]. Nevertheless, out of a population of forty thousand souls, there are less than a hundred members, and the Institution will probably have to close. Many workers, deceived by the phrase 'Mechanics' Institution' ask what is the point of teaching them their trade, and believe that the masters want to find out all about the workers' 'know-how' and afterwards turn them out. A similar prejudice has injured the Manchester Mechanics' Institution; in the latter town the workers also complain that they do not have an adequate share in the running of the Institution.[109] Mr Black,[110] a Bolton doctor, tried to give a series of free lectures on anatomy; no one turned up to them. Someone told me that to attract English workers into the Mechanics' Institution it was necessary to give them a few pints of ale every evening.

Mr Smith told me: 'If I could only have a heart-to-heart talk

[106] On the early maturation of girls employed in cotton factories see Friedrich Engels, *The Condition of the Working Class in England*, translated and edited by W. O. Henderson and W. H. Chaloner, 2nd ed. 1971, pp. 183–4.

[107] For the political significance of Robert Peel's visit to Lancashire in 1828, see R. Walmsley, *Peterloo: The Case Reopened*, Manchester, 1969, pp. 441–6.

[108] For the Bolton Mechanics' Institution founded in 1825, see Mabel Tylecote, *The Mechanics' Institutes of Lancashire and Yorkshire before 1851*, Manchester, 1957, p. 57 and *passim*.

[109] These complaints are discussed in Tylecote, *op. cit.*, pp. 134–6.

[110] This was James Black, physician, of 36 Bradshawgate, Bolton (E. Baines, *History, Directory and Gazetteer, of the County Palatine of Lancaster*, Liverpool, 1824, vol. I, p. 553).

with Francis Place for a couple of hours, I would disillusion him on a large number of matters. I would show him that the millenium is still a long way off.' I told him that in my opinion the root of the trouble lay in the workers' lack of a good education, and that there was no hope of any improvement while they were dominated by religious fanatics. I asked him what he thought of the Bible. 'Look at this portrait,' he replied, showing me a likeness of Thomas Paine.

He told me that there were certainly a good number of free-thinkers in Bolton; some of them held these opinions because they were enlightened; others, less admirable, wished to rid themselves of all religious restraints. Most of them did not dare confess their beliefs, as employers did not like workers who were known to be freethinkers because they were more difficult to control. The majority are favourable to Catholic Emancipation.

In good times, the weavers hardly bother their heads about politics at all, but when times are bad they begin to dabble in politics, in the belief that the government is responsible for their distresses. Parliamentary reform has been under discussion for a long time. At the present moment, Irish affairs are beginning to attract attention. There is complete indifference to foreign affairs.

Bolton is very well provided with Sunday schools, but it is questionable whether they are harmful or useful for they serve to perpetuate sectarian disputes. Bolton has always been a nest of Orangeism, but things have much changed in this respect recently. On Sundays it is forbidden to walk in the streets during divine service. The Boroughreeve and the constables patrol the town, seize those who don't look like gentlemen and take them to church by the scruff of the neck; sometimes they are fined by the magistrates. But they hold their hand when they find someone who argues back.

The condition of the manufacturing population. Competition from the Irish is extremely damaging to day-labourers and weavers; many Irish weavers emigrate to Bolton. As for the spinners, they are almost always recruited from amongst the children who have been brought up to labour in the cotton mills. There are very few Irish amongst them.

When a spinner reaches the age of forty or forty-five he is usually worn out. He will be sacked at the first opportunity and if he has no savings he is reduced to hawking boot-polish, collecting rags, entering the 'poor-house' or sweeping the streets.

The weavers of quilts do not earn more than 12s a week, and their boy assistants get 4s.

The number of hours of actual work is twelve, but at Wigan, a few miles from Bolton, they still work from thirteen to fifteen hours [a day]. Mr Smith considered that a communal canteen where they might all eat together would not suit the workers. Their aim is to earn and to spend as much as possible.

Birth control,[111] which alone would ensure the welfare of the working classes, has still not made any progress among them. [Richard] Carlile's work *Every Woman's Book* does not meet with any approval.[112]

There are few Irish in Bolton in comparison with the rest of Lancashire because they used to be too badly treated there. The main reason for this was their Roman Catholicism. These prejudices are less strong today, but when the Irish are mentioned in England they are still spoken of with great contempt even by working men. When Doherty was appointed secretary of the Manchester spinners' committee it caused a great scandal.[113]

It was in 1803, during the war which followed the Peace of Amiens, that weavers' earnings began to fall, and this fall has continued ever since; at that time they were around 30s to 40s per week. Now a weaver does not get more than 8s a week; he is paid as follows. 60 reed, Bolton count, standard: 7s a cut, or 24 yards, 120 shots in an inch 6/4 wide. The day-labourer who works for a weaver receives only 5s 3d: he has to give the weaver 25 per cent. Some weavers, who were able sometimes to buy back three or four looms out of their savings, managed to make a reasonable living by employing day-labourers. A man cannot weave much more than one piece of cloth in a week.

[111] 'La doctrine de la population' in the text.
[112] Carlile's birth-control pamphlet was first published under this title in 1826 (N. E. Himes, *The Medical History of Contraception*, London, 1936, pp. 220–1).
[113] For John Doherty, one of the most active trade unionists in the early nineteenth century, see S. and B. Webb, *The History of Trade Unionism, 1666–1920*, London, 1920, pp. 117–18; G. D. H. Cole, *Attempts at General Union . . . 1818–1834*, London, 1953, *passim*; A. Aspinall, ed., *The Early English Trade Unions*, London, 1949, p. 314 and R. G. Kirby and A. E. Musson, *The Voice of the People: John Doherty, 1798–1854, Trade Unionist, Radical and Factory Reformer*, Manchester, 1975.

The weavers of fancy fabrics are better paid but at the same time their outgoings are also greater.

It is possible that the poverty of the weavers arises to a certain extent from the introduction of the power loom. It would appear from visits to power loom factories that no former hand loom weavers are employed there, the only employment being for very young girls.

The weavers' plight has more likely been caused by the great influx of Irish hand loom weavers, and, what is more important, by the excessively high birth-rate among the weavers' families. It is a way of life which has many pleasant features, for it leaves the weaver, working in his own home, considerable independence. Besides, it is a trade which is easily learnt. It takes six months to train a weaver—the proof of this is in the House of Correction.[114] A ten-year-old child can be put to the loom; it is difficult to employ them otherwise, for in many trades only children who are following their fathers' footsteps are admitted.

If one were to calculate the average weekly wage of all the men, women and children employed in weaving, it would probably not work out at more than 4s. Nevertheless, on the way to Bolton we met hundreds of men who, we were told, were mostly weavers, going to attend a foot race near Manchester. They would make up lost time by night work.

Spinners' wages do not come on the average to more than 18s (I think the figure is too low), although some of them earn up to 30s. Women, who are hardly ever employed except as piecers, earn from 7s to 8s. The nominal wage is severely reduced by the system of fines, which leads to cruel extortion by the masters. The workers complained about it recently, but they were not even given a hearing.

Another abuse is even more flagrant. The employers build rows of houses and force every one of their spinners, even lads of sixteen living with their parents, to rent one. The rent comes to 7 guineas a year which is deducted from their wages in monthly instalments—an abuse arising from not paying wages weekly, which is strongly resisted by the employers (*Glasgow Gazette*).

Altogether, these various deductions are a method of reducing wages, a reduction to which the workers are opposed.

---

[114] *The Annual Register* (1818), p. 128, states that the time allowed to teach a prisoner how to weave calico at the New Bailey prison in Manchester was only three weeks.

Sometimes it is with such profits on lodging and food for their workers that large firms get out of difficulties while smaller ones make losses. At the same time such employers avoid the inconvenience of strikes and lock-outs as well as the poor rate they have to pay when the workers are idle (Mr Simpson).

Spinners usually get married at the age of twenty or twenty-one. There is always the alternative of sending the children to work in the cotton mill, or of going on the parish.

For some time past the Bolton magistrates have been getting harsher: they will not order relief unless the family has a weekly income of less than 2s per week.

The poor rates are now 2s 6d in the £ on the assessed value of property, a rate which is equivalent to two-thirds of the economic rent.

The trade of spinner is easily learned. One can train a young man up into a reasonably competent spinner in one year. Among the working-class families one can expect a child to be born every two years, and the death rate is not heavy for their houses are healthy.

Way of life. Every family has a separate house. Only the Irish live more than one [family] to a room.

The house of Mr Smith, in the centre of the town in a newly-built neighbourhood with two bedrooms, costs £6 a year plus 12s in rates and taxes.

The weavers usually eat porridge made with milk for lunch and supper, with potatoes and bacon for dinner.

The spinners, of course, live rather better. Bread, normally 2d a pound, at the moment is 2½d; beer (wholesale) is 1s 4d a gallon; the best (retail) is from 5d to 7d a quart (4 quarts to a gallon) or 2½d to 3½d a pint (drunk in the public houses 3d or 4d).

Potatoes are 8d for 20 lb wholesale, or 240 lb for 6s 6d. They were 5s [for 240 lb] for a long time, but it is probable that they will now go even higher. Coal is from 5s to 10s a ton. The low cost of provisions has kept the workers alive during the past three years [1825–1828]. A dearth this winter would be terrible.

14 October   The working class: conversations with John Kennedy and others. The workers are earning enough to live on at the moment; if wages were higher, they would work less. Their sole aim always is to keep body and soul together.

There are savings banks in Manchester quite unknown to the

public. When a man has laid something by, he joins with a neighbour and [by pooling their resources] they build a small house,
until one of them becomes the sole proprietor.

Mr [*sic*] [John] Dalton told us that there was near Manchester
a society of weavers who had made a thorough study of botany.

Mr John Kennedy[115] considers 40's to be the average count of
cotton yarn spun in Manchester and 20s as the average wage of a
spinner.

The *Courier* of 14 October states that at Glasgow the weavers
earn from 8s to 10s a week and spinners from 24s to 25s.

Smith told me that at Bolton the average rate of wages [for
spinners] was only 18s. In fact, the further one travels from Liverpool to the north the lower the wages. Mr Kennedy thinks that
workers are usually incapable of passing from one branch of the
trade to the other. He says that a forty-year-old spinner is not
exactly worn out, but that he has no longer got the same agility as
a young man and consequently his job goes to a younger man.

Mr Kennedy is a Scot by origin and has made a fortune in
cotton spinning in Manchester. He now lives in retirement in a
charming house at Ardwick Green. He thinks that cotton-spinning
mills are frequently set up merely as a means of investing surplus
capital and without the slightest regard to the state of demand.
Men behave like a flock of sheep: they follow the stream without
worrying about where they are going. A man establishes a factory
simply because he cannot earn more than 5 per cent on his capital.
Sometimes he is lured by the prospect of beginning with the most
up-to-date machinery. Sometimes he wishes to get ready a factory
for his son; sometimes sheer vanity prompts him to wish to have a
factory more grandiose than those of his neighbours. Plentiful
capital is almost always the precursor of a period of poverty,

[115] For John Kennedy (1769–1855), one of the most successful and
enlightened of the early Manchester factory spinners, see C. H. Lee,
A Cotton Enterprise, 1795–1840, Manchester, 1972, pp. 10–12, 151–3 and
William Fairbairn, *A Brief Memoir of the late John Kennedy Esq.*, Manchester, 1861 (reprinted from the *Memoirs of the Literary and Philosophical
Society of Manchester*, 1859–60). It may be worth noting with regard to
Kennedy's comments on the qualities entrepreneurs needed for business
success that it was a common aphorism in Manchester at this time that
'those that begin with moderate capital and cautious habits do best'. For
a discussion of the small beginnings and cautious habits of local businessmen in the first half of the nineteenth century, see V. A. C. Gatrell,
'The commercial middle class in Manchester, *c.* 1820–1857', Cambridge
Ph.D. thesis, 1971, pp. 139–53.

because the low rate of interest stimulates this kind of forced investment, and results in the flooding of the market with goods.

This state of affairs makes the position of the millowner a very hazardous one. Mr Kennedy considers that the great majority of those who have invested their capital in the cotton industry have been ruined. He told me that sixteen years ago, in 1812, towards the end of the war, there were no more than seven cotton mills belonging to their original owners. He has never seen a firm established with a large capital which has ever succeeded. The only men who have made fortunes have been those who started with nothing. They lived only for their businesses, and brought up in habits of strict economy, people like this are the only ones who possess the resources for tiding themselves over periods of crisis. The principal Manchester manufacturers are men of this kind.

It is a very common fault among [cotton] manufacturers to make over-ambitious changes. The necessary changes should be introduced without renewing the core of the machine. Above all the manufacturer should draw on his own practical experience and not change things merely for the sake of change. Mr Houldsworth operates with machines which are twenty or thirty years old, and so does Mr Kennedy.

He thinks that improvements are going on all the time and that this imposes on the manufacturers the duty of constant vigilance if they are to succeed.

Spinning has not been profitable for a year; fine counts only have been in some demand. The difficulty of selling the yarn has led to the setting up of several power loom factories; spinners have set to work to weave their own yarn because cotton cloth can be sold anywhere, whereas yarn cannot.

Whatever may be the losses of individual cotton manufacturers it is quite clear that society does not lose; on the contrary, society benefits through the continuous lowering of prices brought about by mechanical improvements.

Mr Kennedy confirms what Parkes told me, that very few engine-makers make fortunes. It is remarkable that no great fortune has been founded in Sheffield.

In 1825 there were very few bankruptcies among owners of cotton mills in Manchester. The same is true of Glasgow.

Mr Kennedy has published two articles in vol. III of the *Memoirs and Proceedings of the Manchester Literary and Philosophical*

Society: one on the cotton trade, and the other on the Poor Laws.[116]
His opinion on the subject of the Poor Laws is that they have not
done any harm to the interests of the country and that they maintain the self-respect of the working classes: If we had not had these
laws,' he said, 'what would we have done with the people during
periods of crisis, what would have become of us in 1819 when
distress was rampant among the population and when the people
saw the upper classes around them living in luxury?'

Mr Kennedy has discovered that patents were taken out for
spinning machines in 1720 and 1730 and for carding machines
almost as far back. A steamboat had been tried out on Loch
Lomond in 1786 (see *The History of Glasgow*).[117] Nevertheless,
these inventions did not become economic propositions until long
after they had been devised; this is proof of the slowness with
which new machinery is introduced.

'Piece-work', he said, 'has increased the production of our
workers much beyond anything which we could have hoped for.
But at the same time it has ruined their characters.' 'How's that?'
I asked him. 'Yes,' he replied, 'piece-work has made them more
unruly. Formerly, when a worker saw a gentleman, he doffed his
hat. Now he keeps it on his head.' 'Do you think that is altogether
a bad thing?' 'As far as I am concerned, no, but it hurts [the self-
esteem of] our aristocracy; you know how men cling to their
privileges and prejudices!'

Yesterday, on our way back from Liverpool, an ordinary working
man stopped the coach, and as there was no vacant place outside,
was getting ready to travel inside, when the coachman told him to
leave the place for one of the gentlemen outside and to travel outside himself.

Mr Houldsworth's factory.[118] The women working at the spindle

[116] 'Observations on the rise and progress of the cotton trade, in Great
Britain, particularly in Lancashire and the adjoining Counties' and 'An
inquiry into the effects produced on society by the Poor-Laws', *Memoirs
of the Literary and Philosophical Society of Manchester*, vol. III, 1819. pp.
115–38, 430–46.

[117] James Cleland's *Annals of Glasgow*, 2 vols., Glasgow, 1816. Vol. II
of this work contains a long account of steamboats (pp. 393–401).

[118] This was almost certainly Thomas Houldsworth (1771–1852), merchant and master cotton-spinner at Manchester and Pontefract. At this
time Houldsworth was M.P. for Pontefract. In 1825 the address of the
firm was given as 50 Little Lever Street, off Stevenson Square, but a later
account located the spinning mill at Friday Street near Shudehill. (E.
Baines, *op. cit.*, vol. II, 1825, pp. 217, 312; F. Boase, *op. cit.*, vol. I, 1892,

and fly frames, with 170 spindles, earn from 18s to 20s a week. The [male] spinners, with mules of 320 spindles, earn between £2 and £4 a week clear. But workers capable of turning out the fine counts are not easy to find. They must have long experience of and a perfect acquaintance with the machine. Several of Mr Houldsworth's workers have been with him for between twenty-five and thirty years. The firm is obliged to dismiss many bad workers before finding a good one.

The temperature [in the mill] is no greater than 75°F i.e. from 18° to 20° Réaumur; a degree of heat greater than this would be harmful rather than helpful, as sweat on the workers' hands spoils the yarn. Mr Houldsworth told me that the workers themselves were responsible for allowing the heat in the workrooms to reach an excessively high level, that it was impossible to get them to open the windows, and that he was forced to do it himself when he came into the workrooms. The counts spun are from 100 to 240.

The English character. Mr Martin[119] of Manchester described to me the most outstanding trait of the English character by saying that an Englishman never expressed opinions on subjects which he did not understand.[120] This is perfectly true, except for certain political matters which arouse his passion. A striking thing is the uniformity of manners. It follows that you very rarely meet a gentleman with bad manners.

At every turn you meet an Englishman who expresses joy at the improvement in manners and opinions which the change in Anglo-French relations has had. There was a time when seven-eighths of the nation believed that a Frenchman had no brains.

The manufacturing classes: the masters. I was told that there is not in the whole of Lancashire, a family which has been to the forefront

---

cols. 1548–9; J. L. Carvel, *The Coltness Iron Company*, privately printed, 1948, pp. 25–7.) It may also have been Thomas Houldsworth's nephew, Henry (b. 1797), of Ardwick Green, Manchester. Henry Houldsworth gave evidence before the Factories Inquiry Commission (*First Report*, D. 2, pp. 102–3). D'Eichthal had introductions to both men.

[119] This was probably Charles Martin, commission twist dealer of the partnership of Martin & Hartwright, twist merchants and importers of raw silk, of 15 Pall Mall, Manchester (Baines, *op. cit.*, vol. II, 1825, p. 235).

[120] This was already a commonplace. Samuel Johnson said: 'A Frenchman must be always talking, whether he knows anything of the matter or not; an Englishman is content to say nothing, when he has nothing to say', James Boswell, *Life of Dr Johnson*, London, 1791, vol. II, p. 326.

for more than two generations. Children are brought up in habits of idleness and luxury, and so, when the family fortunes suffer a check, they are incapable of retrieving the situation.

Mr Robert Thomson[121] told me that it is England's misfortune to depend too much on foreign trade. Nevertheless, whatever the inescapable sufferings of the population may be, the people are certainly better off than they were before the establishment of the cotton industry. Besides, one should not be afraid of such misfortunes—uncertainty is part of the human condition: 'Nothing sticks in the world.'[122] Nothing stands still. Everything is either progressing or declining.

According to the *Courier* of 20 September [1828] (taken from the *Manchester Courier*), exports of calicoes to the U.S.A. were:

	July–August 1827	*June–July* 1828	*Decrease*
Plain	2,528,000 yd	1,236,000 yd	1,292,000 yd
Printed	5,300,000 yd	2,712,000 yd	2,589,000 yd

In the same period, calico exports to Brazil were as follows:

	July–August 1827	*June–July* 1828	*Increase*
Plain	2,568,000 yd	4,922,000 yd	2,358,000 yd
Printed	2,008,000 yd	4,426,000 yd	2,416,000 yd[123]

I had a long interview with Mr Mitchell,[124] head of a spinning firm, on the subject of the causes of commercial crises. He appeared to be in whole-hearted agreement with me in the opinion that there had been an increase in the capacity of manufacturing establishments quite beyond the needs of demand, both as a result of improvements in machinery and also from a desire to invest further capital.

He said that piecemeal improvements in machinery, as distinct from fundamental innovations, were going on all the time but they

[121] The proprietor of the Adelphi Mill in Glasgow.

[122] In English in the original.

[123] It has not proved possible to trace these figures in the *Manchester Courier*.

[124] There were several Mitchells employed in the cotton industry in the Manchester area at this time but it is likely that the person interviewed by d'Eichthal was William Mitchell of Mitchell & Co., cotton-spinners of Holt Town, a developing Manchester suburb at this time (E. Baines, *op. cit.*, vol. II, 1825, p. 238).

could be adopted only gradually by the old mills and then only in so far as the cost of the change could be recouped. . . . He thinks that the old-established factory owners have always disliked changing their methods of working, and even today many of them who have known prosperous times cannot bring themselves to adopt those economies without which there can be no profits under present conditions. He states as a fact that many cotton mills were founded for the sole purpose of providing an outlet for capital by people who were completely ignorant of that line of business, and even today the same thing is going on. 'When the rate of interest is low,' he said, 'it's a misfortune for us, because capitalists, in order to get a better return on their capital, use it to build new mills.'

During the years 1826 and 1827 most of the cotton operatives in Glasgow were working half time or less. In 1828 they were all fully employed.

Mr Simpson of Bolton told me that, within a radius of 10 miles of Manchester, people are sometimes fifty years behind that town. What then of foreigners? Nothing can take the place of such an agglomeration of industry and of tradition among the workmen. Take away the manager (the best of them are often the most hidebound) from his accustomed surroundings and he will no longer be able to accomplish anything; it is necessary to have people who have grown up among machines. The English have moulded their workmen after the fashion of their machines.

When the rate of interests falls, capitalists withdraw their liquid assets and set them to work in undertakings with which they are in no way familiar, in particular in cotton mills. At the moment, new dwelling houses are being built, although many of them remain empty. Everyone prides himself on doing better than his neighbour.

John Kennedy witnessed the foundation of Manchester; most of those who established businesses have been ruined. Nevertheless, the country has continued to gain. Successive falls in interest rates have acted as a stimulus to the establishment of new concerns as an investment for capital, and this has led to cut-throat competition. In 1814 there were no more than seven [cotton] firms still belonging to their original owners.

A great number of Scotsmen have raised themselves from nothing in Manchester: witness the careers of Messrs John Kennedy and M'Connell; in Glasgow Mr Done [i.e. Dunn].

Mr [John] Dalton told me that in commercial towns, in fact, children shared equally in the wealth of their fathers.

16 October The journey from Manchester to Leeds cost us 14*s* inside. The country between Manchester and Leeds is the wildest I have ever seen. For some miles it is quite empty and the hills are very high. But as you approach Halifax the country becomes very populous, and when you travel through the area at night it is tempting to think you are in a fairyland. It is lit up by the gas-lights of the factories, the lights of the weavers' cottages and the glow of the forges. In a way, then, the countryside can be seen at night.

Leeds, 18 October   Mr [Benjamin] Gott (woollen cloth mill).[125] When he showed us over his splendid establishment, Mr Gott called our attention to the tidy appearance of his workers: he used them as an example to prove to us that great exertions do not have the effect of corrupting morality. The father of a family works surrounded by his children; the mother is also employed in the mill; but usually the men work away from the women.

He assured us that their behaviour was beyond reproach; and besides, if they had misbehaved, they would be sacked. He also pointed out to us that the temperature was not particularly high, and that this kind of work was in no way harmful to the health of the operatives. I believe implicitly that if all employers looked after their workers like Mr Gott, work in manufacturing industry would be harmful neither to health nor to morals. Nevertheless my hostess, Mrs Hirst, told me that when a young girl has worked in the mills it is a very poor recommendation for her if she wishes to take up domestic service.

I was told that a woollen weaver earns from 15*s* to 16*s* per day [*sic*].

The conversation came round to the subject of social changes which have taken place since the 1790s. At that time there were twenty or thirty first-class families which set the tone; the heads [of these households] had received a classical education. All that has gone, and today there is hardly one house in which one would find cultured companionship. It is extremely difficult to complete

[125] For Benjamin Gott (1762–1840) see W. B. Crump, *The Leeds Woollen Industry, 1780–1820*, Leeds, 1931 and H. Heaton, 'Benjamin Gott and the Industrial Revolution in Yorkshire', *Economic History Review*, vol. III, 1931–2, pp. 45–66.

the quota of subscribers to the Assembly Rooms.[126] Mr Grieg (a vigorous old gentleman aged seventy-two)[127] told me that in Manchester there were perhaps hardly eight leading families which were second-generation.

Commercial fluctuations over the past thirty years are the cause of this. Those who have struggled successfully to survive are men who have risen from nothing, who were capable of devoting their whole time to business. All the leading men today had this kind of background.

Leeds, 19 October My hostess, Mrs Hirst,[128] tells us that the people of Leeds are known far and wide for their uprightness and their religious sentiments. Nowhere else are more chapels and charitable foundations to be found. No time is lost in amusements: the theatre hardly makes a profit.

There was an attempt to set up a race-course, but the employers opposed it, because horse-races are an opportunity for debauchery for the workers and prevent them from working a full week. People are so engrossed with business that they have no time for the pursuit of pleasure. Those who are well enough off take their holidays away from Leeds during the summer. Besides, leisure time is devoted to furthering the cause of some local public body.

Mr Bischoff [129] tells me that the people must not be allowed to amuse themselves, because their favourite amusements always end up in drunkenness. Mr Edward Baines[130] tells me that [prevailing]

---

[126] This is an interesting commentary on R. G. Wilson's *Gentleman Merchants: The Merchant Community in Leeds 1700–1830*, Manchester, 1971.

[127] This was Samuel Greg (1756–1834), master cotton-spinner at Quarry Bank Mill, Styal, near Wilmslow, Cheshire (Frances Collier, *The Family Economy of the Working Classes in the Cotton Industry, 1784–1833*, Manchester, 1964, pp. 38–46 and E. R. R. Green, 'Samuel Greg of Quarry Bank: an Ulster pioneer of the Lancashire cotton industry', *Textile Quarterly* (Belfast), vol. VI, No. 2, pp. 80–3).

[128] Possibly the wife of William Hirst (1777–1858), author of *The History of the Woollen Trade for the Last Sixty Years*, Leeds, 1842. He was a prominent Leeds woollen manufacturer who had suffered heavily in the crash of 1825.

[129] Probably James Bischoff (1776–1845), author of *A Comprehensive History of the Woollen and Worsted Manufactures*, 2 vols., London, 1842 (*Dictionary of National Biography*).

[130] Either Edward Baines senior (1774–1848), proprietor of *The Leeds Mercury* or his son (later Sir) Edward Baines junior (1800–90), editor of *The Leeds Mercury* and the historian of the cotton industry.

religious sentiments conform so exactly to the melancholy and taciturn nature of the English that it will take centuries to change them. Nevertheless, everyone is agreed that there is now a majority in favour of Catholic Emancipation.

Sheffield, 21 October   We visited the cutlery factory of Rodgers & Co., the steel-works of Nailor & Sanderson, the file works of Turton, the Ibbetson brothers' saw file, steel plate and copper pan works, a steel forge and steel wire works, a silverplate works, etc.

In these various factories, human muscle is still the prime mover; they are not very large, and many of the operations are carried out by hand which, it would seem, could easily be done by machinery (for example, [we saw] a punch or cutting machine for steel and copper plates; after each blow the punch had to be re-set; steel wire is still made by simply hammering it).

Mr Ibbetson[131] told us he had been concerned for a long time with the problem of mechanising the operation of several of the processes carried out at Sheffield. He had even got a machine ready at that very moment which could perform in one day the work which it would take twelve men a month to do; a machine of this sort was capable of depopulating the town. He had hesitated to introduce it for a long time; he had tried to introduce it in the United States, but he would prefer, if the machine proved a success, that his native country should enjoy the benefit of it. He showed us a steam engine and a building which had been got ready for this purpose.

He stated that the obstacles to the introduction of machinery in Sheffield were of two kinds:

1. *The raw material* to be worked up, steel, was of such varying quality that a machine which operated with an unvarying action could only be applied to it with great difficulty. He had nevertheless seen files of French origin which had been produced by machinery. They left nothing to be desired.

2. *The smallness of the market.* Machines could be introduced only by breaking down the job so that there was considerable subdivision of labour; this would mean a market extensive enough to

---

[131] For William Ibbetson of the Globe Works, Sheffield see G. I. H. Lloyd, *The Cutlery Trades*, London, 1913, pp. 272, 312 and Friedrich Engels, *The Condition of the Working Class in England . . .*, Oxford, 1971, pp. 249–50.

keep the machines more or less fully employed. Now it would be difficult for a Sheffield manufacturer to achieve sales big enough to keep a large mechanised works going all the time.

When *the introduction of machinery* is under discussion, people are using an inexact phrase. Machinery has existed from the beginning of industrial history, and constant attempts have been made to extend its spheres of action. In Sheffield itself, for example, it is very likely that the tools or machines in use today are much superior to those which were in use twenty years ago, and that much labour has been saved thereby. In the making of plated metal goods, for example, we were shown a kind of lathe which is called *the engine*. By using this the workmen carry out many operations formerly done by hand. These improvements are introduced piecemeal, as capital becomes available to the industrialists for the purpose and as the state of trade and the growth of their businesses gives them the expectation of being able to recoup their capital investment. No machine has been brought to perfection all at once. Even the block-making machine,[132] which in its complete layout is the most perfect ever invented, had its predecessors. The [newly-invented] machine is confined to certain kinds of products before it is applied to the manufacture of a wider range. Thus, the present-day power loom as used in the weaving of simple calicoes is still not capable of being used for the weaving of fancy fabrics nor for woollens (except worsteds) nor for silk. Nevertheless it appears that a patent was taken out for a power loom as early as 1740. There have been constant references to the introduction of machinery for spinning cotton. But we must not forget that at that period, besides the development of Britain's domestic wealth, there had just opened in North America not only an enormous market but a vast source of raw materials. The workhouses had to be emptied to find workers. Mr [William] Radcliffe states that in 1803 he was driven to perfect the process of weaving and to invent his dressing machine in order to be able to weave all the yarn spun in England.[133]

[132] 'Machine à poulies' in the text. For the history of block-making machinery see E. A. Forward, 'Simon Goodrich and his work as an engineer', *Transactions of the Newcomen Society*, vol. III, 1922–3, pp. 7–9; J. W. Roe, 'Interchangeable manufacture', *ibid.*, vol. XVII, 1936–7, pp. 167–8 and H. W. Dickinson, 'The Taylors of Southampton', *ibid.*, vol. XXIX, 1953–5, pp. 169–75 and discussion, pp. 177–8.

[133] William Radcliffe, *Origin of the New System of Manufacture, Commonly Called 'Power-Loom Weaving'* ..., Stockport, 1828, pp. 19–29. For Radcliffe (1760–1841), see *Dictionary of National Biography*.

There have been no doubt occasions on which the introduction of a new machine has been responsible for depriving some workers of their livelihood for some time, but this has never been permanent. Doubtless also, once society becomes accustomed to using machines [in the production of goods] and possesses the technical 'know-how', persons will be found ready to anticipate that growth of demand for their products which alone justifies their multiplication. Such persons injure their own interests and those of others; indeed, very few [new] manufactures intended purely as an investment for capital have succeeded. The glut which results from this overproduction soon halts this kind of speculation, and the local population soon finds work again.

In the works owned by Nailor and Sanderson making cast and forged steel, there are furnaces of which the bottom opens out into a cellar 15 ft deep. The fuel lies on a simple grille surmounted by a chimney (two furnaces in each chimney). The air blast is so violent that it is frequently necessary to close the cellar vent-holes.

Businessmen in Sheffield tend to be very short of ready cash. Mr Michaelson told me that he often sold people iron to a greater value than their own capital, but those were respectable persons who did not indulge in speculation. Mr Kennedy had already assured me that the same state of affairs existed among makers of steam engines, as if it was impossible to earn a living making tools [i.e. capital equipment].

Workers' wages. Cutlers earn from 14s to 28s a week; filemakers 8s to 9s. In Mr Ibbetson's workshops, the workers' average wage is 27s, although some get from 2 to 3 guineas. Mr Ibbetson is gradually getting rid of the drunkards so that his workers are a pretty regular set, but Mr Turton told me that good filemakers worked only three days a week and spent the rest of the time drinking.

There are some well-educated men among the workers. One of Mr Ibbetson's workers is a first-rate mathematician; there are also five or six lay preachers among them and some great orators. We saw posters stuck up in the streets expressing the thanks of the Britannia metal workers for support received from the public during their last strike against their employers, which ended in an increase in wages.

GUSTAVE D'EICHTHAL
(1802–1886)
an intellectual portrait

I

Though he was physically unprepossessing, and was small in stature, though he was sickly as a child and subject to nervous breakdowns as an adult, Gustave d'Eichthal early showed great promise. At the Lycée Henri IV he was an outstanding scholar among schoolfellows who themselves later achieved distinction. During the most formative years of early adulthood he was successively the first disciple of Auguste Comte and a leader of the Saint-Simonian sect, playing a significant part both in its organisation and in the evolution of its doctrine. The young d'Eichthal was held in high regard by a number of his contemporaries, including Auguste Comte, John Stuart Mill, Thomas Carlyle and Francis Place.

In his subsequent career, however, he never quite fulfilled the promise of his youth. He himself recognised this, and died murmuring to his eldest son that he still had much to do. He knew his own failings, for he found study and writing difficult and worked only in bursts. His mood alternated between extreme optimism and deep depression and throughout his life he reproached himself for his timidity and lack of success as a proselyte. He often found personal relations difficult and for long periods in middle and old age he felt himself misunderstood, spurned, a preacher in the wilderness. Yet throughout his life, in all his different intellectual pursuits, there runs a unifying thread. He was a dreamer who dreamed of ending what he regarded as an existential crisis. First as a Comtian, then as a Saint-Simonian and afterwards throughout his long life, he found mankind hesitating at the crossroads, thought he glimpsed the future path and beckoned his reluctant contemporaries to follow him. He, like other more famous 'Prophets of

Paris', turned his back on politics, on violent revolution and taught by the word rather than the sword. Typical of so many of his romantic generation, he had a deep-felt sense of all-pervading structural crisis and sought to end it, above all through a new synthetic religion. Little remembered though d'Eichthal is, he was thus representative of the influential group of messianic thinkers that flourished in Paris in the first half of the nineteenth century.

There are other reasons why it can be claimed that d'Eichthal's name and achievements have been unjustifiably forgotten.[1] He and his family are significant, firstly, for the light their experience throws on the problems faced by Jews in the changing atmosphere of the late eighteenth and early nineteenth centuries and in the increasing toleration of Jews in western Europe and especially France. He was one of the first generation of Jews in the post-emancipation period to play a part in Gentile society and was one of a small group of assimilationist Jews who not merely ceased to be orthopraxis but converted to Christianity. He even sought to reconcile Judaism and Christianity in a new religion. D'Eichthal is interesting, secondly, for the rôle he played in two of the most seminal of early nineteenth-century intellectual schools, Comtism and Saint-Simonism. D'Eichthal is worthy of our attention for a third reason. After his break with the Saint-Simonians and until his death in 1886 he took an interest in Greece, its language and legacy, in ethnology, and particularly the racial problem and the origin of different civilisations, and in biblical exegesis and the religious question. These pursuits brought him some minor importance in the intellectual life of nineteenth-century Paris.

---

[1] His son, Eugène, left a sympathetic portrait of his father in his *Quelques âmes d'élite (1804–1912), esquisses et souvenirs*, Paris, 1919, especially pp. 15–48. This apart, the only studies devoted to d'Eichthal are two lectures given after his death, and subsequently published, which dealt with two aspects of his work, his hellenism and his Old Testament criticism: le Marquis de Queux de Saint-Hilaire, 'Notice sur les services rendus à la Grèce et aux études grecques par M. Gustave d'Eichthal', in Gustave d'Eichthal, *La Langue grecque, mémoires et notices, 1864–1884*, Paris, 1887, pp. 1–103; Maurice Vernes, *M. Gustave d'Eichthal et ses travaux sur l'Ancien-Testament*, Paris, 1887, 59 pp. D'Eichthal's attitude towards Judaism and his involvement in Saint-Simonism have been discussed in Barrie M. Ratcliffe, 'Crisis and identity: Gustave d'Eichthal and Judaism in the Emancipation period', *Jewish Social Studies*, vol. XXXVII, 1975, pp. 122–40, and Barrie M. Ratcliffe, 'Saint-Simonism and Messianism: the case of Gustave d'Eichthal', *French Historical Studies*, vol. X, 1976, pp. 484–502.

II

In the years following Jewish emancipation in France Gustave d'Eichthal and his family were part of a small group of wealthy Jews, some of whom abandoned Judaism but most of whom assimilated into Gentile society and achieved some prominence there. There are a number of reasons to explain why we know relatively little about this assimilationist minority. For one thing there is a lack of statistical data on the extent of the decline in religious observance, of marriage with non-Jews, of conversions among different groups, and between different communities. For another, assimilation is not an easy word to define. Its meaning can range from adopting the language of the country of residence in religious ceremonies, a relaxation of dietary and other laws and participating more fully in Gentile culture, to the abjuration of Jewish faith and even conversion to Christianity. Jewish historians have tended to ignore those who converted since they left the mainstream of Jewish life. For many of their orthopraxis contemporaries, as for some Jewish scholars later, those who left Judaism were guilty of abandoning a fortress still under siege, for in the early nineteenth century Jews in many parts of Europe were still subject to intolerance and even persecution.[2] Many too, resented the proselytising of a minority of those who converted to Christianity and who sought to convert Jews, even founding orders to work among the poor.[3] On the other hand, it has sometimes been suggested that assimilation was an easy process, that even conversion was, as that cynic Heine called it, 'an entry ticket to European culture'. Thus the wave of conversions among wealthy Jews in Berlin in the early nineteenth century—Rachel Varnhagen suggested that half the members of the Jewish community converted[4]

[2] The young Heine condemned converts in his bitter poem 'Almanson', written in 1823 while the historian Heinrich Graetz condemned the comportment and conversion of the Salon Jewesses as the consequence of their infection with 'moral depravity'. H. Graetz, *History of the Jews from the Earliest Times to the Present Day*, vol. v, London, 1892, p. 448.

[3] Pierre Pierrard, *Juifs et Catholiques français*, Paris, 1970, pp. 22–3. In France the best known of these were the brothers Théodore-Marie and Alphonse-Marie Ratisbonne, sons of a wealthy Strasbourg banker, who founded the Congregation of Notre-Dame-de-Sion. See Théodore Ratisbonne, *Mes souvenirs*, published by the Congregation of Notre-Dame-de-Sion, 1966.

[4] Carl Cohen, 'The road to conversion', *Leo Baeck Yearbook*, vol. VI, 1961, p. 264. It should be added that of course only the upper echelons

—has received the name *Gefallsucht*, which suggests that the reason for it was the need to be accepted in Gentile society. Yet assimilation and conversion, whether seemingly rapid and large-scale as in Berlin or a more gradual erosion of tradition and belief as in Paris, was never undertaken lightly or merely as a result of a fashion, social or intellectual. In many if not most cases, it was the consequence of considerable soul-searching and led to strains and even breaks of family ties and friendships. It reflected what was for many a crisis of identity. It was the product not of sudden impulse but of a long process of attrition: social and cultural assimilation in both France and Germany date back to the early eighteenth century and even beyond. Assimilation and conversion took place, above all, among the wealthy, educated minority who had the privilege of being more acceptable to Gentile society. Thus the Jewish bankers, financiers and stockbrokers in Paris in the first half of the nineteenth century, with the exception of James de Rothschild and one or two others including the Sephardim Moïse Millaud,[5] abandoned traditions and faith and married into Christian society.[6] For the d'Eichthals the crisis of adaptation was first posed not by the French Revolution and the legislation of the 1790s that freed Jews from many of the constraints previously placed upon them but by the widening commercial horizons and growing contacts with gentile society and by the *Aufklärung* of the eighteenth century. Then for the first time a small number of Christians openly questioned and even abandoned their religion and were thus a group into which Jews could assimilate without having to abjure their faith and convert to Christianity.[7] The *Aufklärung* also posed an intellectual challenge, for the Jewish faith had to be justified to both adherents and outsiders in the light of reason. It was in the wealthier and freer communities, especially in the flourishing port of Bordeaux but also in Lorraine, that the first signs of a decline in the spiritual importance of Judaism and a weakening of rabbinical

---

of the three thousand Berlin Jews abandoned their faith, and that even among these many retained their links with the Jewish community. Many stayed within Judaism and moved towards Reform, while still others stayed orthodox and opposed every effort at innovation. Michael A. Meyer, *The Origins of the Modern Jew: Jewish Identity and European Culture in Germany, 1749–1824*, Detroit, 1967, pp. 149ff.

[5] *L'Univers israélite*, XXVIIe année, 1 November 1871, obituary notice.

[6] Léon Poliakov, *Le Développment de l'antisémitisme en Europe aux temps modernes (1700–1850)*, Paris, 1968, pp. 218–19.

[7] Léon Poliakov, *ibid.*, pp. 208–9.

authority are to be seen.[8] Gustave d'Eichthal's maternal grandfather, Salomon Moïse Lévy, was a prosperous linen and woollen
merchant in Nancy in Lorraine who in the eighteenth century
benefited from widening opportunities under the paternal government of Stanislas Leszczynski. Lévy's wife was a Berr, sister of
Berr Isaac Berr who was a leading member of the community in
Lorraine, appealed for emancipation before the Constituent Assembly and participated in Napoleon's Grand Sanhedrin in 1806.[9]
Gustave's mother, who was born in 1780, grew up in an orthopraxis family, strongly influenced by the generous ideals of the
philosophes, where the new vistas opened up by emancipation were
enthusiastically debated. She was to bring up her own children
'under the double inspiration of Moses and Voltaire'.[10]

More interesting perhaps is the rise of the d'Eichthal family in
Germany, which on a lesser scale paralleled that of the Rothschilds
in that the successful founder of the dynasty spawned sons who
migrated to different parts of western Europe to follow financial
and industrial careers.[11] Unlike the Rothschilds, who remained
conspicuously faithful to their religion, the d'Eichthal family, in
different ways and at different times, shed old ways for new. It was
Aron Elias Seligmann (1747–1824) who founded the family fortune.

[8] S. Posener, 'The social life of the Jewish communities in France in
the eighteenth century', *Jewish Social Studies*, vol. VII, 1945, pp. 195–232.
See also Arthur Hertzberg, *The French Enlightenment and the Jews*, New
York, 1968, especially chapters VI and VII.
[9] Gustave d'Eichthal himself described Berr's role in the 1790s in
Israel Bederride, *Les Juifs en France, en Italie et en Espagne, recherches sur
leur état depuis leur dispersion jusqu'à nos jours, sous le rapport de la législa-
tion, de la littérature et du commerce*, Paris, 1859, 602 pp.
[10] 'Notes autobiographiques', Fonds d'Eichthal, *Bibliothèque de
l'Arsenal* 14408, fo. 4.
[11] The Seligmann family were created barons in 1814 and took the title
d'Eichthal. There is regrettably no study of the family, and our information is drawn in part from the *Neue Deutsche Biographie*, vol. IV, pp. 386–
387, and, above all, from Gustave d'Eichthal's manuscript notes in the
Fonds d'Eichthal, *Bibliothèque de l'Arsenal*, 14408, fos. 4, 9 and 10.
Although there are studies which trace the rise of the Court Jews in
eighteenth-century Germany, there is regrettably no study of the remarkable explosion of Jewish banking talent in south-western Germany in the
late eighteenth and early nineteenth centuries, in such centres as Frank-
furt, Fürth, Karlsruhe, Mayence, Munich and Würzburg, talent which
played a leading rôle not only in German banking but in financial centres
such as Antwerp, Brussels, London, Paris, Vienna and, as Barry Supple
has shown, even New York ('A business élite: German Jewish financiers
in nineteenth-century New York', *Business History Review*, vol. XXXI,
1957).

Originally from a small village near Heidelberg, he became a tobacco manufacturer and salt factor, made money supplying the armies of the Elector Palatine but made his fortune when one of his patrons became Elector of Bavaria. He followed the Elector to Munich where he set up as a banker. Such success was won at a price; his wife felt unable to alter her customary Jewish way of life. Following Talmudic precepts she continued to hide her hair and she obtained her husband's permission to stay in Mannheim rather than live in Munich. He came to visit his wife faithfully ever year and nineteen children resulted, ten of whom survived into adulthood.

The second generation of d'Eichthals by their careers and marriages show how a dynasty of merchant bankers set up a family network in different financial centres in Germany and France. The eldest son, Arnold (1772–1838), became a banker in Augsburg, and though he later went bankrupt his son Auguste also became a prominent financier and entrepreneur. The second son, David (1776–1851), had the most spectacular career, forsaking the successful bank he had established in Karlsruhe to become an industrialist. In 1810 the Grand Duke of Baden persuaded him to invest in an ailing cotton factory being run by the famous engineer and industrialist, Johann Georg Bodmer.[12] At first David d'Eichthal ran the enterprise jointly with Bodmer but gradually it became his sole responsibility. This was no small-scale factory but a large water-powered cotton mill in a disused monastery at St Blasien in the Black Forest. Its ownership made d'Eichthal one of the largest manufacturers of his day, though he remained very much an outsider among Baden industrialists because of his Jewish origins and difficult character. Not satisfied with turning out high-quality yarn, he added a small-arms factory and an engineering works to the complex. When the young Gustave d'Eichthal visited St Blasien in October 1819 he found the buildings magnificent and described the church as one that would be considered beautiful even in Paris. The factory, he wrote, employed nearly a thousand workers, and his uncle's house contained furniture, utensils and locks that had been manufactured on the spot.[13] By 1840 David

---

[12] W. O. Henderson, *Industrial Britain Under the Regency: The Diaries of Escher, Bodmer, May and de Gallois, 1814–18*, London, 1968, pp. 7–8.
[13] Letter from Gustave d'Eichthal to his mother, 4 September 1819, Fond's d'Eichthal, *Bibliothèque de l'Arsenal*, 13746, fo. 43. See also 'Par-

d'Eichthal had already 1½ million florins invested in St Blasien, and when he got into financial difficulties in 1845 he transformed the enterprise into a joint-stock company. This, however, did not prevent the company going into liquidation with the mid-century depression.

Yet another son, Simon (1784–1854), also became an important banker and industrialist in Munich. He acted as intermediary for Bavarian state loans to Greece between 1832 and 1837 and along with Ludwig I founded the Bavarian Mortgage and Exchange Bank in 1835. This was established to provide cheap credit for peasants on the security of mortgages, and out of an original capital of 10 million florins d'Eichthal provided 3,347,000. He was one of the first in Bavaria to take an interest in railway construction. Though his first project, to build a line from Munich to Salzburg, was unsuccessful, his second, to construct a railway between Augsburg and Munich, was completed and opened in 1840. A fourth son, Bernard, decided on a scientific career and studied in Paris and Rome as well as in Germany, but he died in 1831.

Louis d'Eichthal (1780–1840), Gustave's father, was destined for a banking career. For this purpose he was sent to Paris when he was seventeen to serve his apprenticeship with the important Jewish banking house of Worms de Romilly. Two other young men were also starting their careers in the same bank: Isaac Rodrigues-Henriques, a Sephardic Jew from Bordeaux who was to abandon Judaism and whose son Olinde was to introduce Gustave d'Eichthal to Comte and Saint-Simon, and Abraham Mendelssohn, son of the celebrated philosopher and father to the composer and pianist Felix Mendelssohn-Bartholdy. In Paris Louis d'Eichthal found the turmoil of ideas and the political and military developments of the Directory and Consulate exciting. He had already had a good grounding in mathematics, physics and chemistry, he attended scientific lectures and was struck by the status that scientists enjoyed in France. Henceforth he was to nurture an ambition that at least one of his sons should follow a scientific career and if possible gain admission to the highly respected Ecole polytechnique.

---

ticulars of the cotton mills and cotton trade of France in 1833 (communicated by Messrs L. d'Eichthal and Son to Sam. Greg and Co.)' and 'Particulars of cotton mills in the Grand Duchy of Baden, April 1833 (correspondence of Mr Melly to Samuel Greg and Co.)', in Factories Inquiry Commission, *First Report*, B.P.P., 1833, D. 2, pp. 39–40 and 43.

Though he spent some time in Nancy, where he met and married Fleurette Lévy in 1803, he returned to Paris in 1812 and set up on his own account as a merchant banker. Five children resulted from his marriage, three of whom survived into adulthood: a daughter, Annette, and two sons, Gustave (1804–86) and Adolphe (1806–75). It was Adolphe who joined his father in the family firm and who succeeded him when he retired. He had an exceptional career as a merchant banker, becoming the close associate of the Pereires and James de Rothschild in railway construction during the July Monarchy. Though the depression and revolution of 1847–8 put d'Eichthal's firm in financial difficulties he recovered and prospered during the Second Empire thanks to his close ties with the Pereires and their successful Crédit Mobilier. As recognition of his ability and respectability he was nominated a regent of the Bank of France, the first Jew to be given a share in the direction of this bastion of financial orthodoxy.[14] In the 1840s he was the youngest of the regents and the only free trader among them.

For the wealthy and successful among the three thousand Jews in Paris[15] the problem of adaptation and assimilation was more marked than elsewhere. There was a greater social contact with Gentile society, the atmosphere was freer, and within the Jewish community there was a discernible relaxation of religious ties and some alienation of the rabbinate.[16] For a variety of reasons Judaism in France was weakened in the early nineteenth century. The Consistories, and especially the Central Consistory, were starved of funds, while the rabbinate was not only understaffed but further weakened by the presence of chief rabbis who were mostly elderly, who had insufficient knowledge of the ways of Gentile society and, in some cases, of its language. The result was that while some ties were merely loosened, others were irremediably severed in conversions to Christianity, and even where outward forms and rituals

[14] Letter from Adolphe to Gustave d'Eichthal, 30 January 1839, Fonds d'Eichthal, *Bibliothèque de l'Arsenal*, 13749, f. 139. It may be noted that James de Rothschild obtained a seat for his son, Alphonse, only in 1855.

[15] Out of a city of six hundred thousand inhabitants. S. Posener, 'Les Juifs sous le Premier Empire', *Revue des études juives*, vol. XCII, 1932.

[16] On the continuing decline of religious observance among Jews in France, and especially in Paris, and on the introduction of a number of religious cermonies copied from or strongly influenced by Catholic ritual into Jewish religious observance, see Michael R. Marrus, *The Politics of Assimilation: A Study of the French Jewish Community at the Time of the Dreyfus Affair*, Oxford, 1971, especially pp. 51–84.

were observed, their spiritual meaning lost its intensity for many. This slackening of religious observance followed the pattern that was developing in Gentile bourgeois society and may, indeed, have owed something to the indifference of the Catholic society in which some Jews had contacts.[17]

The d'Eichthals also had the example of a number of their friends and relations who were assimilating into Gentile society and even abandoning their faith. Aron Elias d'Eichthal converted to Christianity in 1811 and Simon d'Eichthal became a Catholic in 1819. Louis d'Eichthal kept up his friendship with Abraham Mendelssohn, who like him had become a merchant banker and who also lost his faith and became a Christian. Mendelssohn's father, Moses, protégé of Lessing and philosopher of repute, had argued that Judaism was a *Vernunftsreligion*, that there was no contradiction between religious belief and critical reason, had sought to bring his co-religionaries into contact with the philosophy of the Enlightenment and to effect a rapprochement between Jews and the society in which they lived. He therefore began to translate the Bible into German, the first Jew to do so since Saadia Gaon, and he set up a school for Jews (the Berlin Jüdische Freischule) where not merely Jewish but general subjects were studied. His son, Abraham, was a true child of the Enlightenment, did not believe in the revelations of the Bible, and ceased to be a practising Jew. Abraham Mendelssohn's sisters also abandoned Judaism: Henriette, a governess in Paris, became a Catholic, after considerable soul-searching, at the behest of her employers, while his intellectual sister, Dorothea, was first an enthusiastic Lutheran and then an equally assiduous Catholic. Abraham Mendelssohn made his house a meeting-place for Berlin intellectuals, and Alexander von Humboldt set up a laboratory and observatory in his garden.[18] He brought up his children as Lutherans, secretly at first so as not to offend their grandparents, and had them baptised in 1816. He did this partly because he had experienced the disabilities Jews suffered and he wanted his children to be more integrated into Gentile society and partly because like Lessing he believed that one civilised religion was as good as another.[19] He was persuaded to

[17] Adeline Daumard, *La Bourgeoisie parisienne de 1815 à 1848*, Paris, 1968, pp. 347–51.

[18] H. E. Jacob, *Felix Mendelssohn and his Times*, London, 1963, pp. 7–8.

[19] He described his views on religion in a letter to his daughter Fanny in 1820. This is reproduced *in extenso* in Sebastian Hensel, *The*

take the final step of converting to Christianity—which he did soon after the baptism of his children—by his brother-in-law, Jakob Bartholdy, who had become a Prussian diplomat and Lutheran and who was to leave Mendelssohn his fortune. Another friend and fellow banker, Isaac Rodrigues-Henriques, who had earlier been a member of the Grand Sanhedrin and had defended Jews against an attack by de Bonald in 1806, also ceased to observe the dietary laws, the Sabbath or Passover, whilst his eldest son, Olinde, married a Roman Catholic.

Once in Paris the d'Eichthal family ceased to be orthopraxis. Though they made an effort to have their children taught Hebrew, they soon gave up and Gustave was later to regret his ignorance of the language.[20] The sons were also given an education in French schools, as this was one of the preconditions for integration into French society. Only during the 1790s had Jewish children begun to attend *lycées* and other schools,[21] and it was the children of the well-to-do who generally did so. Thus Isaac Rodrigues-Henriques sent his son, Olinde, to the Lycée Charlemagne, and Olinde later went on to take a doctorate at the University of Paris. Elie Halévy, cantor at one of the synagogues though he was, sent his two sons, Léon and Fromenthal, to the same school. In October 1813 Gustave d'Eichthal was sent to a private Catholic boarding school where he was a fellow pupil of Isidore Geoffroy Saint-Hilaire, son of the naturalist, and Victor Lanjuinais.[22] Five years later he entered the Lycée Henri IV, one of the best-known schools in the country, and his brother joined him there soon afterwards. Here his close friends were Lanjuinais and Saint-Marc Girardin, destined for a career as a writer and politician, and here, from 1816 onwards, he was the outstanding pupil of his year. He was made to suffer for his origins because he was quickly nicknamed 'the Jew' and 'the Wandering Jew'.[23] His formal education was also the

---

Mendelssohn Family, 1729–1847, 2 vols., London, 1884, vol. 1, pp. 79–81.

[20] Notes autobiographiques, Fonds d'Eichthal, *Bibliothèque de l'Arsenal*, 14408, fo. 10.

[21] S. Posener, 'The immediate economic and social effects of the emancipation of the Jews in France', *Jewish Social Studies*, vol. 1, 1939, pp. 271–326.

[22] Notes autobiographiques, *loc. cit.* He described this boarding school as 'une des plus famées, une des plus comme il faut de Paris'.

[23] Journal de Gustave d'Eichthal, Fonds d'Eichthal, *Bibliothèque de l'Arsenal*, 14717, p. 40.

occasion for the family'a final break with Judaism. The headmaster of Gustave's boarding school, Jean-Baptiste Le Comte, persuaded his parents to bring up their children as Catholics, and they were baptised in the parish church of Deüil, near Versailles in July 1817, with Le Comte and his wife acting as godparents.[24] His parents were also baptised a few months later. This was not the gesture of a moment. One of the first books that Gustave d'Eichthal had to read, and which he regularly read through childhood, was a French translation of the Bible illustrated with reproductions of Raphael paintings.[25] Nor was the step without repercussions, for some family ties were severed, as with the Lévys in Nancy.[26] When in 1836 Gustave d'Eichthal fell in love with Augusta de Laemel, daughter of his father's youngest sister, Sophie, he was prevented from marrying her by the Laemel family, who had remained orthopraxis, and by his father who insisted the girl convert to Catholicism.[27] When he did marry it was to a Jewess—Félicité Rodrigues-Henriques, who came from a Sephardic family of stock-brokers who had also converted to Catholicism.[28]

For the young Gustave d'Eichthal Catholicism was not just a convenient passport to gentiledom. He embraced it with fervour because he, like Abraham Mendelssohn's composer son, Felix, belonged not to his father's generation, which subjected everything to the acid test of reason, but to transform the 'inner Saul into a Paul'.[29] As he confessed in 1832:

à treize ans je suis devenu chrétien; j'ai abreuvé mon coeur, sans le pouvoir rassasier, des joies du mysticisme et de l'extase. J'ai

[24] 'Extrait des registres des baptêmes de l'Eglise paroissale de notre Dame de Deüil', Fonds d'Eichthal, *Bibliothèque de l'Arsenal*, 14405.

[25] Gustave d'Eichthal later described how he thrilled at the drama presented in the Bible in his confession of faith to the Saint-Simonians in 1832. Manuscript in d'Eichthal's hand, dated 2 March 1832, Fonds d'Eichthal, *Bibliothèque de l'Arsenal*, 14408, fo. 7.

[26] Notes autobiographiques, *loc. cit.*

[27] Correspondence between Gustave d'Eichthal, Sophie de Laemel and Louis d'Eichthal, 1837–8, Fonds d'Eichthal, *Bibliothèque de l'Arsenal*, 13748 and 13749. Augusta de Laemel thus shared the fate of Jettchen Gebert in Georg Hermann's novel of that name.

[28] Acte de Mariage, Fonds d'Eichthal, *Bibliothèque de l'Arsenal*, 14405, fo. 11.

[29] It might be said that his conversion was similar to that of Théodore Ratisbonne (1802–84) whose state of mind while he worked at the Fould Bank in Paris between 1818 and 1820 was very close to d'Eichthal's the previous year. Théodore Rattisbonne, *op. cit.*, pp. 17–18 and 116–18.

aimé la chasteté, la tempérance, la pudeur. J'ai conquis avec les
martyres la palme de béatitude. J'ai prié avec les solitaires et
vaincu les ruses du Démon. . . . Et j'avais éprouvé aussi les
angoisses de la damnation. J'avais tremblé pour moi-même et
pour ceux qui m'étaient chers, devant la perspective des éternels
chatîments. Enfin j'avais souffert du christianisme tout ce qu'il
en fallait pour m'en détacher, dès qu'une foi plus consolante me
serait présentée.[30]

Many among the prosperous Jews in Paris in the nineteenth
century found religion had lost much of its spiritual meaning, yet
they remained outwardly orthopraxis because it was a badge of
their Jewishness, a link with previous generations. D'Eichthal
abandoned Judaism but remained a Jew. Despite his conversion,
he, like a number of others who left Judaism, like Börne and Heine,
was not lost to Judaism and his Jewishness remained an important
element in his career.

There is an old Talmudic saying that 'a Jew who has sinned still
remains a Jew' and d'Eichthal never forgot or denied his origins.
In 1837 he confessed that memories of the religious devotion of
both his grandmothers had left him with a deep attachment to his
people.[31] Besides, others did not allow him to to forget his origins,
and he met with anti-Semitism on a number of occasions. One of
his reasons for joining the Saint-Simonian movement was just this
prejudice, and he himself suggested that it might have been the
most important consideration.[32] As a member of the sect he was
partly responsible for the interest Saint-Simonians took in Jewish
affairs.

Perhaps the best instance of d'Eichthal's continuing concern for
the condition of the Jews came in 1836–7 when he spent six months
trying to persuade the Austrian government to grant toleration to
Jews. The situation of the half a million Jews in the Austrian
Empire was indeed unenviable, intolerance having reached a peak
during the reign of Francis II when Jews were heavily taxed and
Jewish marriages and areas of settlement restricted. Between October 1836 and March 1837 d'Eichthal visited Prague and Vienna.[33]

[30] Manuscript of 2 March 1832, Fonds d'Eichthal, *Bibliothèque de
l'Arsenal*, 14408, fo. 7.
[31] Extract of a letter to ?, n.d. (1837), Fonds d'Eichthal, *Bibliothèque de
l'Arsenal*, 14393, fo. 3.
[32] Gustave d'Eichthal and Ismayl Urbain, *Lettres sur la race noire et la
race blanche*, Paris, 1839, pp. 12–13.
[33] Manuscript in the hand of Gustave d'Eichthal dated 10 May 1837,

and was both dismayed by the restrictions Jews suffered and impressed by the intellectual ferment he found, especially among the well-to-do Jews in the capital. In Vienna he not only found the large number of baptised Jews he found elsewhere but he met for the first time the Reform movement in Judaism. He saw some dangers in Reform and shared the fears of conservatives that it would be the first stage along the road to the abandonment of the Jewish religion and identity and that it might cause a rift between the Jews of Germany and the still traditional and conservative communities of eastern Europe. But he was enthusiastic about the enlightened spirit and the toleration of other creeds that the movement showed and impressed by the warmth of religious sentiment shown by Reform leaders.[34]

He arrived in Vienna on 19 October and three days later he wrote to Chancellor Metternich offering him a copy of his book *Les Deux Mondes*[35] and requesting an audience.[36] This was secured on 26 October. It was d'Eichthal's intention to discuss his views on Jews and Judaism and the question of improving their status in the Empire, but Metternich was much more interested in the Saint-Simonian movement. He claimed to have been the only European statesman to have appreciated the importance of the sect and to have read their publications. He asked d'Eichthal how such talented young men could have abandoned the practical for the mystical. Only during the second hour of their discussion did d'Eichthal

---

Fonds d'Eichthal, *Bibliothèque de l'Arsenal*, 14408, fo. 5; journal de Gustave d'Eichthal, 19 October 1836–10 March 1837, *ibid.*, 14718.

[34] He wrote to his brother: 'J'ai causé avec quelques uns de ces hommes; et je puis déclarer qu'il n'y a point sur la terre de foi religieuse aussi énergique, aussi chaleureuse et en même temps aussi patiente aussi résignée que celle de ces hommes; je dois les aimer car je me suis retrouvé tout entier en eux et jusque dans leur amertume.' Letter from Gustave to Adolphe d'Eichthal, 10 October 1836. Fonds d'Eichthal, *Bibliothèque de l'Arsenal*, 14393, fo. 4.

[35] *Les Deux Mondes . . . servant d'introduction à l'ouvrage de M. Urquhart, 'La Turquie et ses ressources'*, Leipzig, 1837. This was a translation of David Urquhart's book originally published in London in 1833. D'Eichthal's activities in Austria have been discussed by Michael Graetz in 'Une initiative saint-simonienne pour l'émancipation des juifs: lettres de Gustave d'Eichthal sur son voyage en Autriche', *Revue des études juives*, vol. CXXIX, 1970, pp. 67–84. Unfortunately, Graetz did not use all the d'Eichthal papers and seems to believe that d'Eichthal wrote *Les Deux Mondes*. . . .

[36] Copy of a letter from Gustave d'Eichthal to Metternich, 22 October [1836], Fonds d'Eichthal, *Bibliothèque de l'Arsenal*, 13758, fo. 30.

manage to steer the conversation towards the Jewish problem.[37]
The matter was delicate, since protocol demanded he say nothing
that seemed to require a response; and though at the time he found
that Metternich admitted the historical and religious contribution
the Jews had made, showed some sympathy towards their cause
and gave some vague assurances, he later discovered that Metternich—perhaps out of malevolence, more likely because of d'Eichthal's demeanour—had ascribed to him bizarre and erroneous
notions about founding a new religion.[38] Though d'Eichthal made
further efforts to gain a second audience,[39] these were without
success. He was received by the Archdukes Charles and Louis[40]
but these audiences too were fruitless.[41]

Whilst he was in Vienna it was being suggested in Jewish circles
that one way to improve the condition of the Jewish population
would be to remove the onerous tax burden borne by all Jews in
the Empire and that this might be best done by the Jewish community itself offering to pay a lump sum equivalent to so many
years' revenue from the tax. Such a project was suggested to
d'Eichthal by his uncle, Leopold de Laemel, a Prague banker, and
by Leopold von Wertheimer. Laemel pointed out that since some
of the wealthiest Jews in Bohemia had abandoned their faith the
tax burden on the remainder had increased, and since the poor
were always the most steadfast in their faith there was a danger that
the Jewish population there would be reduced to 'a proletarian
mass'.[42] D'Eichthal enthusiastically took up this project and, as

[37] Letter from d'Eichthal to his brother, 28 October 1836, Fonds
d'Eichthal, *Bibliothèque de l'Arsenal*, 14393, fo. 27. Metternich was later
to express his appreciation of the Saint-Simonians to Michel Chevalier.
Letter from Chevalier to Arlès-Dufour, 30 August 1840, Fonds Enfantin,
Bibliothèque de l'Arsenal, 7704.

[38] Copy of a letter from d'Eichthal to the Archduke Louis, n.d., Fonds
d'Eichthal, *Bibliothèque de l'Arsenal*, 13758, fo. 10.

[39] Draft of a letter to Metternich, n.d. (12 January 1837), Fonds
d'Eichthal, *Bibliothèque de l'Arsenal*, 13758, fo. 10.

[40] On 13 and 29 November 1836, journal de Gustave d'Eichthal, Fonds
d'Eichthal, *Bibliothèque de l'Arsenal*, 14718.

[41] D'Eichthal did not feel, however, that his efforts were entirely in
vain for he felt—with what accuracy we cannot tell—that his appeals had
counted for something in the alleviation of some of the restrictions on
Jews in Vienna early in 1837. Letter from Sophie de Laemel to Gustave
d'Eichthal, 22/23 February 1837, Fonds d'Eichthal, *Bibliothèque de
l'Arsenal*, 13748, fo. 169.

[42] Letter from Leopold de Laemel to Gustave d'Eichthal, 12/13
January 1837, Fonds d'Eichthal, *Bibliothèque de l'Arsenal*, 13748, fo. 158.

Salomon Rothschild was away from Vienna at the time, wrote to James de Rothschild in Paris suggesting that his firm, the greatest Jewish banking house, act as guarantor for the raising of the necessary funds among the Austrian Jewish community. In his letter he argued that after discussion with leading Jews and with influential persons in the administration he had come to the conclusion that the only way to improve the condition of Jews in the Empire was the payment of an indemnity to the Austrian government. One reason for this was that since the more prosperous Jews were given greater toleration they were less interested in the fate of their co-religionaries. Another reason was that popular prejudice was still powerful and that there was an anti-Semitic element even in government and court circles. Moreover, the financial position of the Empire would not allow any reduction in taxes that would either lower revenue or put a greater tax load on the rest of the population. In this situation the offer of an indemnity by the Jewish community might well be favourably received. Besides, when slaves had been liberated in the British West Indies, compensation had been given to slave owners, and French *émigrés* who had had land sequestered during the Revolution had also been compensated by the Bourbons.[43] By mischance this letter never reached Rothschild and d'Eichthal left Vienna without getting any further, though he was to raise the matter again in October 1837.[44] In the event it was not until ten years later that the Austrian government began the process of gradually abolishing the tax on Jews.[45] The only visible result of d'Eichthal's efforts to improve the lot of Austria's Jews was the article he had inserted in the *Journal des débats* in August 1837.[46] In this he described the unhappy situation of Jews in the different provinces of the Empire and discussed the circular issued by Count Karl Chotek, governor-general (*Oberstburggraf*) of Bohemia, which proposed to accord fuller civil rights to the better-off Jews in the province. James de Rothschild congratulated him on this article, had it published in the *Augsburger*

---

[43] Letter from Gustave to Adolphe d'Eichthal, 13 December 1836, copy of a letter to Baron James de Rothschild, 6 December 1836, Fonds d'Eichthal, *Bibliothèque de l'Arsenal*, 13758, fos. 14 and 20.

[44] Copy of a letter from Leopold von Wertheimer, 10 October 1837, Fonds d'Eichthal, *Bibliothèque de l'Arsenal*, 13759, fo. 11.

[45] Letter from Sophie de Laemel to Gustave d'Eichthal, 22 August 1846, Fonds d'Eichthal, *Bibliothèque de l'Arsenal*, 13745, fo. 156.

[46] *Journal des débats*, 9 August 1837.

Allgemeine Zeitung[47] and soon afterwards invited him to his country residence at Ferrières.

D'Eichthal also showed an interest in the future of the Jewish religion. In common with many Jews in Paris he was strongly influenced by the first writings of the post-emancipation period which showed the growing self-respect among the Jews. These writings, addressed to the general public, attempted to show the grandeur of the Mosaic Code, the contribution Judaism had made to Christianity and might still make to civilisation. A number of Jewish apologists emerged about this time. In Germany there was Isaac Bernays and the founder of the *Zeitschrift für jüdische Theologie*, Abraham Geiger. In France the assimilationist Léon Halévy published his *Résumé de l'histoire des juifs modernes* in 1828, but by far the most important of those who sought to rescue Jews and Judaism from the calumnies heaped upon them over the centuries was Joseph Salvador (1796–1873). This sadly neglected Jewish intellectual[48] abandoned the medical career he was studying for when he read of the anti-Jewish riots in Germany in 1819[49] and henceforth devoted himself to rehabilitating the history and religion of the Jews and to tackling what contemporaries called 'the religious question'. He became one of the most original of Jewish thinkers in the nineteenth century, whose work was greeted with enthusiasm, especially by assimilationists.[50] The first task Salvador set himself was to assert the originality and continuing relevance

[47] Letter from James de Rothschild, 14 August 1837, Fonds d'Eichthal, *Bibliothèque de l'Arsenal*, 13759, fo. 17.

[48] Regrettably there has been no study of Salvador or his achievement since the two biographies published in 1881, the second of which relied heavily on the first: Colonel Gabriel Salvador, *J. Salvador, sa vie, ses oeuvres et ses critiques*, Paris, 1881; James Darmesteter, *Joseph Salvador*, Versailles, 1881, which first appeared in the *Annuaire de la Société des études juives*, 1880. It may be noted that the editor of the liberal *Archives israélites* published three appreciative, if sometimes critical, articles on Salvador: année XXI, 1860, pp. 98–106, 165–74 and 215–22. See also obituary notices in the *Archives israélites*, XXXIVe année, 15 April 1873, pp. 248–50; *Univers israélite*, April 1873, p. 492.

[49] He described the impact of his reading about persecution of Jews in his *Paris, Rome, Jérusalem, ou la question religieuse au XIXe siècle*, 2 vols., Paris, 1860, vol. I, pp. 240–7.

[50] The assimilationist James Darmesteter, for example described how he discovered 'avec surprise et plaisir' that Salvador's ideas were very similar to his own. Darmesteter, *op. cit.*, p. 4. For Darmesteter see Michael R. Marrus, *The Politics of Assimilation: A Study of the Fremch Jewish Community at the Time of the Dreyfus Affair*, Oxford, 1971, pp. 100–10.

of the Mosaic Code.[51] Thus in his *Loi de Moïse* published in 1822, Moses became the founder of the first known republic who gave the Jews a constitution based on equal rights for all and who established the rule of law.[52] In his second work Salvador developed this theme and also set out to show how much Christianity owed to Judaism.[53] His third book, *Jésus Christ et sa doctrine*, attempted as others were doing elsewhere, to place the life of Christ in its historical context, showing the debt owed to Jewish prophets and to the religious sects of Judea. At the same time he tried to justify the rôle of the Jews in the trial and condemnation of Christ.[54] The logical continuation of this book was his next work which described the destruction of Jerusalem, the end of the Jewish state and the Roman occupation. Here he praised the heroism of Jewish resistance, portrayed as an early nationalist movement.[55] His final and most developed publication was *Paris, Rome, Jérusalem*, which was published in 1860. Once again, Salvador praised Judaism as the trunk of which Christianity and Mohammedanism were the branches, a trunk whose strength remained intact. A new epoch had begun with the French Revolution which had radically altered the political and social system of Europe and yet left untouched the established religions. Europe had thus entered upon a period of spiritual crisis. Salvador claimed that a new religious revival was preparing which would gain much from Judaism. It was typical of his writing, as it was of those of others who were proferring remedies for the spiritual crisis at this time—including, as we shall see, d'Eichthal himself—that the precise manner whereby the new religion was to emerge or exactly what it would borrow from Judaism were not discussed.

Though it was not until 1836 that d'Eichthal read any of Salvador's works, they had an immediate impact. On his return to

---

[51] A number of historians in early nineteenth-century France had used the past for political reasons, and particularly to find the unfolding of liberty or the triumph of the people. See Stanley Mellon, *The Political Uses of History: A Study of Historians in the French Restoration*, Stanford, 1958 and Jacques Barzun, 'Romantic historiography as a political force in France', *Journal of the History of Ideas*, vol. II, 1941, pp. 318–29.

[52] *Histoire des institutions de Moïse et du peuple hébreu*, 3rd ed., Paris, 1862, vol. I, preface, pp. 1–3; vol. II, pp. 330ff.

[53] *Ibid.*, vol. I, pp. 383–94.

[54] *Jésus Christ et sa doctrine*, Paris, 1838, vol. I, p. 333.

[55] *Histoire de la domination romaine en Judée et de la ruine de Jérusalem*, 2 vols., Paris, 1847.

France from Austria in March 1837 he hastened to meet this 'prophète méconnu jusqu'ici, mais prophète',[56] and he was as impressed with Salvador in person as he had been with his writings.[57] He hailed Salvador's later publications[58] and recommended his books to friends.[59] D'Eichthal and Salvador kept in touch after 1837 and there may well have been a two-way influence on the later publications of the two men. Thus Salvador was one of the few who encouraged d'Eichthal to undertake his work of biblical exegesis which d'Eichthal considered to be parallel to Salvador's. Certainly his aim and conclusions were strikingly similar. Like Salvador, d'Eichthal believed not only that it was important to bring Judaism and the Jewish people closer to Gentile society but that the Jewish people had made and could still make a significant contribution to western civilisation. In 1838 he admonished his father for failing to understand his continuing attachment to Judaism:

> Le Judaïsme c'est pour vous le culte de quelques barbes crasseuses que vous avez entendu hurler autrefois dans la synagogue de notre village. Le Judaïsme c'est pour moi la manifestation la plus élevée de la révélation divine, la source et la base du Christianisme et l'Islamisme, et qui, après avoir enfanté ces deux religions nommées, doit achever cette initiation du monde en les réconciliant.[60]

In the 1830s he believed that the Jewish people were a bridge between east and west, that they could help reconcile western Christianity with eastern Mohammedanism and he continued to

[56] Letter from d'Eichthal to Enfantin, 31 March 1837, Fonds d'Eichthal, *Bibliothèque de l'Arsenal*, 14407.

[57] Letter from d'Eichthal to ? ('ma tante'), 2 April 1837, Fonds d'Eichthal, *Bibliothèque de l'Arsenal*, 13759, fo. 13. According to his journal (*ibid.*, 14718) he visited both Salvador and Chief Rabbi Marchand Emmery on 29 March. His notes on Salvador's *Histoire des institutions de Moïse* are to be found in *ibid.*, 7826, fos. 16–29.

[58] *Jésus Christ* . . ., for example, in letters to Freslon, 22 September 1841, Fonds d'Eichthal, *Bibliothèque de l'Arsenal*, 14389, and to Enfantin, 25 January 1838, *ibid.*, 14407, fo. 31.

[59] To his lifelong friend and correspondent, John Stuart Mill, who replied that the *Loi de Moïse* had made 'a very mixed impression' but that *Jésus Christ* . . . made a 'wholly favourable' one. Mill added that he found Salvador nearer the truth than even Strauss and had recommended his book to several people. Letter from Mill to d'Eichthal, 10 January 1842, Fonds d'Eichthal, *Bibliothèque de l'Arsenal*, 13756, fo. 49.

[60] Copy of a letter from Gustave d'Eichthal to his father, 25 April 1837, Fonds d'Eichthal, *Bibliothèque de l'Arsenal*, 13749.

believe that the Mosaic Code had played and could still play an important rôle in the progress of humanity.[61] Thus when in the new dawn that d'Eichthal, like so many others, felt had arrived with the February Days of 1848, he proclaimed the need to establish a new religious democracy. The first step in this would be the erection of a statue of Moses in the Place de la Concorde.

D'Eichthal, moreover, continued to take more than a passing interest in the civil and religious condition of the Jews. He continued to applaud the Reform movement and in 1838 wrote to a friend that in his opinion the Jewish faith had been the only religion that had made any progress during the previous thirty years.[62] In 1882 he was still applauding assimilationist moves, like the formation of a Jewish group in Russia in that year whose aim was the adoption of Russian as the language of all Jews in the empire and the acceptance of military service.[63] He maintained close relations with a number of the leaders of the French Jewish community, including Alphonse and Max Cerfberr, Adolphe Crémieux, Isidore Cahen, Isidore Loeb and Zadoc Kahn.[64] In 1865 he met and found he had much in common with Maurice Hess and helped him with the last stages of his translation of Heinrich Graetz's study of Judaism and the origins of Christianity.[65] For a time he worked with the Jewish scholar Salomon Munk. He gave

[61] Thus for example while he was in Vienna late in 1836 he proclaimed that Israel had a special religious destiny as 'l'âme de l'humanité'. Letter to James de Rothschild, n.d. (1836), manuscript entitled 'Ils disaient le Cantique de Moïse et le Cantique de l'Agneau', Fonds d'Eichthal, *Bibliothèque de l'Arsenal*, 7826, fo. 2. In 1838 he wrote a long letter to Enfantin critical of the failure of Saint-Simon to grasp the rôle of the Jews in the formation of Christianity. Letter of 25 January 1838, *ibid.*, 14407, fo. 31.

[62] Letter from Gustave d'Eichthal to Ismayl Urbain, 8 September 1838, Fonds d'Eichthal, *Bibliothèque de l'Arsenal*, 13741, fo. 26.

[63] Journal de Gustave d'Eichthal, entry for 25 May 1882, Fonds d'Eichthal, *Bibliothèque de l'Arsenal*, 14724.

[64] When d'Eichthal died the *Archives israélites* published a warm obituary which said that 'il gardait pour la croyance de ses ancêtres qu'il avait quittée une profonde estime, et pour ceux qui la professaient une sincère affection; c'est dans ces sentiments qu'il s'intéressa, sans en partager les convictions, au Recueil que nous rédigeons, et qu'il nous honora plus d'une fois de ses savantes communications et de ses intéressants entretiens.' Notice by Isidore Cahen, XLVIIᵉ année, 15 April 1886, p. 116.

[65] The work was *Sinaï et Golgotha, ou les origines du Judaïsme et du Christianisme*, Paris, 1867. Journal de Gustave d'Eichthal, entries for 16 September, 19 December 1865, 3 January and 1 March 1866, Fonds d'Eichthal, *Bibliothèque de l'Arsenal*, 14721.

him funds to cover some of the costs of one of his books,[66] while Munk helped d'Eichthal in his work on the Pentateuch.[67] When the Société des études juives was set up in 1880, d'Eichthal was a founder member.

Gustave d'Eichthal also showed a concern for the state and status of Jewish communities in the Near East. As he explained to Adolphe Crémieux, he was born a Jew and in his youth had suffered from the anti-Semitic prejudice that was still to be found in Paris, and part of his family had remained orthopraxis and lived in countries where Jews were still oppressed. His interest in anything that might improve the condition of Jews in the world was thus a natural one.[68] During a stay in Algeria in 1838 he was struck by the poverty of the Jewish community in the capital and attempted to interest the Central Consistory in their cause.[69] After the Damascus affair of 1840 he initiated discussions with the Pereires, Max Cerfberr, Adolphe Crémieux and other leading Jews to see what could be done to safeguard the position of Syrian Jews in the future.[70] In 1839 he took up the question of Jerusalem and Palestine, which was just beginning to interest a few Jews in the west. The problem was, above all, one of the rights of the Jewish population in an area under the control of the Pasha of Egypt. The problem was also becoming one of a homeland for Jewish settlement, because the 1840s saw the early gropings towards Zionism, a number of romantic, impractical projects for Jewish settlements in which the future of Jerusalem and Palestine were discussed.[71] D'Eichthal suggested that the Central Consistory approach Mehemet Ali with the proposal that Jerusalem and Palestine be declared neutral, independent of both Egyptian and Turkish control.[72] The idea

---

[66] This was Munk's *Mélanges de philosophie juive et arabe*, Paris, 1857–9, 2 vols. Journal de Gustave d'Eichthal, entry for 8 January 1867, Fonds d'Eichthal, *Bibliothèque de l'Arsenal*, 14722.

[67] Journal de Gustave for 19 September 1872, Fonds d'Eichthal, *Bibliothèque de l'Arsenal*, 14724.

[68] Letter, n.d. (August 1839), Fonds d'Eichthal, *Bibliothèque de l'Arsenal*, 13759, fo. 15.

[69] Letter to Alphonse Cerfberr, 29 September 1838; Journal de Gustave d'Eichthal, Fonds d'Eichthal, *Bibliothèque de l'Arsenal*, 14719; letter from Joseph von Wertheimer to d'Eichthal, 6 October 1839, *ibid.*, 13749.

[70] Journal de Gustave d'Eichthal, entry for 7 February 1841, Fonds d'Eichthal, *Bibliothèque de l'Arsenal*, 14719.

[71] Walter Laqueur, *A History of Zionism*, London, 1972, pp. 46ff.

[72] He first had the idea on 21 July 1839; journal de Gustave d'Eichthal, Fonds d'Eichthal, *Bibliothèque de l'Arsenal*, 14719.

was that in this manner not only would liberty of worship and the sanctity of Jewish holy places be ensured but those of Christians and Muslims as well.[73] The Holy Land would thus be a secure place of pilgrimage for believers from all three religions. He also envisaged his plan would be a step towards the reconciliation of these faiths, perhaps in the new synthetic religion he hoped for. It would also be an alternative to the suggestions that Palestine become an exclusively Jewish homeland.[74] Though he felt that this was a suggestion that could come from a Christian or a Muslim he believed that coming from the leaders of the Jewish community in France it would help to prove the spirit of conciliation that animated French Jewry. D'Eichthal approached leading members of the Central Consistory, including Crémieux, its vice-president, and the Cerfberrs.[75] They took his initiative seriously enough to place it before a full meeting of the Consistory. Though his project was rejected in 1839 he took it up again in 1864–5 when he approached the *Archives israélites* as well as a number of prominent Jews including Isidore Cahen, Maurice Hess, Lévy Bing and Louis Königswarter.[76] He reiterated his proposal in a letter entitled 'Rome et Jérusalem' which was published in *Le Temps* in November 1867,[77] and although this had little impact outside his circle part of his letter was reproduced in the *Archives israélites*[78] and d'Eichthal attempted to interest Jules Baroche, minister of justice, in his plan.[79]

[73] Letter from d'Eichthal to Crémieux, n.d. (August 1839), Fonds d'Eichthal, *Bibliothèque de l'Arsenal*, 13759, fo. 15. The idea was not entirely original, for there was some discussion of it at the time, for instance in the *Augsburger Allgemeine Zeitung*, 18 August 1839.

[74] He believed such plans for a Jewish homeland to be retrograde and the work of 'juifs supersticieux'. It was at this moment that Sir Moses Montefiore requested permission to purchase land in Palestine. *Journal des débâts*, 6 August 1839.

[75] He saw Alphonse Cerfberr on 13 August and Crémieux on 23 August. Journal de Gustave d'Eichthal, Fonds d'Eichthal, *Bibliothèque de l'Arsenal*, 14719.

[76] Letter from Gustave d'Eichthal to Ismayl Urbain, 15 June 1864, Fonds d'Eichthal, *Bibliothèque de l'Arsenal*, 13742, fo. 169; journal de Gustave d'Eichthal, entries for 1, 20 and 31 May 1865, *ibid.*, 14722.

[77] *Le Temps*, 6 November 1867; letter from Gustave d'Eichthal to Ismayl Urbain, 3 November 1867, Fonds d'Eichthal, *Bibliothèque de l'Arsenal*, 13743, fo. 21.

[78] Letter from Gustave d'Eichthal to Ismayl Urbain, 23 November 1867, Fonds d'Eichthal, *Bibliothèque de l'Arsenal*, 13743, fo. 22.

[79] Journal de Gustave d'Eichthal, entry for 18 November 1867, Fonds d'Eichthal, *Bibliothèque de l'Arsenal*, 14723.

Thus, despite his conversion to Christianity and despite his later attachment to the Saint-Simonian sect, d'Eichthal continued to show a concern not merely for the future of Jewish communities but for the future of Judaism. Though his endeavours always had an idiosyncratic twist and brought but little result, his assimilationist outlook was shared by a number, and certainly some of the most influential, of his Jewish contemporaries, and his belief in the rôle Judaism might yet play was shared by others like Joseph Salvador and James Darmesteter later in the century who remained practising Jews.[80]

III

In the 1820s the young d'Eichthal, in common with many of his generation in Paris, was searching for a guide, a purpose, a profession. For a time he lost his religious faith and for a short period became a freemason.[81] He remained undecided on a career and at different times tried a scientific, a philosophical and a business one. But on two occasions he thought he had found the leader to follow and a set of beliefs in which he could find a mooring of purpose and certainty. This was when he came under the spell first of Auguste Comte and later of the Saint-Simonians. D'Eichthal played a minor rôle in Comtism and a more significant rôle in Saint-Simonism, two of the most influential of nineteenth-century intellectual movements that had as many affinities with each other as they had bitter differences.

His first intention on leaving the Lycée Henri IV was to enter the Ecole polytechnique, the engineering school, entry to which was through competitive examination. The driving force behind this was less d'Eichthal's ambition than his father's, for Louis d'Eichthal, remembering the scientific education of his youth and the prestige acquired by scientists during the revolutionary and Napoleonic periods, nurtured a desire that both his sons follow scientific careers. It was whilst Gustave was preparing for the entrance examination that he came into contact with Auguste Comte, six years his elder, who was still struggling to make his name and to make ends meet. Some time in 1822 a friend of the

[80] For the extent of this assimilationist element in the Jewish community later in the century, see Michael R. Marrus, *op. cit.*, especially chapters V and VI, pp. 86–164.

[81] Fonds d'Eichthal, *Bibliothèque de l'Arsenal*, 14405, fo. 13.

family, Olinde Rodrigues, suggested that Comte would make a good mathematics tutor for Adolphe d'Eichthal.[82] Listening in at the lessons, Gustave was impressed by Comte's ability and was soon being taught himself—not mathematics but Comte's positive philosophy. He became, at the age of eighteen, Comte's first disciple, and spent most of 1823 with him.[83] He later described to Comte the impact that their relationship had on him: '. . . You have exercised so decisive an influence upon me that I would be incapable of eradicating the marks even if I wanted to.'[84] For a moment, indeed, he contemplated following a philosophical career himself and under Comte's inspiration wrote a scientific treatise that Comte showed to his friend, the naturist Henri de Blainville. Both agreed that the work had some merit and that d'Eichthal was worthy of a scientific career.[85] For Comte as well the relationship evidently had some significance, for his widow was later to remark that, when she and Comte married, d'Eichthal was the person for whom he had the greatest affection and that her husband had regretted through his life that their close ties had been broken.[86]

In January 1824 d'Eichthal's grandfather died and Louis d'Eichthal was called to Munich to help settle the estate. Invited to accompany his father, Gustave accepted because he felt that it would give him the opportunity of learning the language, discovering German intellectual trends and introducing Comte's ideas to Germany. In Berlin he made contact with a number of scientists and philosophers. At the university he attended the physics and meteorology lectures given by Paul Erman and handed Erman a copy of the essay, *Système de politique positive*, that Comte had just

[82] Notes autobiographiques, dated 25 July 1868, Fonds d'Eichthal, *Bibliothèque de l'Arsenal*, 14408, fo. 10.

[83] Draft of a letter from Gustave d'Eichthal to ?, n.d., cited in 'Matériaux pour servir à la biographie d'Auguste Comte: correspondence d'Auguste Comte et Gustave d'Eichthal', edited with an introduction by Pierre Laffitte, *Revue occidentale*, 1896, 2nd series, vol. XII, pp. 186–276 and 345–388. Copies of all Auguste Comte's letters to d'Eichthal are to be found in the Fonds d'Eichthal, *Bibliothèque Thiers*, carton IV.

[84] Letter from Gustave d'Eichthal to Comte, 23 March 1824, cited by Pierre Laffitte, *loc. cit.*, pp. 191–3.

[85] Letter from Auguste Comte to d'Eichthal, 1 May 1824, *ibid.*, pp. 196–203. Unfortunately, the manuscript of this work has not survived.

[86] Letter from Auguste Comte's widow to d'Eichthal, 15 March 1866, *ibid.*

published.[87] He met Friedrich Bucholz, who agreed to publish parts of Comte's essay in his monthly political journal.[88] Finally, he made contact with Hegel, who was also teaching in Berlin, had several conversations with him and gave him a copy of the essay of which Hegel apparently thought highly.[89] D'Eichthal began to study German philosophy, started to read Herder[90] and Kant[91] and translated the latter's *Idee zur einer allegemeiner Geschichte in weltbürgerlichen Absicht.*[92]

Berlin, however, was also the occasion of a cooling of the relationship between Comte and his disciple. D'Eichthal was under pressure from his father to take up a profession and, while he himself contemplated becoming Comte's collaborator, Comte was unenthusiastic.[93] He therefore decided on a commercial career and began his apprenticeship with the Arnold Mendelssohn banking house in Berlin in November 1824. He stayed there until May 1825 but once in France again continued his apprenticeship by working in an import house in Le Hâvre and was therefore less in contact with Comte than before. The links were not entirely severed, for it was he who suggested that Comte give a public lecture course to make his ideas more widely known;[94] and when in April 1826, soon after beginning the lectures, Comte had his mental breakdown it was d'Eichthal who helped to pay for his medical expenses, as he gave him financial help on other occasions. When he visited

[87] Letter from Gustave d'Eichthal to Adolphe, 17 May 1824, Fonds d'Eichthal, *Bibliothèque de l'Arsenal*, 14396, fo. 3.

[88] Letters from Gustave d'Eichthal to Auguste Comte, and from Auguste Comte to d'Eichthal, cited by Pierre Laffitte, *loc. cit.*

[89] D'Eichthal noted of Hegel that 'il aimait beaucoup l'esprit pratique des français; il l'était fort peu lui-même'. Undated manuscript, Fonds d'Eichthal, *Bibliothèque de l'Arsenal*, 14408, fo. 10. See also the letter from Auguste Comte to d'Eichthal, 10 December 1824, cited by E. Littré, *Auguste Comte et la philosophie positive*, Paris, 1863, 687 pp., pp. 152–8.

[90] Letters from Gustave d'Eichthal to Comte, 6 and 18 June 1824, cited by Laffitte, *loc. cit.*

[91] Letter to Comte, 22 August 1824, cited by Laffitte, *loc. cit.*

[92] Letter from Gustave d'Eichthal to Comte, 10 December 1824, cited by E. Littré, *op. cit.*, pp. 152–8.

[93] Letter from Comte to d'Eichthal, 1 May 1824, cited by P. Laffitte, *loc. cit.* D'Eichthal was later to claim that the rift was partly the result of Comte's quarrel with Saint-Simon which took place at this time. See his note inserted in *Le Globe*, 13 January 1832.

[94] Letter from Gustave d'Eichthal to Adolphe, 20 April 1826, Fonds d'Eichthal, *Bibliothèque de l'Arsenal*, 14396, fo. 30.

England in 1828 he took with him copies of Comte's 1824 essay and gave a copy to John Stuart Mill. His doctrinal estrangement from Comte was completed when in 1829 he became progressively more involved in the Saint-Simonian movement, then at its most dynamic and fertile stage.[95]

Comte and d'Eichthal had long had contacts with Saint-Simon and the Saint-Simonians. Comte had acted as secretary to Saint-Simon for a time and had remained in close touch with him until 1824. After Saint-Simon's death Comte had contributed to *Le Producteur*, then under the editorship of Cerclet, and already the journal of the Saint-Simonians led by Olinde Rodrigues. Though Comte began his quarrel with this group as early as 1826, when he accused them of using his ideas without acknowledgement, he had already introduced d'Eichthal to them. He had taken d'Eichthal to meet Saint-Simon in 1823 and Saint-Simon had told him to remember that the most important facet of life was not science but religion.[96] D'Eichthal was, on his own admission,[97] unimpressed by the philosopher, but after 1825 he was kept abreast of developments because Olinde Rodrigues was a close friend of the d'Eichthal family, and because he became a subscriber to *Le Producteur*.[98] Besides, there was much in Saint-Simonian theories that d'Eichthal found attractive; the rôle ascribed to science and industry, ideas on banking and credit, the importance that was increasingly

[95] Comte condemned d'Eichthal's new friends in two bitter and cynical letters, written 7 and 11 December 1829, while d'Eichthal attempted a defence of the Saint-Simonians in a letter to Comte of 8 December 1829. See Pierre Laffitte, *loc. cit.* At the end of his life d'Eichthal recognised the debt he owed to Comte when he wrote: 'je lui ai du la notion d'une loi régulière présidant au développement de l'humanité; je lui ai du de m'avoir arraché aux incertitudes et aux angoisses de la foi catholique, à laquelle j'étais alors attaché, mais ces bienfaits furent achetés au prix d'un douloureux sacrifice: la philosophie positive, telle que Comte l'entendait, entraînait la négation de toute foi religieuse et je dus m'y résigner.' Gustave d'Eichthal, 'Sur mes rapports avec le saint-simonisme', dated 14 April 1883, Fonds d'Eichthal, *Bibliothèque Thiers*, carton IV, n.
[96] Notes autobiographiques, dated 25 July 1868, Fonds d'Eichthal, *Bibliothèque de l'Arsenal*, 14408, fo. 9. He gave a slightly different version of this encounter in a letter to Mme. Adam, 21 March 1883, Fonds d'Eichthal, *Bibliothèque Thiers*, carton, IV, w.
[97] Notes by d'Eichthal, cited by Pierre Laffitte, *loc. cit.*, p. 187. He did, however, subscribe to Saint-Simon's *Catéchisme des industriels* in 1824. Receipt signed by Saint-Simon, 2 February 1824, Fonds d'Eichthal, Bibliothèque Thiers, carton IV, a.
[98] Letter from Adolphe d'Eichthal to his brother, 6 April 1826, Fonds d'Eichthal, *Bibliothèque de l'Arsenal*, 13746, fo. 134.

attached to religious sentiments and the solicitude shown for the condition of the working class.

It was only in 1829 that he became fully converted to Saint-Simonism. At the time he was preparing two books, one of which, a work on Great Britain, he never completed. The other was to be a study of government finance and he published the first part of this in May 1829.[99] It caused something of a stir and led to expressions of appreciation from the Ministry of Finance and from some of his father's business colleagues at the Bourse.[100] The burden of his book was that, contrary to popular prejudice, government borrowing and a national debt were not a burden on the taxpayer but in many ways preferable to levying taxes. D'Eichthal set out to combat the idea that the national debt is a burden the present inherits from the past which ought to be gradually reduced by the re-purchase of bonds through a Sinking Fund. Government borrowing is preferable to extra taxation because it leaves individuals with greater resources while governments can borrow at advantageous rates because they can offer good security. Indirect taxes, however, are costly to levy, raise prices and, argued d'Eichthal, France was already suffering from heavy taxes on necessities. He therefore proposed that in the event of any revenue surplus the government should lower taxes rather than attempt to reduce the national debt and that a government bank be set up to direct national finances.[101]

This work brought d'Eichthal into contact with the Saint-Simonians, since government finance was one of the problems they were discussing in their meetings and their journal.[102] By July 1829 he was a regular attender at their weekly meetings and although at first he found he could not agree with all their ideas he quickly felt

[99] *Lettres à MM. les Députés composant la commission du budget, sur la permanence du système de crédit public, et sur la nécessité de renoncer à toute espèce de remboursement des créances sur l'état*, Paris, 1829, 83 pp.

[100] Letters from Gustave d'Eichthal to his brother, 6, ?, 12 June 1829, Fonds d'Eichthal, *Bibliothèque de l'Arsenal*, 14407, fos. 4–6.

[101] He proposed to discuss this institution in a later work. He never did, but he did publish an article, 'Les Fictions de l'amortissement', *Le Globe*, 12 December 1830 and a pamphlet *Observations sur l'opération du remboursement au pair*, in March 1838.

[102] Manuscript in the hand of Gustave d'Eichthal, Fonds d'Eichthal, *Bibliothèque de l'Arsenal*, 14394, fo. 2. D'Eichthal cited an 1826 article on loans in *Le Producteur* (op. cit., p. 24, n. 3). His book obviously owed much to English writings on government finance and the ideas put forward by Jacques Laffitte.

that they had something important to say, and he was attracted, like so many others, by the intelligence and personality of the man who was emerging as a leader, Prosper Enfantin.[103] By October he was converted and was writing to his brother in London that he, too, would certainly join on his return to Paris.[104]

Once he embraced Saint-Simonism d'Eichthal devoted himself wholeheartedly to it until he finally left the Sect in 1832.[105] He made a not insignificant contribution, and the experience left an indelible mark on the rest of his career. As Saint-Simonian expenses increased, d'Eichthal became one of the major benefactors and his involvement cost Louis d'Eichthal at least 100,000 francs.[106] It was chiefly because of d'Eichthal's financial help that Enfantin was able to resign from his post at the Caisse hypothécaire and devote himself entirely to Saint-Simonism. It was then that Enfantin moved to No. 6 rue Monsigny, to an apartment chosen by d'Eichthal because the offices of Le Globe were in the same building.[107] Because of his banking connections d'Eichthal was given joint direction of Saint-Simonian finances along with Isaac Pereire, an undertaking that was to cost his family dear when, following the collapse of the sect, creditors demanded payment of the debts it had incurred.[108] His knowledge of both Germany and

[103] Letters from Gustave d'Eichthal to his brother, 23 July and 4 August 1829, Fonds d'Eichthal, *Bibliothèque de l'Arsenal*, 14407, fos. 10 and 11. Adolphe d'Eichthal's response was to call many of the Saint-Simonians' ideas 'false, ridiculous, immoral'. *Ibid.*, 13746, fo. 160.

[104] Gustave d'Eichthal to his brother, 6 October 1829, *ibid.*, 14407, fo. 13. He told John Stuart Mill at the end of November that he had just completed six weeks' intensive study of the doctrine and was now a convinced Saint-Simonian—letter to John Stuart Mill, 23 November 1829, pp. 39–68, *John Stuart Mill: correspondance inédite avec Gustave d'Eichthal (1828–1842, 1864–1871)*, translated with an introduction by Eugène d'Eichthal, Paris, 1898.

[105] D'Eichthal described the rôle he played in Saint-Simonism in unpublished notes in the Fonds d'Eichthal, *Bibliothèque Thiers*, carton IV, n. and o.

[106] Letter from Gustave d'Eichthal to Sophie de Laemel, n.d., Fonds d'Eichthal, *Bibliothèque de l'Arsenal*, 13748, fo. 169.

[107] Gustave d'Eichthal, 'Mon rôle dans le saint-simonisme', dated June 1883, Fonds d'Eichthal, *Bibliothèque Thiers*, carton IV, o.

[108] Letter from Gustave d'Eichthal to Victor Lanjuinais, 22 April 1837, Fonds d'Eichthal, *Bibliothèque de l'Arsenal*, 73759, fo. 11. In 1857 d'Eichthal claimed that his involvement in the sect had cost his family 150,000 francs. Letter to Arlès-Dufour, 17 March 1857, *ibid.*, 13752, fo. 121. The liquidation of the Saint-Simonian debt took many years and it came before the courts for the last time only in 1860. Journal, entry for June 1860, *ibid.*, 14721.

Britain proved invaluable. It was d'Eichthal who introduced the Saint-Simonians to the German philosopher Lessing. Lessing had been the patron and friend of Moses Mendelssohn and Abraham Mendelssohn gave d'Eichthal a copy of his *Erziehung des Menschengeschlechts*, a revolutionary theological work which postulated that God educated the human race through revelation and through reason, in 1824. This book was translated by Eugène Rodrigues and played some rôle in the evolution of the sect's religious beliefs.[109]

D'Eichthal played a part in the propaganda activities of the sect: he helped edit and wrote articles for their journal *L'Organisateur* and he wrote pamphlets and contributed pieces to their paper, *Le Globe*. More important, he undertook proselytising work in England. During his visit there in 1828 he had formed a friendship with John Stuart Mill, less than two years his junior and already making a name for himself in London. Soon after his full conversion, d'Eichthal set about the task of converting Mill and at that moment Mill was perhaps more willing to listen than he might have been for he had just traversed a crisis in his life and had broken with the Benthamites.[110] There followed a long interchange of letters between the two men.[111] Though Mill never became a fully-fledged Saint-Simonian, there is ample evidence that the correspondence with d'Eichthal and the writings he read not merely exercised a fascination upon him but left an imprint on his thinking. There are passages in his *Autobiography* where he confesses he nearly became a Saint-Simonian.[112] The nearest he came

[109] Manuscript in the hand of Gustave d'Eichthal, Fonds d'Eichthal, *Bibliothèque de l'Arsenal*, 14408, fo. 10.

[110] For Mill and d'Eichthal and Saint-Simonism, see Iris W. Mueller, *John Stuart Mill and French Thought*, Urbana, Ill., 1956, especially chapter III, pp. 48–91; D. R. Hands, 'John Stuart Mill and the Saint-Simonians', *Journal of the History of Ideas*, vol. VII, 1946, pp. 103–12; Richard K. P. Pankhurst, *The Saint-Simonians, Mill and Carlyle: A Preface to Modern Thought*, London, n.d. (1957). The importance of Mill's mental crisis in his intellectual career has been emphasised by R. J. Halliday, *John Stuart Mill*, London, 1976 and B. Mazlish, *James and John Stuart Mill*, London, 1975.

[111] A not quite complete edition of this correspondence appeared as *John Stuart Mill: correspondance avec Gustave d'Eichthal (1828–1842, 1864–1871)*, edited with an introduction by Eugène d'Eichthal, Paris, 1898. The complete original correspondence is to be found in the Fonds d'Eichthal, *Bibliothèque de l'Arsenal*, 13756.

[112] See *Autobiography*, London, 1873, 313 pp., pp. 163–8. It may be noted that in contrast to Mill's knowledge and views the general tenor of

was when he wrote a series of seven articles entitled 'The spirit of the age' published in the *Examiner* in 1830–1. At about this time, too, Mill became fascinated with France and his many other contributions to the *Examiner* deal exclusively with French politics and culture. Once Thomas Carlyle had shown a sympathtic attitude towards the Saint-Simonians, d'Eichthal began a similar correspondence with him.[113] His major effort, however, was the proselytising mission to England he made with Charles Duveyrier from December 1831 to March 1832. When Carlyle met him for the first time he was favourably impressed, describing him as 'a little, tight, cleanly pure lovable Geschöpfchen: a pure martyr and apostle, as it seems to me, almost the only one (not "belonging to the Past") I have met. . . . His eyes narrow and some distorted; but his mind open, his heart noble.'[114] D'Eichthal and Duveyrier sought not mass conversions but to convert men of influence, journalists and politicians, as well as intellectuals like Mill and Carlyle.[115] They achieved scant success and in any case their work was cut short by the French government's closure of Saint-Simonian lecture rooms in Paris and its decision to bring the leaders to trial. Both returned to Paris where d'Eichthal presented an overly optimistic report to his fellows[116] and made a speech for the defence at the trial proceedings.[117]

British attitudes towards France and matters French was one of indifference and even outright hostility. For a discussion of these views see Gerald Newman, 'Anti-French propaganda and British liberal nationalism in the early nineteenth century: suggestions toward a general interpretation', *Victorian Studies*, vol. XVIII, 1975, pp. 385–418.

[113] D. B. Cofer, *Saint-Simonism in the Radicalism of Thomas Carlyle*, New York, 1931; Eugène d'Eichthal, 'Carlyle et le saint-simonisme', *Revue historique*, vol. LXXXIII, 1903, pp. 292–306.

[114] Cited by Richard K. P. Pankhurst, *op. cit.*, p. 98.

[115] Evidence of this is to be found in the 'Notes et correspondance relatives à la mission saint-simonienne en Angleterre en 1830–32', Fonds d'Eichthal, *Bibliothèque de l'Arsenal*, 14385.

[116] *Oeuvres de Saint-Simon et d'Enfantin*, Paris, 1865, etc., 47 vols., vol. III, pp. 81–100.

[117] *Ibid.*, vol. XLVII, pp. 405–27. One passage in his speech is a very good summary of the attraction of Saint-Simonian doctrine and of Enfantin for the romantic generation of 1830: 'On nous a dit que nous ferions bien de nous retirer chacun dans notre famille pour y reprendre nos fonctions de l'ancien monde, pour redevenir négociants, médecins, ingénieurs. . . . Cette vie mesquine, cette vie étroite, cette vie sans poésie était pour nous un insupportable fardeau. Nous rêvions quelque chose de mieux, quelque chose de grand. . . . Nous n'avons plus les joies du guerrier; nous n'avons plus de croisade à faire, de nouveau monde à

D'Eichthal also played some part in the schisms and leadership changes between 1831 and 1832, for he backed Enfantin in his quest for the sole leadership and helped force the departure first of Bazard and, later, of Rodrigues. He was throughout Enfantin's greatest supporter and became 'le fils aimant et aimé d'Enfantin, bien souvent son confidant et son conseil, le soutenant alors que tous semblaient l'abandonner . . .'[118] In the bitter debates on a new morality and future relations between the sexes that took place during the second half of 1831 d'Eichthal was Enfantin's staunchest supporter, not merely because he had fallen under the spell of his undoubtedly magnetic personality but because he saw in Enfantin's ideas a courageous effort to end the hypocrisy and depravity that he felt hid behind conventional morality.[119] After the dissolution of the sect Enfantin was himself to acknowledge that d'Eichthal had always been the first to approve and encourage the changes that took place in Saint-Simonism between 1830 and 1832.[120]

---

découvrir; le temps même est passé des expéditions napoléoniennes; nous n'avons plus ni solennités, ni temples, ni tournois, ni chants, ni fêtes. La vie est terne et monotone aujourd'hui, et Dieu a mis dans le coeur de beaucoup d'hommes une énergie qui ne peut se ployer à cette contrainte. Nous avons cependant été plus heureux que beaucoup d'autres; car beaucoup sont réduits à chercher dans des joies désordonnées un aliment à l'activité brûlante qui les remplit. Nous, nous avons rencontré un Homme qui nous appelant à lui, nous a révélé une vie nouvelle. . . . Nos vies ne font plus qu'une même vie; nos destinées sont communes, nous sentons que nous sommes appelés à faire ensemble une chose glorieuse, Sainte, divine. . . .'

[118] Gustave d'Eichthal, 'Sur mes rapports avec le saint-simonisme', dated 14 April 1883, Fonds d'Eichthal, *Bibliothèque Thiers*, carton IV, n.

[119] Gustave d'Eichthal ,'Sur la part que j'ai prise aux travaux du saint-simonisme', n.d., *ibid.*, carton IV, o. It might be added that Bazard's schism was not merely a matter of doctrinal differences—as it is generally made out to be—but, as with Olinde Rodrigues, a few months later, a question of his wife's fidelity: it was revealed that his wife had been unfaithful with Margerin. It was Margerin's scandalous conduct whilst he was on a mission to Belgium that led to his expulsion from the sect (cf. the version given by Sébastien Charléty, *Histoire du Saint-Simonisme*, Paris, 1965, ed., p. 106). Margerin later returned to Catholicism and became a professor at the Catholic university of Louvain—note by d'Eichthal on Mme Coignet's article on Saint-Simonism in the *Nouvelle revue*, dated 3 February 1883, Fonds d'Eichthal, *Bibliothèque de l'Arsenal*, 14387, fo. 138. For personal factors in Rodrigues' schism see Barrie M. Ratcliffe, 'Les Pereire et le Saint-Simonisme', *Cahiers de I.S.E.A.*, vol. v, 1971, pp. 1215-57.

[120] Letter from Enfantin to Emile Barrault, 4 February 1833, *Oeuvres de Saint-Simon et d'Enfantin*, vol. VIII, Paris, 1865, p. 217.

In the evolution of Saint-Simonian ideas between 1829 and 1832 d'Eichthal was one of those who welcomed and played a part in the growing mysticism of the sect and his religious excesses earned him the nickname of 'the Jewish Tyrtaeus' from Michel Chevalier.[121] The fact that he had a Jewish background was also important. One of the persistent stories after the dissolution of the sect was that it had had large numbers of Jewish adherents and that this had given a peculiarly Jewish slant to it. For this reason Saint-Simonism was later attacked by anti-Semites.[122] While this is largely mythical,[123] it is true that half a dozen Jews played a rôle in the sect, that the place of Jews and Jewish women were discussed in their meetings and that there were philosemitic aspects to their doctrine. Gustave d'Eichthal had a hand in this.[124] It was his idea that the Saint-Simonians should send a prosleytising mission to the largest synagogue in Paris. The Jews of antiquity, he argued, had opened the doors of their synagogue to Christ and his disciples who had condemned them, surely now they would open their doors to apostles who came to rehabilitate them.[125] Enfantin agreed, and d'Eichthal and Emile Barrault saw Marchand Emmery, Chief Rabbi, as well as other Jewish luminaries, like Cahen, director of the Jewish school in Paris. They then visited the synagogue during the New Year celebrations and were sympathetically received, but

[121] For d'Eichthal's religious excesses see his letters in the Fonds Alfred Pereire, *Bibliothèque nationale*, 24609, pp. 495–7; letter from Enfantin to Bailly, April 1830, *ibid.*, 24608, pp. 42–52; d'Eichthal's profession of faith of 16 December 1832 in *Oeuvres de Saint-Simon et d'Enfantin*, vol. XIV, part II, pp. 112–13; his report of his vision of 2 March 1832 in manuscript in Fonds d'Eichthal, *Bibliothèque de l'Arsenal*, 14390, fos. 1–2; and published in *Oeuvres de Saint-Simon et d'Enfantin*, vol. VI, pp. 184–96.

[122] Zosa Szajkowski, 'The Jewish Saint Simonians and socialist anti-semites in France', in *Jews and the French Revolutions of 1789, 1830 and 1848*, New York, 1970, pp. 1091–118; Georges Weill, 'Les Juifs et les Saint-Simoniens', *Revue des études juives*, vol. XXXI, 1895, pp. 261–280.

[123] This has been argued in Barrie M. Ratcliffe, 'Some Jewish problems in the early careers of Emile and Isaac Pereire', *Jewish Social Studies*, vol. XXXIV, 1972, pp. 189–207.

[124] Gustave d'Eichthal was to claim in 1836 that 'l'ex-Saint-Simonisme a été le pacte d'alliance des Juifs et des Chrétiens'. Gustave d'Eichthal to Adolphe 10 October 1836, Fonds d'Eichthal, *Bibliothèque de l'Arsenal*, 14393, fo. 20.

[125] 'La Juive', Ménilmontant, 9 September 1832, Fonds d'Eichthal, *Bibliothèque de l'Arsenal*, 14390, fos. 4–5.

when they went again at Yom Kippur, dressed in full Saint-Simonian regalia, they were, not surprisingly, less well received.[126] D'Eichthal also played some part in Saint-Simonian attempts to reconcile western civilisation with that of the Near East, attempts of growing importance in the sect, which spawned Michel Chevalier's *Système de la Méditerranée* as well as the search for a female messiah in north Africa.[127] It was d'Eichthal who first put forward the notion that the female messiah that the Saint-Simonians were beginning to look for in 1831–2 would be not a gentile but a Jewess.[128] And if he was in the forefront of those in the sect who advocated women's liberation he was so partly because of his experience of Jewish family life.[129]

In Saint-Simonism d'Eichthal found the security, the faith, the mission he had been searching for. He was therefore one of the last of the leaders to abandon the sect in its collapse of 1832 and he remained despite the pleas and threats of his family and friends. Late in 1831 his family were complaining that the credit of the d'Eichthal bank was in danger because of rumours of family ties with the Saint-Simonians.[130] In 1832 his father's illness was the occasion of a renewed attempt to persuade him to leave.[131] He only did so the following November[132] and it is testimony to the electric atmosphere and emotional strain of the Saint-Simonian experience that d'Eichthal immediately suffered a major nervous breakdown.[133]

[126] Manuscript notes by Gustave d'Eichthal, 6 March 1832, Fonds d'Eichthal, *Bibliothèque de l'Arsenal*, 14390, fo. 5, see also 'Les Souvenirs de Lambert-Bey', *Archives israélites*, 1864, pp. 211–15.

[127] He later claimed that it was Enfantin and himself, who above all others, had tried to tackle this question. Letter to Mr Freslon, 22 September 1841, Fonds d'Eichthal, *Bibliothèque de l'Arsenal*, 14389.

[128] 'La Juive', *loc. cit.*

[129] Manuscript notes by Gustave d'Eichthal, 26 April 1832, Fonds d'Eichthal, *Bibliothèque de l'Arsenal*, 14390, fo. 3; notes autobiographiques, *ibid.*, 14408, fo. 10.

[130] Letter from Gustave d'Eichthal to Louis d'Eichthal, 11 December 1831, Fonds d'Eichthal, *Bibliothèque de l'Arsenal*, 14407, fo. 18.

[131] Correspondence between Isaac Rodrigues and Gustave d'Eichthal, June and July 1832, *ibid.*, 14390, fos. 21–3.

[132] For the anguish he felt, see his manuscript notes for the farewell speech to the sect of 3 November 1832 and his letter to Hoart, 9 November 1832, *ibid.*, 14390, fos. 6 and 7.

[133] He had already suffered a breakdown the previous March. See his journal, *ibid.*, 14717, p. 39. It is a curious irony that scholars have pulled a discreet veil over the sexual mores and problems of the Saint-Simonians when they themselves devoted so much of their endeavour to the question

Through the highly charged atmosphere of a messianic sect, through the friendships he made and kept, the Saint-Simonian experience had a powerful impact on the rest of d'Eichthal's

---

of relations between the sexes. In the case of Gustave d'Eichthal it is clear that his devotion to Enfantin and his religious exaltation were partly sexual in origin. His personal papers contain frequent lamentations at what he at least regarded as his manifold sexual problems, chiefly his powerful, if irregular, drives. Only in his seventieth year could he note with relief in his diary 'la sécrétion sexuelle vient de cesser, ou à peu près, et me laisse un repos que je n'ai jamais connu'. Journal de Gustave d'Eichthal, entry for 22 November 1873, Fonds d'Eichthal, *Bibliothèque de l'Arsenal*, 14724. These drives he ascribed variously to his conversion to Catholicism and ill-advised clandestine reading during puberty, to enforced sexual abstinence or to problems with his urethra, which he twice had operated on, without any success, though this did not prevent him from advising close friends to follow his example, telling them 'faites-vous explorer'. Gustave d'Eichthal, 'Notes sur ma vie', *ibid.*, 14408, fo. 10. With François Lallemand of Toulouse, who carried out the first of these operations, he carried on a long correspondence on different aspects of sexual drives, including 'pertes seminales' (a subject on which Lallemand published a three-volume work entitled *Des pertes seminales involontaires*, 1836–42) and masturbation, which d'Eichthal described as 'plus néces-saire qu'on ne le croit . . . quelquefois le seul remède à la folie'. Letter of 24 April 1838, *ibid.*, 13759, fo. 12. Moreover, d'Eichthal admitted that his sexual problems were an element in his enthusiasm during his Saint-Simonian phase: 'C'est ma propre histoire sous ce rapport qui dans le saint-simonisme m'a fait m'associer avec tant de chaleur à l'entreprise d'Enfantin et le soutenir même dans ce qui ne me paraissait pas définitive-ment soutenable'. Gustave d'Eichthal, 'Notes sur ma vie', *loc. cit.* He later admitted, too, that his famous vision of 2 March 1832, when he claimed that Jesus lived in Enfantin, was partly inspired by his feelings for his cousin Frédérique von Kerstorf, who had fallen in love with him, come to Paris in the hope of marrying him but returned home to Munich a couple of weeks previously. 'Frédérique', note in d'Eichthal's hand, n.d., *ibid.*, 14394, fo. 3 and letter from Gustave d'Eichthal to Aglaé St-Hilaire, 16 November 1835, *ibid.*, 7722, fo. 14. Similarly, his final break with the Saint-Simonians was partly motivated by his growing frustration at the enforced celibacy of their retreat at Ménilmontant. In the note that was read to the Saint-Simonians on his departure he announced: 'Enfin après quinze jours d'agitation et de souffrance j'ai eu *ma nuit*. Secoué de désirs, dans un transport irrésistible, loin d'une femme, j'ai coïté avec mon lit, et alors du calme m'est revenu, ma tête s'est débarrassée, mes idées se sont précisées'. *Ibid.*, 14390, fo. 6. When he left he not merely shaved off his Saint-Simonian beard but broke his celibacy by returning to the brothel he had previously frequented and thereby 'la principale cause de mon état *d'agitation physique* et surtout *morale* se trouve par là dis-paraître [*sic*]'. Letter from Gustave d'Eichthal to Charles Lambert, 12 November 1832, *ibid.*, 7722, fo. 66. For a general discussion of attitudes towards what the French gave the term 'onanism' see Angus McLaren, 'Some secular attitudes toward sexual behaviour in France: 1760–1860', *French Historical Studies*, vol. VIII, 1974, pp. 604–25.

career. He continued to defend Saint-Simon and the Saint-Simonians from subsequent attacks and saw himself continuing Simonian work in many of his later writings. In old age he even began the task of collating material for a definitive work on Saint-Simon and on the sect.[134] Three years before his death he restated his faith in the importance of Saint-Simonism:

> Le saint-simonisme, dans ses deux stages, celui du fondateur et celui de l'École, n'a pas été une utopie, une abstraction comme la doctrine de Fourier ou celle d'Owen, il est né, pour ainsi dire, du sein même de l'histoire, il en a suivi tous les développements et s'est efforcé de s'y associer. Il a eu en vue les mêmes faits que les contemporains, seulement il en a mieux étudié, mieux prévu, mieux déterminé les conséquences, c'est ce qui lui a donné son caractère prophétique . . . Quant à nous, dans les études auxquelles nous nous sommes livrés depuis 50 ans, dans le prodigieux spectacle des évènements auxquels il nous a été donné d'assister nous avons toujours trouvé la justification des idées capitales émises par Saint-Simon et par ses disciples et, aujourd'hui même, l'état de crise profonde dans lequel se trouvent la France et le monde entier nous paraît ne pouvoir trouver sa fin que dans l'application et le développement des principes posés par le saint-simonisme.[135]

IV

D'Eichthal's Saint-Simonian experience marked him, his sense of mission remained throughout his life. For him the malady of the century was not material or social but spiritual and religious. One of his chief preoccupations after 1832, therefore, was to carry on and complete the work begun by Saint-Simon in his *Nouveau Christianisme* and continued by Enfantin and the sect. He devoted much energy to biblical criticism and the search for a religion that would reconcile and synthesise the three great religions of the Mediterranean basin—a grandiose task that was, of course, beyond his capabilities. His work was in any case troubled by other difficulties. He rightly felt that his religious writings were the least understood of his achievements, and he was dogged throughout by a feeling of loneliness, by fits of deep depression, by real or imagined maladies. Throughout his life he was to complain of 'une

---

[134] The manuscript notes for this work are in the Fonds d'Eichthal, Bibliothèque Thiers, carton IV.

[135] Gustave d'Eichthal, 'Sur mes rapports avec le saint-simonisme', dated 14 April 1883, Fonds d'Eichthal, *Bibliothèque Thiers*, carton IV, n.

énorme fatigue cérébrale, de la somnolence, de la difficulté de travail'.[136] The result was that though he had a number of publications between 1832 and 1886 most were fragmentary, essays rather than full-scale works. He died murmuring to his eldest son 'j'avais encore beaucoup à faire'[137] and left a large number of manuscripts, projects begun but never completed.[138]

This lasting concern to solve the religious problem together with his prickly disposition meant that d'Eichthal ploughed a solitary furrow for most of his life after his break with the Saint-Simonians. But he had other interests which brought him into closer communion with his fellows. He took an interest in race and in what contemporaries called ethnology. The heady days of February and March 1848 rekindled his enthusiasm for practical reform and spurred him, as they did so many other intellectuals, into attending and calling meetings, public and private, as well as writing pamphlets suggesting reforms. His first interest after leaving Ménilmontant, however, resulted from the trip he made in 1832-3 to Italy and Greece.[139] This was his philhellenism and interest in Greek studies. On more than one occasion, d'Eichthal was to claim that it was the success of his work in this sphere which gave him the greatest feeling of being understood and appreciated.[140]

He was attracted to Greece, whose civil war had ended in 1832, because it exercised a fascination over all the young and idealistic in western Europe, and he arrived in the country anxious to make some contribution to the success of the new régime. He had, moreover, a good chance of putting his energy to good use, for his cousin Wilhelm, son of Simon d'Eichthal, the Munich banker, was in Nauplion negotiating the Bavarian State loan to Greece. Besides, his arrival in September 1833 coincided with the appointment of the leader of the French party, John Kolettes, as minister of the interior, and Kolettes became d'Eichthal's patron. There already

[136] Journal of Gustave d'Eichthal, Fonds d'Eichthal, *Bibliothèque de l'Arsenal*, 14721.
[137] Eugène d'Eichthal, *Quelques âmes d'élite*, p. 47.
[138] He listed these manuscripts in a letter he wrote to Eugène d'Eicththal on 29 March 1879, Fonds d'Eichthal, *Bibliothèque de l'Arsenal*, 14401, fo. 1.
[139] There is a note on d'Eichthal's visit to Greece in his manuscript, 'Système de la Méditerranée', Fonds d'Eichthal, *Bibliothèque Thiers*, carton IV, s.
[140] For instance his journal entries for 5 May 1868 and 17 July 1880, Fonds d'Eichthal, *Bibliothèque de l'Arsenal*, 14723 and 14724.

was a large foreign contingent manning the upper echelons of the civil service, and the Greek government stood in need of the knowledge of banking, European banking circles and government finance that he possessed. Finance was the most serious problem facing the Regency. The year 1832 had been the most costly of the war: the contraction of the National Income that resulted would take years to make good, and in a desperate attempt to obtain funds the government had alienated public lands for a fraction of their true value. At the same time the 7 May 1832 Treaty signed by Russia, France and Great Britain required the new Greek State to service the foreign loan out of the first receipts of the treasury. When d'Eichthal arrived in Greece, then, the Regency was faced with a budget deficit, with state income badly depleted and, given the delicate political situation, with little chance of making any radical reform of a tax system where taxes were farmed out. Finance was under the tutelage of a board of control which worked independently of all ministries and which was directed by a Frenchman, Artémonis J.-F. de Régny. This board of control attempted to check illegal sales of public lands, and began inquiring into sales that had taken place during the war; the government took a particular interest in the land question, particularly the allocation of land to those who had helped Greece win its freedom.[141]

D'Eichthal directed his energies towards the problem of government finances and the land question, and for six months following his arrival he made a study of the topography and resources of the country. He suggested to his father and brother that they set up a bank in Nauplion[142] and persuaded his brother to take up the question of establishing a steamboat service between Marseilles and Nauplion, Constantinople, Smyrna and Alexandria.[143] Finally, he suggested to Kolettes that a statistical bureau (Bureau d'Economie politique) be set up to look into the land question and offered his services. Both proposal and offer were accepted and on 21 May 1834 he was officially nominated a member of the bureau along

---

[141] John A. Petropulos, *Politics and Statecraft in the Kingdom of Greece 1833–1843*, Princeton, N.J., 1968, chapters IV and V, pp. 153–270.

[142] Letter from Adolphe to Gustave d'Eichthal, 10/11 March 1835, Fonds d'Eichthal, *Bibliothèque de l'Arsenal*, 13748, fo. 60.

[143] Autobiographical notes by Gustave d'Eichthal (1875), Fonds d'Eichthal, *Bibliothèque de l'Arsenal*, 14394, fo. 1; le Marquis de Queux de Saint-Hilaire, 'Notice sur les services rendus à la Grèce et aux études grecques par M. Gustave d'Eichthal', in Gustave d'Eichthal, *La Langue grecque, mémoires et notices, 1864–1884*, Paris, 1887, pp. 1–103.

with another young Frenchman, Alexandre Roujoux, an ardent republican who had left France after fighting in the July Days, and Nicholas Poneropoulos, a French party politician and merchant.[144] In letters to his family and friends he spoke enthusiastically of the task he was undertaking.[145] He envisaged encouraging European immigrants to settle uncultivated areas of Greece, particularly Messina and Elis because of their proximity to Europe, the fertility of the soil and the presence of coal reserves.[146] D'Eichthal submitted his ideas on colonisation and the establishment of model communities to the Greek government, and the Bureau itself suggested that Messina and Elis would be the best areas.[147] In June 1834 he helped the Bureau draw up the Regency's abortive law on the distribution of public land to ex-soldiers and the indigent and himself drew up a bill for the general concession of public lands, though it took a year before the final bill was passed as the Dotation Law of 7 June 1835.[148]

D'Eichthal, however, was unable to proceed with his colonisation schemes. Early in October 1834 he was denounced as an ex-Saint-Simonian who held dangerous views about society. The occasion for this was the presence in Greece of three ex-Saint-Simonians to whom he had given financial help. Although, because he was protected by Kolettes, he was not relieved of his post, his position was weakened. The final blow was the fall of Kolettes in May 1835 which was followed by d'Eichthal's own resignation and his departure for France the following month.[149]

[144] Copy of a letter from Gustave d'Eichthal to the French minister for foreign affairs, 11 June 1834, Fonds d'Eichthal, *Bibliothèque de l'Arsenal*, 13759, fo. 16; letter from d'Eichthal to Charles Duveyrier, 17 March 1834, cited by Saint-Hilaire, *loc. cit.*, pp. 24–8. D'Eichthal was sworn in on 19 May, according to his journal entry, *loc. cit.*, 14717.

[145] He wrote to Charles Duveyrier: 'cette oeuvre si positive, si certaine à laquelle je me suis attaché jette une douce lueur sur mon avenir. . . . Sur cette terre désolée, des villes, des monuments, des routes, des moissons, sur cette terre solitaire des ports des vaisseaux à rames, à voile, à vapeur, tout cela danse incessamment devant mes yeux.' Cited Eugène d'Eichthal, *op. cit.*, pp. 30–1.

[146] Letter from Gustave d'Eichthal to Aglaé St-Hilaire, 26 May 1834, Fonds d'Eichthal, *Bibliothèque de l'Arsenal*, 7722, fo. 10.

[147] Letter from Gustave d'Eichthal to Charles Duveyrier, 26 May 1834, cited by St-Hilaire, *loc. cit.*, pp. 28–30.

[148] John Petropulos, *op. cit.*, pp. 236–8.

[149] Copy of a letter from Gustave d'Eichthal to the Greek minister of the interior, 3 June 1835 and journal, Fonds d'Eichthal, *Bibliothèque de l'Arsenal*, 13759, fo. 16 and 14717.

Though his stay in Greece was quite a brief one and though he never returned, it had an impact on his later career. He remained a friend of Kolettes, who served for a time as Greek ambassador in Paris, and his brother acted as Greek consul-general. The d'Eichthal bank also helped float Greek bonds on the French market[150] and arranged study missions to Greece by French engineers. Gustave d'Eichthal remained a philhellene but it was not until the 1860s that he again took an active interest in Greek affairs. His interest revived when in February 1864 he met Egger, who was Professor of Greek literature at the Sorbonne, and Renieri, a French hellenist.[151] From then onwards he was convinced that there was a pressing need to encourage the study of both the language and literature of Greece since Greek civilisation was still a vital element in western, and particularly French, culture.

One aspect of his efforts to promote the Greek language was his, rather impractical, suggestion that Greek be adopted as an international language, as the language of diplomacy, perhaps as a first step towards European federation.[152] One of the obstacles to this proposal was that, though Greek was very much part of secondary education in Europe, it was taught as a dead language and pronounced differently from country to country. D'Eichthal therefore began to press for the teaching of Greek as a living language and for the adoption of contemporary Greek pronunciation. He secured an interview with Victor Duruy, the education minister, who told d'Eichthal that he would be in favour of the introduction of modern Greek pronunciation provided the Academy supported the idea.[153] At d'Eichthal's behest the Academy set up a commission to report on the question, and since the committee included among its members Egger, Brunet de Presle and Dehèque who all shared

---

[150] See E. Driault and M. Lhéritier, *Histoire diplomatique de la Grèce de 1821 à nos jours*, Paris, 1924, vol. II, p. 174.

[151] Journal of Gustave d'Eichthal, entries for 6 and 8 February 1864, Fonds d'Eichthal, *Bibliothèque de l'Arsenal*, 14722.

[152] *De l'usage pratique de la langue grecque*, signed by Gustave d'Eichthal and Renieri, Paris, 1864. It is possible that d'Eichthal took the idea for the pamphlet from an article by Renieri in *Le Spectateur de l'Orient* (February 1855, pp. 358ff.). This is what Renieri claimed after d'Eichthal's death, though he admitted that his friend had greatly developed his idea. Letter from Renieri to Mme d'Eichthal, 24/25 April 1887, Fonds d'Eichthal, *Bibliothèque de l'Arsenal*, 14407, fo. 73.

[153] Letter from Gustave d'Eichthal to Ismayl Urbain, 5 May 1864, *ibid.*, 13742, fo. 126; journal, entry for 24 September 1864, *ibid.*, 14722.

d'Eichthal's views, it reported favourably.[154] The proposal could not be implemented, however, because of the resistance of teachers of Greek and because of the problems raised by the differences between ancient and modern Greek.

Even more impractical was d'Eichthal's idea that Greek should be the official language of Austria. The Empire was to be reformed and one of the things being discussed was the official language the dual monarchy should adopt. D'Eichthal saw Austria, with its mix of peoples, as a microcosm of the whole European and global problem of nationalities and nations, and the language issue as of international significance. In 1865 he went to Vienna and discussed his ideas with Austrian academics. Not surprisingly, his idea evoked no response.[155] Despite these failures he persisted in his idea of Greek as the *lingua franca* of statesmen and scientists, publishing letters reiterating his proposals in the *Revue scienti-fique*,[156] in the Cobden Club publication in England [157] and suggesting to the pacifist Peace Conference that met in Paris in September and October 1878 that they adopt his idea as one of their aims.[158]

More successful was his idea of establishing a society of hellenists and philhellenes whose purpose would be the encouragement of Greek studies in France. Early in 1867 he met with Beulé, secretary to the Académie des Beaux-Arts, Bréal and Brunet de Presle, both professors at the College de France, to plan the association.[159] By April a steering committee of thirty members had been formed and the programme for the Association pour l'encouragement des études grecques en France drawn up.[160] D'Eichthal was to play a

---

[154] Letters from Gustave d'Eichthal to Ismayl Urbain, 30 October and 12 November 1864, *ibid.*, 13742, fos. 146 and 147.

[155] D'Eichthal was in Vienna 10–18 August 1865, journal, *ibid.*, 14722. See also St-Hilaire, *loc. cit.*, p. 72, n. 1.

[156] Journal, entry for 19 January 1884, Fonds d'Eichthal, *Bibliothèque de l'Arsenal*, 14725.

[157] Journal, entry for 6 July 1871, *ibid.*, 14724.

[158] Journal, entry for 2 October, *ibid.*, 14724. This idea was not, of course, greeted with enthusiasm and nothing came of it.

[159] Letters from Gustave d'Eichthal to Ismayl Urbain, 24 and 31 March 1867, *ibid.*, 13743, fos. 7 and 8; journal, entries for 23 February, 19 and 28 March and 1 April 1867, *ibid.*, 14722.

[160] Gustave d'Eichthal, 'L'Association des études grecques et le peuple grec', *Le Temps*, 6 January 1869; Gustave d'Eichthal, *Notice sur la fondation et le développement de l'association pour l'encouragement des études grecques en France (avril 1867–avril 1877), lue à la séance du 5 juillet 1877,*

leading rôle in this learned society, acting as treasurer for a long period and as secretary, besides reading scholarly papers which were subsequently published in its *annuaire*.[161]

In the 1830s and 1840s d'Eichthal took an interest in ethnology and was an early and active member of the Société ethnologique. His chief concern was the racial question. In part his inspiration for this came from current debates on Negro emancipation in England and France but, as was typical of him, he treated the problem not in the narrow sense of freeing slaves but in terms of the rehabilitation of the Negro, of the respective qualities of black and white and of the reconciliation and association of the two races. His inspiration was also partly Saint-Simonian, for under Enfantin the sect had laid growing stress on the union of east and west, of Christian and Muslim, and in 1833 a party of Saint-Simonians had undertaken a trip to north Africa to search for the female messiah that some claimed would be found there.[162] A member of this expedition had been Thomas Urbain, a mulatto from Cayenne, who, the better to understand north Africa, learned Arabic, became a Muslim, was circumcised and in 1840 took a twelve-year-old Arab girl as his wife. Urbain was to have a distinguished career as an interpreter for the French government and as an expert commentator on Algerian affairs.[163] D'Eichthal's interest in race as well as in Islam was stimulated by his growing friendship with Urbain, who acted as his secretary when he was writing his *Deux mondes* in 1836 and thereafter remained a lifelong friend and correspondent. And he pursued his interest in race and

Paris, 1877 (offprint from the *Annuaire de l'association pour l'encouragement des études grecques en France*, 1877, pp. 351–424). Egger gave public recognition to d'Eichthal's rôle in the foundation and early work of the association in an article in the *Revue des deux mondes*, 1 July 1870.

[161] His contributions to the *Annuaire* were collected together by his son and published as Gustave d'Eichthal, *La Langue grecque, mémoires et notices, 1864–1884*, Paris, 1887, 426 pp.

[162] For a bibliography on the Saint-Simonians and Algeria and the Suez Canal, see Jean Walch, *Bibliographie du Saint-Simonisme*, Paris, 1967, pp. 90 and 96.

[163] Urbain described his stay in Egypt in the *Revue de Paris*, July 1852 and he left a full account of this and of his life in 'Notice autobiographique', dated 9 July 1871, Fonds d'Eichthal, *Bibliothèque de l'Arsenal*, fo. 76. In view of the undoubted interest of his writings on Algeria and of his manuscripts at the Arsenal it is a pity no one has yet made a study of Urbain.

Africa by reading the accounts of European explorers like Mungo Park who described the warm hospitality accorded him by Africans, or Hugh Clapperton who gave a sympathetic description of the culture of the western Sudan, as well as the accounts of administrators like Baron Jacques-François Roger who had been governor of Senegal and who admired many aspects of African life and culture.[164] D'Eichthal also made a lengthy visit to Algeria in 1838 to study Mohammedanism and the different races in Algiers. The consequence of his concern about the racial problem was the publication in 1839 of some of the letters that he and Urbain had exchanged on the question.[165]

In this work d'Eichthal showed that he shared the view of many of his contemporaries that race was the basic determinant of culture and human character, a dangerous view that in other hands was used in racialist arguments. The major thesis he put forward, however, was that black and white were not antagonistic but complementary, each bringing his own contribution to mankind. Though he considered—wrongly—that the Negro had no political or scientific achievements, he felt he had qualities which would enable him, in association with white man, to make an important contribution to the progress of humanity. The white he called the male race and the Negro the female. He wrote to a friend of the qualities of the Negro:

> s'il n'offre point le développement spontané des qualités scientifiques et politiques, le noir a par contre les sentiments et les qualités domestiques, développées au plus haut degré, et c'est par là surtout *qu'il est femme.* Pour celui qu'il aime il est obligeant et serviable jusqu'au dévouement, fidèle jusqu'au sacrifice. Sa poésie respire la douceur des sentiments intimes, et il a une adoration de fétichiste pour les fleurs et toutes les gracieuses merveilles de la nature. Or ce contraste entre la Race blanche et la Race noire est précisément celui que nous retrouvons dans les natures opposées de l'homme et de la femme, l'une essentiellement dévouée, domestique, délicate; l'autre essentiellement dominateur, politique, scientifique; l'une cherchant à concentrer le monde dans

---

[164] Copy of a letter from Gustave d'Eichthal to St Chéron, 17 August 1839; letter from Gustave d'Eichthal to Ismayl Urbain, 16 October 1839, *ibid.,* 13759, fo. 15, 13741.

[165] *Lettres sur la race noire et la race blanche* by Gustave d'Eichthal and Ismayl Urbain, Paris, 1839, 67 pp.

sa vie intime, l'autre cherchant à étendre sa propre vie jusqu'aux sphères les plus lointaines.[166]

This description of feminine qualities would hardly please present-day feminists, but they would approve d'Eichthal's plea for the liberation of both women and the Negro, both of whom he felt western man had enslaved.

It would be wrong to dismiss these reflections on racial characteristics as not only based on scant information but bizarre. It would be so because information about African peoples south of the Sahara, except along the west coast of equatorial Africa and to some extent at the Cape, was still very limited despite great increases in knowledge in the first three decades of the nineteenth century.[167] More, in a century when the Negroes that the white man knew best were those whom they had transported, enslaved and humiliated and those in west African polities which had been influenced by slaving and slavers, when racial theories and attempts to classify, grade and explain the origins of races were extremely damaging to Africans, especially Negroes, d'Eichthal—despite his ignorance of many African achievements and history—was sympathetic to what he regarded as the African's qualities.[168] Indeed, his views on the complementarity of the attributes of Negro and Caucasian were similar in many ways to the views of the greatest nineteenth-century African apologist and nationalist, Edward Wilmot Blyden.[169] He even went as far as advocating mixed marriages to produce mulattoes blessed with the qualities of both races—the kind of qualities d'Eichthal found in his friend Urbain.[170]

[166] Letter from Gustave d'Eichthal to Freslon, 22 September 1841, Fonds d'Eichthal, *Bibliothèque de l'Arsenal*, 14389.

[167] Philip D. Curtin, *The Image of Africa*, Madison, Wis., 1964, especially chapter IV, 'Towns and elephants', pp. 198–226.

[168] It should be noted, though, that there was some evidence in the first decades of the nineteenth century of a greater appreciation of African arts and crafts, and that his view of the essential qualities of the Negro was not far distant from that of some missionaries who regarded Africans as natural Christians and of W. R. Greg, who in 1843 wrote that 'the European is vehement, energetic, proud, tenacious and revengeful: the African is docile, gentle, humble, grateful, and commonly forgiving. . . . The one is to the other as the willow is to the oak.' Cited by Philip D. Curtin, *op. cit.*, p. 327.

[169] Edward Wilmot Blyden, *Christianity, Islam and the Negro Race*, new ed., Edinburgh, 1967.

[170] *Lettres sur la race noire et la race blanche*, pp. 12–13. It should perhaps be added that Blyden did not approve of mixed marriages, for he was against miscegenation and a strong advocate of racial purity.

Although one of his friends asked him, if the white man was the male and the Negro the female, what sex was the North American Indian,[171] most of d'Eichthal's circle greeted his *Lettres sur la race noire et la race blanche* with enthusiasm. One of his friends, the deputy Victor Lanjuinais, promised to raise the racial question in the next session of the Chamber.[172] John Stuart Mill congratulated him on his book and added:

> Je suis depuis longtemps convaincu que non seulement l'orient par rapport à l'occident mais encore la race noire par rapport à la race blanche, offrent des différentes caractéristiques ... des rapports plus intimes et plus sympathiques entre ces mondes et ces races ne doivent pas etre seulement à leur profit, mais aussi au notre; que si notre intelligence et notre activité sont plus développées, ils possèdent, eux, les qualités dont nous avons le plus besoin pour servir de contrepoids aux notres, c.à.d. cet amour du repos, cette aptitude aux jouissances de la vie materielle et par suite cette extrême sensibilité sympathique qui distinguent la race noire.[173]

The book also brought d'Eichthal into contact with a heterogeneous group of savants from different disciplines who in 1839 formed the Société ethnologique, the first purely scientific ethnological society ever to be established.[174] It was the first body to set about the task of collecting and assimilating data from outside Europe on race and culture. It called its field ethnology what we would now call anthropology. Since the chief interest of the society was race, it is not surprising that when W.-F. Edwards, the society's founder and first president, met d'Eichthal he invited him to join them.[175] Not only did d'Eichthal do so but during the 1830s he

[171] Letter from Stéphane Mony to Gustave d'Eichthal, 28 June 1839, Fonds d'Eichthal, *Bibliothèque de l'Arsenal*, 13749, fo. 198.

[172] Letter from Victor Lanjuinais to Gustave d'Eichthal, n.d. (1839), *ibid.*, 13749, fo. 197.

[173] Copy of a letter from John Stuart Mill to Gustave d'Eichthal, 14 January 1839, *ibid.*, 13741, fo. 61. Mill's reference to the relations between east and west is a reference to d'Eichthal's *Deux mondes*.

[174] A group in England led by Thomas Hodgkin had already set up the Aborigines' Protection Society, but this had a dual purpose as a political pressure group and as an ethnological society.

[175] Letter from Gustave d'Eichthal to Ismayl Urbain, 23/25 September 1839, Fonds d'Eichthal, *Bibliothèque de l'Arsenal*, 13741, fo. 62. D'Eichthal wrote that he accepted the invitation with enthusiasm because 'il y a quelque chose de grand à tirer de là. Il n'y a aujourd'hui ni politique, ni religion hors de la *Science des Races*'. W.-F. Edwards had published one of the most important racist theories of history and society in the nineteenth century (*Caractères physiologiques des races humaines*, Paris, 1829).

played a significant rôle in the Society's activities. Until 1846 he acted as its assistant secretary and from then until 1852 as its secretary.[176] In 1846 he instituted a series of discussions on the characteristics of the black and white races[177] and contributed papers on the links between ancient Egypt and America and Polynesia[178] and on the Buddhist origins of civilisation in Mexico.[179] But his best known papers to the Society were those he gave on the Fulbe.

Here, d'Eichthal tackled a problem that exercised scholars throughout the nineteenth century and which remains unresolved today: the origins of the Fulbe (Fulani) people of west Africa. The Fulbe, successful State-builders and pastoralists, had largely non-negroid features, and the question of their origins was already evoking debate among French scholars when d'Eichthal wrote. He put forward the theory that the Fulbe could be traced back to Malaya and claimed that they had arrived in Africa via Madagascar and Merowe, bringing with them an important cultural heritage.[180] Such a theory of long-range migration appears less eccentric when we compare it with some of the other efforts to explain the origins of the Fulbe, which included tracing them to Persia, Bohemia, India, Arabia and even to Jews.[181] He also believed that the Fulbe had made an important contribution to west African civilisation. Converted to Islam by Arabs, they brought this religion, superior to polytheism, to the other peoples of the western Sudan. D'Eichthal's theories were later taken up by racists to show that what achievements west Africans had were not the work of the Negro but

[176] Journal, entries for 30 January 1846 and 23 January 1852, *ibid.*, 14719 and 14720.

[177] Meetings of 23 April, 14 and 29 May, 25 July 1847, Journal, *ibid.*, 14720.

[178] Letter from Gustave d'Eichthal to Ismayl Urbain, 1 February 1843, *ibid.*, 13741, fo. 134. This work was later issued in fuller form as *Etudes sur histoire primitive des races océaniennes et américaines*, Paris, 1845, 173 pp.

[179] Journal, entries for 27 March and 8 May 1846, Fonds d'Eichthal, *Bibliothèque de l'Arsenal*, 14719. This was to be published as *Etudes sur les origines bouddhiques de la civilisation américaine*, Paris, 1865, 86 pp.

[180] D'Eichthal published a first sketch of his theory in 'Recherches sur l'histoire et l'origine des Foulahs ou Fellans', *Bulletin de la Société de géographie*, November 1840. Fuller versions were given to the Société ethnologique and published in its *Mémoires*, vol. I, 1841 and ès a book, *Histoire et origine des Foulahs ou Fellans*, Paris, 1841, 296 pp.

[181] Philip D. Curtin, *op. cit.*, pp. 411–12, n. 65; Robert Cornevin, 'Histoire des peuples de l'Afrique noire', thèse pour le doctorat ès lettres, Paris, 1960, especially chapter IV, 'Les Peuls', pp. 345–81.

of a non-negroid people. There is no evidence, however, that this was in any way his purpose. One outcome of this work and his slender book on race was that in 1849 d'Eichthal, along with four others including his friend Isidore Geoffroy Saint-Hilaire, was invited by the minister of education to be a member of a committee to advise on an expedition to Africa to be undertaken by L.-L. Ducouret.[182] The committee worked out the route that Ducouret was to undertake, a route so long that had he attempted it he would almost certainly not have survived. Worse, Ducouret, who had travelled in Africa and the Middle East, claimed to have discovered the Niam-Niam people—Negroes with tails—and to have actually touched the tail of one of them in Mecca. The committee, it appears, were innocent enough to believe him and it was one of the objects of this government-funded expedition to find the Niam-Niams. It was thus perhaps all to the good that when in 1850 Ducouret landed in Morocco he promptly took a house, servants and a mistress and went no farther.

D'Eichthal devoted much of his energies, especially in his later years, to the religious question and to a related interest, biblical exegesis. The west, he continued to believe, was undergoing a period of crisis where religious sentiment had weakened, where the ties with classical civilisation, with the Jewish, Greek and Roman traditions, had loosened.[183] He complained that

> Notre education nous dispose trop à sacrifier le passé à l'avenir, la conservation à la Réforme, l'hérédité à l'élection, la famille à l'Etat, la nature à l'industrie. L'humanité a perdu la mémoire. Elle ne songe plus à se retourner vers ses ayeux pour leur demander l'origine des temps présents et le secret de l'avenir.[184]

He therefore believed it important to 'renouer la chaine des temps',[185] to strengthen and re-establish the links between the present and the past. The goal he set himself was to show the legacy left by the great civilisations of the Mediterranean basin, to show the ties between them and to establish the contributions each

---

[182] Letter from the Ministère de l'Instruction publique et des Cultes to Gustave d'Eichthal, 12 July 1849, Fonds d'Eichthal, *Bibliothèque de l'Arsenal*, 13751, fo. 167.

[183] Gustave d'Eichthal, *La Sortie d'Egypte* . . ., Paris, 1850–72, p. i.

[184] Letter from Gustave d'Eichthal to ?, January 1837, Fonds d'Eichthal, *Bibliothèque de l'Arsenal*, 13758, fo. 16.

[185] Gustave d'Eichthal, *Les Evangiles*, Paris, 1863, 2 vols., vol. i, pp. lxi–lxii.

—and especially the Jews—had made. This was one reason why he retained an interest in things Greek, why he published a pamphlet on the three great Mediterranean peoples and Christianity in 1865,[186] and why he devoted so much attention to biblical criticism.

The explanation of this preoccupation lies partly in his own personality—as a child he had felt God was present in everything and had feared walking on grass for fear of hurting him[187]—in the religious sentiments of that romantic generation of 1830,[188] in the religious syncretism that was particularly powerful in the nineteenth century.[189] His chief inspiration, though, was Saint-Simonism.[190] He retained his faith in the Saint-Simonian metaphysico-theological theory of history; he continued to believe that history was moving towards an imminent dénouement that would bring the period of crisis to an end, and he continued to believe in the synthetic religion of mankind that Eugène Rodrigues had envisaged in his preface to Lessing's *Erziehung des Menschengeschlechts*. He was not the only ex-Saint-Simonian who went on searching for a synthetic religion for all humanity. Jean Reynaud advocated a new religion in his *Terre et Ciel*[191] while Pierre Leroux spent his last years as a mystic searching for a regenerated Christianity. His view of religion was more spiritual than the Saint-Simonian social religion, arguably the weakest of their theories. Besides, while Saint-Simon had claimed that the study of the Bible sullied the imagination, bound men to outdated dogmas and led them to neglect present-day problems, d'Eichthal believed such study would be profitable, and in 1838 criticised this aspect of *Nouveau Christianisme*.[192] A further stimulus to his religious writ-

---

[186] *Les Trois Grands Peuples méditerranéens et le christianisme*, Paris, 1865, 48 pp.

[187] Manuscript in the hand of Gustave d'Eichthal, n.d., Fonds d'Eichthal, *Bibliothèque de l'Arsenal*, 14394, fo. 6.

[188] Henri Tronchon, *Romantisme et Préromantisme*, Paris, 1930, especially chapter I, pp. 1–23.

[189] D. G. Charlton, *Secular Religions in France 1815–1870*, Oxford, 1963, pp. 135–44 and *passim*.

[190] He freely admitted this debt. In 1875, for example, he wrote of Saint-Simon: 'J'ai reçu de ce maître . . . et durant une vie déjà bien longue, j'ai toujours gardé cette croyance, que l'organisation définitive de la société moderne n'est possible que par le développement et la rénovation du christianisme.' *Mémoire sur le texte primitif du premier récit de la création (Genèse, ch. I–II, 4)* . . ., Paris, 1875, p. 3.

[191] *Philosophie religieuse. Terre et ciel*, Paris, 1854, 441 pp.

[192] Denying that biblical study was retrograde, he added that 'la Bible

ings was undoubtedly his Jewish origins and his continuing regard for Judaism. His belief in an imminent dénouement that would end the current crisis was reminiscent of Hebrew prophecy and messianic expectation. In his researches on the Old Testament and especially on the Pentateuch he tried to show Judaism not as merely preparing the way for Christianity, as a transitory stage in the theological destiny of history, a religion that had already fulfilled its mission, but as a faith that still had a rôle to play. He shared this belief in Judaism with a long line of Jewish apologists, including Joseph Salvador. Indeed, his researches on the Pentateuch were prompted by Salvador's work on the Mosaic Code, and he set out to verify Salvador's general conclusions and to answer critics who had asked how it was that the Mosaic Code had come out of the Sinai desert some thirteen centuries previously. Though Salvador had himself attempted to answer this, d'Eichthal felt that more still needed to be done to convince the general public.[193] His study of the Bible was also influenced by that increasingly scientific approach to Holy Scripture that was one of the most important developments in Christian and Jewish theology in the nineteenth century. He was impressed by the *Wissenschaft des Judentums* in Germany[194] and by the work of Abraham Geiger in particular,[195] as well as by the work of Gentile biblical scholars like David Friedrich Strauss,[196] whose *Das Leben Jesu* created a sensation when it appeared in 1835, and of Catholic scholars in France who

---

est au contraire bien plus propre à élever et ennoblir l'imagination, et elle donne d'ailleurs à la vie matérielle une sanctification que lui refuse le christianisme'. Letter to Enfantin, 25 January 1838, Fonds d'Eichthal, *Bibliothèque de l'Arsenal*, 14407, fo. 31.

[193] Gustave d'Eichthal, *La Sortie d'Egypte . . .*, pp. 2–5 and p. 10. Elsewhere d'Eichthal described the work of Salvador and the Saint-Simonians as parallel, 'car en partant du Mosaïsme il est presque toujours arrivé à des résultats identiques'. Letter to Freslon, 22 September 1841, Fonds d'Eichthal, *Bibliothèque de l'Arsenal*, 14389.

[194] Nahun N. Glatzer, 'The beginnings of modern Jewish studies', in Alexander Altmann, ed., *Studies in Nineteenth-centruy Jewish Intellectual History*, Cambridge, Mass., 1964, pp. 27–45; Christopher Dawson, 'On Jewish history', *Orbis*, vol. x, 1967, pp. 1249–50.

[195] Letter from Gustave d'Eichthal to Dr Geiger, 18 November 1837, Fonds d'Eichthal, *Bibliothèque de l'Arsenal*, 13759, fo. 12.

[196] He regarded Strauss's work on Jesus as completing Salvador's *Jésus Christ et sa doctrine*. Letter to Freslon, 22 September 1841. Littré published his translation of Strauss's book in 1839–40: *Vie de Jésus, un examen critique de son histoire, par le docteur David Frédéric Strauss*, 2 vols., Paris, 1839–40.

were devoting themselves to biblical exegesis even before Ernest Renan published his *Vie de Jésus* in 1863.[197]

His work on the Bible was made easier by his contacts with Jewish scholars which meant he could call on their knowledge of Hebrew and its syntax. Throughout 1844 he worked with Munk on the Pentateuch until Munk was appointed to a post at the Bibliothèque royale.[198] He had the help of the Jewish orientalist Hermann Zotenburg when he was preparing his work on the Exodus[199] and that of Auguste Carrière, professor of Hebrew at the Ecole pratique des hautes-études and at the Ecole des langues orientales, for his work on the Book of Genesis.

The most important aspect of d'Eichthal's biblical exegesis was the work he did on the oldest part of the Old Testament canon, the Pentateuch, which because ancient tradition ascribed it to him is commonly called the Book of Moses. D'Eichthal's inspiration was Salvador's *Histoire des institutions de Moïse*. He regarded the Pentateuch as not only the foundation of the Jewish state and Judaism but—along with the Gospels—as the greatest of mankind's books, that had had a profound influence on the evolution of modern society;[200] when he began his researches he shared the view of many of his contemporaries that the Book of Moses was the work of one man and Salvador's view that it was the great founding constitution of the Israelite polity and religion. His reading of the work of Old Testament scholars soon made him aware that traditional views about the historical origin and authorship of the Pentateuch were being revised. Scholars had early noticed that it contained numerous doublets, discrepancies in linguistic usages and religious ideas, contradictions and antagonisms. Nineteenth-century scholars were realising that it was oral literature that had been written down only at a relatively late stage and that the Pentateuch and the Old Testament in general were to be interpreted as a product of the ancient Near Eastern culture of which Israel was a part. His own researches as well as his reading of the

[197] Harry W. Paul, 'In quest of Kerygma: Catholic intellectual life in nineteenth-century France', *American Historical Review*, vol. LXXV, 1969–70, pp. 387–424.
[198] Letter from Gustave d'Eichthal to Ismayl Urbain, 2 June and 19 October 1844, Fonds d'Eichthal, *Bibliothèque de l'Arsenal*, 13741, fos. 160 and 171; *La Sortie d'Egypte* . . ., p. 3.
[199] Journal de Gustave d'Eichthal, entry for 28 March 1874, Fo d'Eichthal, *Bibliothèque de l'Arsenal*, 14724.
[200] Gustave d'Eichthal, *La Sortie d'Egypte* . . ., pp. 1–2.

work of other biblical scholars convinced d'Eichthal that the Mosaic Law was not the *fons et origo* of the Jewish state and religion but the product of their evolution and that the Pentateuch could best be understood by a comparative study of the different texts that made it up, by a careful interpretation of history and ancient languages. Though he never completed this reinterpretation of the Pentateuch and the Mosaic Code, parts of his work were published.[201]

The first task d'Eichthal set himself was a reinterpretation of the story of the creation given at the beginning of the Book of Genesis. According to this God created light on the first day, the firmament on the second, earth and sea and plants on the third but had not established the sun, the moon and the stars until the fourth. If this were so, it was asked, how was it that night followed day for the first three days? Was it not more logical, too, that the creation of plants should follow rather than precede the sun's creation? D'Eichthal's explanation of these apparent anomalies was that the order given in Genesis was not the original but a revised order made by a later generation. The correct order was the logical one where the firmament was already in existence before the six days and where the sun, moon and stars were created on the first day and the rest followed naturally. The alteration of the order of the creation had taken place during the Babylonian captivity which had brought Judaism into contact with the Persian religion. In Mazdaism light was increate and thus came before God. To prove that the Jewish god was superior to the Persian, Hebrew apologists added as their god's first act the creation of light and, in order to emphasise the importance of this act, the creation of the sun, moon and stars was moved to later in the week. In the opinion of another biblical scholar, Maurice Vernes, d'Eichthal's research and hypotheses on the creation in Genesis were challenging and original.[202]

D'Eichthal sought, secondly, to understand why, in the story of

[201] *La Sortie d'Egypte, d'après les récits combinés du Pentateuque et de Manéthon, son caractère et ses conséquences historiques*, Paris, 1850–72, 75 pp.; *Mémoire sur le texte primitif du premier récit de la création (Genèse, ch. I–II, 4), suivi du texte du second récit*, Paris, 1875, 79 pp. After his father's death, Eugène d'Eichthal published a collection of Gustave's studies entitled *Mélanges de critique biblique: le texte primitif du premier récit de la création dans le Genèse, le Deutéronome, le nom et le caractère du dieu d'Israël, Iahveh*, Paris, 1886, 402 pp.

[202] Maurice Vernes, *M. Gustave d'Eichthal et ses travaux sur l'Ancien-Testament*, Paris, 1887, pp. 8–23.

Moses and the burning bush in the Book of Exodus, God gave himself two different names *Ehyeh* (I am that I am) and *Yahveh* (Jehovah).[203] While many scholars were using etymology to show that the two terms had common roots and therefore a common meaning, d'Eichthal concluded that the existence of the two names was the consequence of a later revision of the original text. In the original there had been only one reply to Moses' question, as to what title God should be known under, but a later and more exacting generation had added another. Since the response *Ehyeh* did not correspond to the question posed and since *Ehyeh* is not found elsewhere in the Old Testament d'Eichthal concluded that the early text had the response *Yahveh*. When Hebrew theologians came into contact with Greek philosophy they realised that there was a lacuna in their dogma. They therefore added a name for their god which defined the essence of divinity and this was the *sum qui sum*, the Hebrew word, *Ehyeh*. Maurice Vernes felt this explanation was not only correct but significant since this textual revision marked a linking of the Jewish tradition with western thought.[204]

Analysing Deuteronomy was the occupation of his last years, for this book he felt constituted the core of the Jewish faith.[205] Nineteenth-century scholars devised a number of source hypotheses about the Pentateuch. Julius Wellhausen, for instance, contended that it was a compilation of four written sources, one of which was Deuteronomy.[206] While this was no longer regarded as originating with Moses, it was still felt to be the work of one pen and to date from the period of the religious reforms ascribed to Josiah. D'Eichthal's study, however, led him to doubt its homogeneity and the single-source view. He concluded it was a compilation from separate sources, some older than others. In particular, the great speech that is ascribed to Moses and which constitutes the first part of Deuteronomy has little in common with the second part which deals with legislation.[207] He questioned not merely the

[203] 'Sur le nom et le caractère du dieu d'Israël, Iaveh', *Revue de l'histoire des religions*, vol. I, 1880, pp. 356–73. This is reproduced in *Mélanges de critique biblique* . . .

[204] Maurice Vernes, *op. cit.*, pp. 28–30.

[205] Gustave d'Eichthal, *Mélanges de critique biblique*, avertissement d'Eugène d'Eichthal, pp. i–iii.

[206] Ivan Engnell, *A Rigid Scrutiny: Essays on the Old Testament*, Nashville, Tenn., 1969, chapter IV, 'The Pentateuch', pp. 50–67.

[207] Deuteronomy, V–XI and XII–XXVI.

unity of this book but the dating that biblical scholars had given it. While agreeing that Deuteronomy was a legitimation of Jerusalem as the only cult centre, of its temple as the only authorised one and of its god as the only true God, he disagreed with most scholars, who put its composition somewhere towards the end of the kingdom of Judah; d'Eichthal put it, instead, some hundred or hundred and fifty years earlier.[208]

D'Eichthal completed his work on the Pentateuch and on the Old Testament with his study of the Exodus in which he discussed its long-term significance and compared the accounts of it in the Egyptian historian Manethon and in the Pentateuch. His study of the New Testament was limited to his work *les Evangiles*,[209] published in 1863. This was a textual comparison of the Synoptic Gospels of Matthew, Mark and Luke and an attempt to discover the original text, which he regarded as the basis of a pragmatic Christianity, such as Saint-Simon had envisaged in his *Nouveau Christianisme*.[210] Though this work was placed on the Index, received some favourable reviews—including one from Sainte-Beuve—and was praised by d'Eichthal's friends,[211] it suffered from being published in the same year as Renan's more original and more controversial *Vie de Jésus*.

As was typical of many of his generation, d'Eichthal was apolitical, though in 1841 he had contemplated taking a seat in the Chamber.[212] For a brief moment in 1848, however, he was swept along in the heady days of February when he thought the Revolution not only heralded political and social change but marked the dawn of a new religious epoch. Late in 1847 he had read *Del primato morale e civile degli italiani* which the Italian cleric Vincenzo

---

[208] Vernes held d'Eichthal's unorthodox hypothesis in high regard— *Une Nouvelle Hypothèse sur la composition et l'origine du Deutéronome, examen des vues de M. G. d'Eichthal*, Paris, 1887. This essay was reprinted in Vernes' *Essais bibliques*, Paris, 1891, 372 pp. Both Vernes' and d'Eichthal's interpretations of Deuteronomy were favourably reviewed by Isidore Loeb in the *Revue des études juives*, vol. XIII, 1886, pp. 153–5.

[209] *Les Evangiles, première partie, examen critique et comparatif des trois premiers evangiles*, 2 vols., Paris, 1863.

[210] *Ibid.*, vol. I, preface; Eugène d'Eichthal, *Quelques âmes d'élite*, p. 36.

[211] Journal de Gustave d'Eichthal, entry for 7 September 1863, Fonds d'Eichthal, *Bibliothèque de l'Arsenal*, 14721; letter from Gustave d'Eichthal to Ismayl Urbain, n.d. (1863), *ibid.*

[212] Letter from Gustave d'Eichthal to Carnot, 17 June 1841 and letter from Trouvé Chauvel, 20 September 1841, Fonds d'Eichthal, *Bibliothèque de l'Arsenal*, 13750, fos. 70 and 74.

Gioberti had published in 1843. Gioberti, a moderate Italian nationalist, had claimed that the Italian people had a cultural and spiritual unity and destiny and a unique contribution to make to civilisation. Italian unity, he claimed, could be achieved through the establishment of a federation of States under the leadership of the Pope. Gioberti thus allied what seemed to many patriots the irreconcilable: liberalism and religion. While d'Eichthal was unimpressed by Gioberti's prolixity and by his chauvinism, he was inspired by his belief in the Pope as a temporal as well as a spiritual leader. It was under Gioberti's inspiration that he wrote a series of articles for the Saint-Simonian journal, *Le Crédit*, in December 1848 and January 1849.[213] Like Gioberti he proclaimed that the Papacy could become the religious and political leader of Christianity, but, unlike Gioberti, insisted that the necessary preliminary to this was doctrinal and organisational reform. During March 1848 he conceived the idea of a 'Démocratie religieuse', setting up a society to work for the creation of a new synthetic religion. A number of ex-Saint-Simonians joined him, including Abel Transon, Cazeaux, Urbain, Jourdan and Isaac Pereire, as did the Abbé des Gouettes.[214] The idea was stillborn; differences and defections, together with the disillusion with the Revolution that set in especially after the June Days, led to the speedy breakup of the group. D'Eichthal never found the like-minded fellows to help him in his quest for the new religion, just as he never reached his goal of a faith that would reconcile and integrate.

Gustave d'Eichthal was sometimes a mystic, always a dreamer, a utopian. Some of his visions, like that of a new religion that would end the crisis of doubt, the alienation of man from himself and his fellows and bring in a new era of harmony, may appear bizarre,

[213] The occasion for these articles was the attempts at reform made by Pius IX. *Les Evangiles* ..., vol. 1, p. xxxviii. *Le Crédit*, 'La Papauté, l'Italie et al confédération européenne', six articles, 12, 18 and 25 December 1848 and 1, 8, 22 and 23 January 1849.

[214] Journal de Gustave d'Eichthal, entries for 12, 15, 17, 28 March 1848, Fonds d'Eichthal, *Bibliothèque de l'Arsenal*, 14720. A similar fate awaited d'Eichthal's efforts in 1849 to form a group to discuss the problem of the reorganisation of European society, whose discussions he guided towards the religious issue. A series of meetings was held, attended by Transon, Quatrefages, Vivien de St Martin, Morpourgo and Lebret. Again, the initial impetus could not be maintained and the twelfth meeting was the last. Journal, entries for 5, 16, 22 and 29 March, 12 and 13 April, 17, 23 and 31 May 1849, *ibid.*, 14720.

best left in deserved oblivion. If some of his ideas show some originality, others of his projects—like that to make Greek a universal language—seem at best impractical, at worst harebrained. Yet what the abundant private papers, correspondence and publications he bequeathed to the Bibliothèque de l'Arsenal and the Bibliothèque Thiers reveal is that d'Eichthal was very much a product of his times, that he shared with many of his fellow intellectuals the belief, so strengthened by the Dual Revolution, that change was possible, that dreams could come true, that the crisis could be ended and utopia reached. He was no more a dreamer than many of his contemporaries. His France pullulated with utopian schemers, with visionaries who planned a restructuring of society, new polities and new religions. Among these dreamers the best remembered are the so-called Utopian Socialists—including Saint-Simon and his disciples—but along with them were many others who dreamed of ending the period of transition that the French Revolution and the new industrialism, and perhaps even the *Aufklärung*, had ushered in. If d'Eichthal pursued the millenium, strived towards the unattainable goal of devising a new religion, he was attempting no more than many others who also yearned for a pantheistic religion and a spiritual unity. Most of these mystics have been forgotten; they acquired neither the notoriety nor the following and they lacked the insight of their more illustrious fellows. Gustave d'Eichthal was one of these. His aims were a widespread inspiration, his generous ideals and his ardent seriousness were widely shared, his failings and disappointments those of many who belonged to the romantic generation of 1830.

INDEX